# Two Little Girls

**THE BERKLEY PUBLISHING GROUP**
**Published by the Penguin Group**
**Penguin Group (USA) Inc.**
**375 Hudson Street, New York, New York 10014, USA**
Penguin Group (Canada), 90 Eglinton Avenue East, Suite 700, Toronto, Ontario M4P 2Y3, Canada
(a division of Pearson Penguin Canada Inc.)
Penguin Books Ltd., 80 Strand, London WC2R 0RL, England
Penguin Group Ireland, 25 St. Stephen's Green, Dublin 2, Ireland (a division of Penguin Books Ltd.)
Penguin Group (Australia), 250 Camberwell Road, Camberwell, Victoria 3124, Australia
(a division of Pearson Australia Group Pty. Ltd.)
Penguin Books India Pvt. Ltd., 11 Community Centre, Panchsheel Park, New Delhi—110 017, India
Penguin Group (NZ), Cnr. Airborne and Rosedale Roads, Albany, Auckland 1310, New Zealand
(a division of Pearson New Zealand Ltd.)
Penguin Books (South Africa) (Pty.) Ltd., 24 Sturdee Avenue, Rosebank, Johannesburg 2196,
South Africa

Penguin Books Ltd., Registered Offices: 80 Strand, London WC2R 0RL, England

This book is an original publication of The Berkley Publishing Group.

First edition: April 2006

Library of Congress Cataloging-in-Publication Data

Reid, Theresa.
    Two little girls : a memoir of adoption / Theresa Reid.—1st ed.
        p.   cm.
    ISBN 0-425-20882-6
    1. Intercountry adoption.   2. Reid, Theresa.   3. Adoptive parents—United States.   4. Adopted children—Russia
(Federation).   5. Adopted children—Ukraine.   I. Title.

    HV875.5.R45 2006
    362.734092—dc22
    [B]
                                                                                    2005054844

PRINTED IN THE UNITED STATES OF AMERICA

10   9   8   7   6   5   4   3   2   1

# Two Little Girls

## a memoir of adoption

### Theresa Reid

BERKLEY BOOKS, NEW YORK

# Contents

# Prelude

"You my mommy!" The little voice pipes from the backseat.

I make eye contact with my three-year-old, Lana, in the rearview mirror, so she knows I'm listening. Her older sister, Natalie, is looking out the window, as if bored by this familiar exchange. But she is very still, listening with her whole body.

"That's right, sweetheart," I say. "I'm your mommy, forever and ever!"

"And I'm your precious baby!"

Smile. "That's right, lovie. You are my precious baby."

"And Nattie, she my sister."

"That's right, honey. Nattie is your sister."

"And she's your precious *big* baby!"

"That's right, sweetheart." No matter how many times we have this exchange, eventually I find I have to talk past a lump in my throat.

My swimming eyes make me a bit of a threat on the road. "You are my precious little baby, and Nattie is my precious big baby, and I am so, so lucky to be your mommy. Being your and Nattie's mommy is the best thing that ever happened to me. It's the best thing that *could* ever happen to me. It's the best thing in the world."

Lana nods, satisfied, and leans back in her seat, smiling. Just as she expected. All's right with her world.

Marc and I have been Lana's parents for just over a year, and she regularly pulls this fact out of her heart and holds it in front of her like a crystal, examining its many facets. The first time she initiated this recitation we were all at home, milling about the bedroom, getting ready for sleep. Lana, who had been with us at that point for about six months, was sitting on the edge of the bed. "You my mommy!" she announced as I walked by.

I stopped before her. "That's right, baby. I'm your mommy."

"And Nattie, she my sister!"

"That's right. Nattie's your sister."

"And Daddy"—she's excited now, a little breathless—"Daddy is my daddy!"

"That's right, sweetheart. Daddy is your daddy."

"We're a *family!*" she crows. "It's a *present!*"

Lana had only recently learned about presents. Her thirty-two months in an orphanage in Ukraine had taught her nothing about gifts. But she has learned, gradually, by receiving gifts herself, and by watching her friends at nursery school receive gifts on their birthdays. Now she is giving the concept a fresh application: family = present. The wisdom of this child gives us pause.

We have been Lana's parents for thirty-two months short of her age, Natalie's for thirteen months short. We adopted our daughters from Russia, in Nat's case, and Ukraine. Nothing we have done in our lives has taught us so much about who we are, and what we can do, and what we can't do.

My husband and I have worked very hard in our lives, and have accomplished a fair amount. He is an endowed professor of pediatrics at an excellent medical school. I earned my doctorate from the University of Chicago, have run a national organization for professionals in the field of child maltreatment, have spoken at national and international conferences on child abuse. We make a good living, live in a lovely home. But with all of our accomplishments and hard work, Marc and I could not do what the poorest, least educated people do tens of thousands of times all across the globe every single day: We couldn't create life.

Our inability to reproduce launched us on a life-transforming quest to become parents by other means. I wrote *Two Little Girls* to make sense of this quest for myself, and to encourage other people to adopt the world's parentless children. Hundreds of thousands of babies and children alive in the world today need loving homes. Of the millions of couples in the U.S. who experience infertility, to the best of our knowledge fewer than seventy-five thousand adopt unrelated children annually—about twenty thousand from overseas. More Americans than ever before express admiration and support for adoptive families; according to one survey, 64 percent of Americans are personally affected by adoption. But relatively few people actually take the plunge. We spend a great deal more money every year trying to create babies through biotechnology than we do trying to adopt the babies who already exist in the world.

I hope that *Two Little Girls* will show that even if you are filled with doubt and confusion, even if towering obstacles—from inside and out—block your path, you can bring one of your dearest dreams to life by adopting a child.

*Two Little Girls* is not always a pretty read. I wanted to tell the truth—both Marc's and my own truths, and the truths that make becoming parents through adoption radically and often painfully different from becoming parents through biology.

When Marc and I finally decided to go out into the world in search of babies, we embarked on our quest in the only way anyone ever does anything: with all of our limitations intact and functioning. As you read *Two Little Girls* you will see our narcissism and our confusion and our questionable motives. They're all there. But I want to say this: *They're all there in biological parents, too.* One of the most disconcerting differences in the two ways of becoming parents is that, in the adoption process, couples' limitations are exposed for all to see. No biological parents have to go through the kinds of self-examination and self-exposure that adoptive parents endure.

You also see our anger. The adoption process itself—the exposure, the scrutiny, the endless hoops, the staggering costs—gives couples lots to be angry about. The strain of the process often creates conflict within couples. Becoming parents through adoption is much more angering than becoming parents through biology.

And then, there's the brutal reality that adoption involves choice. You not only choose to adopt, you choose to adopt a particular kind of child, and even a particular child. Many people in the adoption community soften this gut-wrenching fact by claiming that their adopted children were "meant to be" theirs. Well, it's obvious to Marc and me that Natalie and Lana were meant to be ours, too; but it's just as obvious that we made many painful, highly fraught decisions along the way, many of which involved the word "No."

Saying no to one child (or child profile) and yes to another is a profoundly disturbing choice that all adoptive parents make. The saving myths of love at first sight and meetings that are meant to be can obscure but not erase this reality. Somehow, couples who hope to adopt have to find a balance between their desires and inchoate needs and guesses about their ability to parent, and the possibility of remaining open to joyous surprise. We seekers have to recognize that the unloveliness we think we see in a particular child may be our own unloveliness, leering out at us from a helpless little person; and we have to recognize that there are some children—helpless little children!— whose physical or emotional health presents challenges we are not willing to bring into our own lives. It is heartbreaking that we cannot love them all, that we have to choose; it is deeply disturbing, even wounding. But the fact that our own choices connect us to our particular precious children does not mean that our love for them is not meant to be: Our own halting process, filled with pain and limited by our ability to see, is how what is *meant* to be *comes* to be.

Reading about how Marc and I came to our decisions might make you wince. I present our process raw, and it often appears less than admirable. I hope that, if you are toying with the idea of adopting, you will see that your own doubt and hesitation and confusion and selfish considerations and anger are not evidence that you should not adopt. They are a normal part of the process—at least for those of us who yet have a very long path to sainthood.

A quest. A test—a test of our human desire, will, and limitations. We moved mountains, inside and out, to become our children's parents. In return, they have completely transformed us. When we set out to adopt, we were self-involved singles; today, we are besotted parents turned inside-out by love. Thank God. Natalie and Lana will continue to transform us every day of our lives. Thank God. The pain involved in becoming their parents falls away, like labor pains. Our girls are, without question, our life's greatest gifts.

# 1

## "They Can't Have Children"

Infertility didn't pain us the way it was supposed to. Our pain developed slowly, furtively, striking only after we foolishly believed we had escaped it altogether. According to hundreds of books and articles, our decision to give up on heroic efforts to get pregnant should have been accompanied by terrible grief over the loss of fantasied offspring, a wrenching sense of failure over our inability to perform the fundamental biological function of reproduction. But we didn't feel these things. Our initial decision to have a family was not based on longing; it was rational and abstract. We thought, overall, that our lives would be fuller with children than without: that, on balance, it would be better for us to have kids than not. It's true that, when shopping for Christmas ornaments, I always chose ones with faces, thinking, "Someday a child is going to *love* this one." (And today, indeed, I have a Christmas tree bristling with whimsical faces that delight my girls.) But these thoughts were not laden with emotion. The idea of the children who would be drawn to these ornaments floated far away in a hazy future. Other people's children did not spark yearning; they sparked dark thoughts about the costs of parenthood. We didn't pine for children, dream about them, imagine ourselves with them, fantasize about their traits. We waited so long to start a family because of our lack of passion for the idea. Marc fretted that we'd have a girl who looked like him. I had been fat well into adolescence, and hated the thought of being thick-waisted again, even temporarily. We were satisfied in our challenging careers and carefree lives.

Our friends who were parents swore it was the best experience life had to offer. "They *have* to say that," Marc said. "They can't get out of it now." We weighed, on the one hand, a profoundly important realm of human experience—parenting—against the losses we would incur entering it: our cherished day-to-day independence, untold travel adventures, all of our disposable income, single-minded focus on our careers. After long deliberation, we decided, without much enthusiasm, that kids would be a net gain. So we took the daring step—in our very late thirties—of throwing out the birth control pills.

As any rational person could have predicted, nothing changed. Month after month, despite our best efforts, nothing untoward happened in my body. We hadn't needed the birth control pills after all: Who knows how long I had been taking them out of the sheer fatuous belief that aging didn't apply to me? They were a vanity.

Imperceptibly, our decision to have a child took on a life of its own. Acting on our decision strengthened our commitment to it. Every step we took increased our investment—emotional, intellectual, financial—and made it harder to go back. This is how many wars start, and how people like us, who didn't really *want* a baby, didn't long for a baby, end up looking at pictures of beautiful babies adorning the walls of a fertility clinic.

Our first attempt at *in vitro* fertilization was something of a lark. We had disgustedly abandoned a doctor who had told us unsentimentally how unlikely it was that we would conceive. Our conviction that we would beat the odds made the drama of two shots a day and minute attention to my bodily processes more an adventure than a serious trial. Marc, a physician, took pride in his ability to administer pain-free injections. His attempts to reproduce our Swedish doctor's accent ("Unt now vee see zee ehkgs") lightened our frequent trips to his office. We worried about what we would do if more than one of the eight fat, juicy eggs the doctor harvested became a little embryo. Would we consider "selective reduction"? After all this? But what if it was triplets? Quadruplets?! We wrestled earnestly with these profound ethical issues for days. Another vanity.

A friend warned me that the second time through IVF was harder, and she was right. The novelty was gone, and so was most of the delusional hope. The pictures of the babies on the doctor's wall seemed less like friendly encouragement and more like a perverse joke, a con. All he displayed were the lottery winners. Where were the pictures of all the people—so many more—who never did conceive? On our second try, he harvested only four or five smaller eggs, none of whom would become a baby.

Halfway through our third attempt, Christmas was coming, and our doctor had planned his annual ski trip to the Alps. My period came a couple of days too late to fit comfortably into his vacation schedule, so he suggested calmly that he just keep me suspended in this halfway state—painfully bloated, pumped with male hormones—for a couple of weeks until he returned. Marc and I looked at each other in consternation and said in one voice (mine growing huskier by the hour), "There *has* to be a better way to have a family!" We tossed the expensive needles and vials into the trash. We weren't crushed. We were frustrated. Stymied.

"They couldn't have children." This pitying statement smacks against my ears like a relic from a bygone era, as out of touch as *Father Knows Best.* "*Anybody* can have children," I want to shout. "Scores of thousands of children in the world need loving parents." But I have to admit that it is extremely difficult to get to many of these children. It usually takes a great deal of money to adopt. Even adopting domestically typically costs thousands of dollars. Because of cost alone, some people really *can't* have children, and that is a scandal and a great sadness. I hope a foundation (or two, or twenty) will make a mission of defraying the costs of adoption so loving people of modest means can become parents, and can use their financial resources to raise a child they want rather than to get the child in the first place. Every loving and capable adult should be able to have a child if he or she wants one, because there are many, many children already on Earth who desperately need adult love.

"They couldn't have children." Adoption also takes—in most cases, although there are a few lucky exceptions—considerable stamina. A mom of my acquaintance who has long wished for a second child said to me, beaming at my younger one shortly after we had brought her home, "Oh, gosh, I'd take one too if someone would just *give* me one!" I am afraid that my private reaction to this comment was not as warm as the smile I gave back. We had just spent thousands of dollars and exerted Herculean effort over several years to wrest this child from Ukraine. Life's greatest gems are not just dropped into your lap—at least, not into mine. Still, even allowing that some work is bound to be required to draw down the treasure of another human life, adopting one of the world's orphaned or abandoned children can be so difficult that many good, determined, and capable people just give up.

I have looked for ways to justify this difficulty. Children without parents—little children, tiny babies—are terrifyingly exposed, helplessly dependent upon the character of the adults they encounter. All of those obstacles between prospective parents and abandoned children— these are the mythic trials by fire and water, right? The tests the heroes must endure to prove that they are worthy to be entrusted with the care of a helpless human being. But no. Life is not myth. Life is real, now, and practical. Biological parents are not expected to gain the right to parent through miraculous feats of ingenuity and endurance. And they actually *create* life, without that life's permission—certainly a more awe-inspiring act than assuming responsibility for a being who already exists. All of the obstacles to adoption end up keeping abandoned kids away from the people who would love to love them. It cannot be said that these would-be parents *couldn't* have children, but, especially given the staggering financial commitment, their decision not to have children makes clear economic sense, at least narrowly defined.

For some people, "They couldn't have children" really means "They couldn't have *biological* children, and other people's children won't do." These folks have not been deterred by costs and bureaucratic obstacles; they haven't gotten that far, because they will not seriously consider adoption. As far as I can tell, there are several reasons for this stubbornness. One is superstition. If they cannot conceive a child, they conclude that it is not "meant to be," and give up trying to parent. Another is an unfounded but powerful, and widespread, fear: that they could not love a child not born to them. A third reason for rejecting adoption is narcissism. If having children is all about reproducing *oneself* and one's partner—seeing your own or your partner's eyes twinkling out of another little face—then adoption obviously does not cut the mustard. Finally, there is atavism, and it is found primarily in men, and even in very good men who just cannot escape one part of their animal heritage: a primitive refusal to nurture another male's offspring. I think it is this atavism I am encountering when a woman tells me she would like to adopt, but her husband "just doesn't want to."

One day, as we were engaged in our intellectualized, mechanized effort to conceive a child we thought it worthwhile to have, Cupid's arrow struck me through the heart. It was just like that. It was the sight of a little hand resting with complete trust on the shoulder of a man. It happened to be in Moscow, on our first trip to Russia, as Marc and I waited to go into the Moscow State Circus. Holding his child, waiting for a light to change, this father was as unconscious of that little resting hand as its owner was. But as my eyes lighted on that little hand it became, like magic, a perfect emblem of a kind of intimacy I suddenly wanted with . . . well, not yet *all* my heart, but with most of it. I might as well have been sprinkled with fairy dust.

But the fairy dust couldn't penetrate completely until a shield I didn't know was there had been removed. It was a shield that had separated me from my own mother.

My mother died of cancer when I was twenty-four years old. I was not old enough to lose my mother. Although, like most twenty-four-year-olds, I was busy showing the world how grown-up I was, I needed my mom as much when she died as I had ever needed her.

One year and three days after she died, when it finally felt to me that she had been dead, perhaps, one week, my father remarried. He married a very kind woman who was so insecure that my mother could not be discussed in her presence. Hearing our love for our mother poured out in sorrow unhinged my stepmother's fragile sense of self. So, one year after my mother died, my brothers and sister and father and I stopped talking about her when we gathered together, because my stepmother was always there, and she could not tolerate such talk.

The wall that formed between me and my mother, between me and my own mother-self, was invisible to me, and impenetrable.

My stepmother died of cancer seventeen years after my father married her. At the time, Marc and I were stalled in the adoption process. We had chosen our agencies, we had filled out some paperwork, we had gotten the lay of the land, knew what we had to do next. And then we stopped. We just didn't know if we cared enough to go forward.

I have no ill-will toward my stepmother. She was a good, kind woman, who never did me any harm. But with her death, a spell she had not meant to cast was broken. At her funeral, I felt the wall between me and my mother—a wall I had not even known was there—dissolve and float away into mist. I was freed to be with my mother again, with her-in-me. All of a sudden, my clarity was perfect. I wanted with all my heart to be a mom. I called Marc from the airport on my way home from my stepmother's funeral and said, "I want to be a mother. We have to do whatever it takes." The next day, we put our shoulders to the boulder and started to push.

As it happened, my clarity about becoming a mom was born the same week as Natalie.

Adoption is an extremely difficult path. In the "adoption community" they aptly call the process the "adoption journey." This journey begins sometime after you have tried to conceive, but before you have given up—when the inkling of possibly needing to adopt first presents itself. The steps you take down this road, as infertility treatments fail and the longing for children persists, lead you into a maze of branching questions. Each question, of course, requires an answer, a decision—and this inescapable element of choice is the hardest and most unnatural aspect of adoption.

One of the first question is, Do you want a child who looks like you? Our gut reaction was, "Yes, we do." So many happy transracial families have been created through adoption in the last ten years that we felt politically incorrect about caring that our child looked like us. But we had lots of reasons for being so retro. Privacy was one: We wanted to retain the prerogative of disclosing our adoption status to the world. Why would we share our most intimate personal business with passing strangers? Every parent of a child with a different skin color in America has been jarred by the impertinence of strangers' questions: "Is that child yours?" "Where did you get that child?" "What happened to his *real* parents?" We didn't want to have to deal with questions like these. It happens that we regularly give up this privacy. When she was three or so, Natalie approached a dazed homeless man on the beach in Chicago to announce that she had been born in Russia. She tells anybody, anytime. There's a bit of status involved. Her kindergarten heartthrob demanded of me one day, "Was Natalie *really* born in Russia?"

"Wow," he breathed, when I confirmed her claim.

That year Natalie wanted her daddy and me to come to class on her birthday to share her adoption story and book with her class. So privacy is something we regularly divest ourselves of; but we have it if we want it.

Another, more subtle reason for choosing to adopt a child who looks like us was denial. Yes, we wanted the ability to obscure from the world that our family was created through adoption; but we also wanted, quietly, to obscure this fact to ourselves. This inclination did not arise from shame, but from the sense that, if we were not reminded, every time we looked at her, that she did not come out of us, then we could just quietly elude all those "adoption issues" that dozens of experts say are unavoidable. For parents, the most insistent of these issues is that there are other people out there who have a huge stake in your and your child's life, strangers to whom you and your child owe a vast, unpayable debt. Who *wouldn't* want to try to escape such a debt, mind-boggling in its complexity? Having children who look like you, you can pretend—even to yourselves—that you created them, that you can go merrily on your way and never have to cope with adoption issues. Of course, this only works while your kids are very young; once they achieve some comprehension, and you begin to share their story with them, the illusion is dispelled. You *didn't* create them, and you wish you had. The birth parents (in all closed adoptions and sometimes in "open" ones) are a ghostly presence in both of your lives. But we were still operating under the delusion that we could make all this go away when we checked the box marked "Caucasian."

Uncomfortable as it was to admit that we wanted a child who looked like us, it was many times more difficult to assert that we wanted a perfectly healthy child. I have seen versions of this sheet several times now, the sheet with three columns: "Yes," "Will Consider," "No," and a list of twenty-five or so possible afflictions that abandoned or orphaned children might suffer. Mental retardation. Crossed eyes. Club foot. Cleft palate. Cleft lip. Mother used drugs. Mother used alcohol. Born of rape. Born of incest. Premature. Missing or stunted limbs.

If I were pregnant, my answer to these questions would have been nurturing. I would have eaten carefully and exercised regularly; I would have refused alcohol, and avoided paint fumes and insecticides and emotional upset. I would have done everything in my power to safeguard my baby's health *in utero*. Everyone would have applauded me and extolled these wonderful early signs of my maternal vigilance. But I wasn't pregnant. We were adopting. And our utterly common desire for a perfectly healthy child could not be expressed positively. It was expressed as a series of "No's."

With every check mark we made in the "No" column, we felt criminally deficient in the capacity to love, in generosity of spirit. With each "No" we checked, the image of a specific child floated before our eyes, a child we would refuse to consider even trying to love. And we checked "No" almost everywhere: not even "Will Consider," just "No."

This negative expression of our heart's desire was one of the unexpectedly agonizing steps in adoption. But we had to admit that we wanted a healthy child. Who doesn't? Who gets pregnant saying, "It's all the same to us if this child is unhealthy"? If a child were born to us mentally or physically disadvantaged, we would love that child with all our hearts, or part of us would die trying. But it's a rare pair who approaches parenthood with a Zen-like detachment regarding their baby's capacities. Neither of us is that kind of saint. We had devoted our professional lives to helping hurt children. In our private lives, we wanted—like everyone else—to build a healthy, happy family. They gave us the choice!—or the illusion of choice, which was just as unnerving. We consulted our hearts, looked each other in the eyes, and checked No, No, No, No, No, No, No.

So we have decided: We want to adopt a healthy Caucasian child. Will he or she be born here in the U.S. or abroad? Like thousands of other people after the nightmare cases of Baby Jessica and Baby

Richard saturated the news media in the early 1990s—cases in which young U.S.–born adopted children were wrenched away from their adoptive parents because one or both birth parents wanted them back—we quickly made the decision to go overseas. The disruption of adoption by birth parents is, despite lavish media attention to the outlying cases, quite rare and almost always avoidable. But we wanted the certainty that no anguished birth parent could inflict a catastrophic blow to our hearts. We would go far, far away and bring home a child whose birth parents could never hope to find her—and who, not incidentally, could never hope to find her birth parents.

For that was another considerable advantage of international adoption, it seemed to us at the time: that our child could never find her birth parents. We read stories in the media about "searchers"— adopted adults who devoted their lives to finding their birth parents. An entire movement—the "search" movement—has emerged to support adoptees' reunions with their biological families. Indeed, nearly every U.S. adoption agency today insists on some degree of openness between birth and adoptive families—a compassionate response to the "bad old days" of secrecy and shame. We recoiled from the prospect of our child's searching for her "real" parents. What an outrage! What a nightmare! We took it personally, even in the abstract. Imagine being rejected like that after having given everything you had to parent that child.

While we were in the midst of the adoption process a physician, a small, intense, driven woman, well-known for her pioneering work in child advocacy, cornered me at a professional conference to tell me all about her search for her birth parents. It consumed her; she devoted all of her non-work hours to this quest. I was overwhelmed by her passion, her intensity about it. I wanted to ask, "What's the matter with you? What was wrong with your adoptive family?" I wanted a guarantee that Marc and I would not be subjected to such punishing rejection. Another colleague, a better friend, a soulful, beautiful woman, adored her adoptive parents, but told me about the sad longing in her core, which came, she said, from having been adopted. I protested: "But I have a sad longing in *my* core, too. How do you know yours is from adoption? Mine isn't—I don't know what it's from." My friend wasn't a searcher, but she was convinced: Although she loved her parents with all her heart, her emotional pain was rooted in adoption.

Now, having parented my girls for several years, I have very different, more complicated feelings about biological family reunions. I know that they can be healthy for everyone involved, including the adoptive parents. But at the time, Marc and I shared an illusion that surely motivates some searchers: that the reunion of birth parents and birth children would be like the reunion of passionate lovers who had been forced apart. Together again, they would be complete, whole, at perfect rest. They would need no one else, including us. We doting adoptive parents would be out in the cold, childless again. Of course we wanted to protect ourselves emotionally from such heartrending betrayal. We wanted it to be impossible for our child and her birth parents to find each other.

We also turned toward international adoption because more healthy babies and children are available overseas. I am sad to say it, but it is true: Although my professional work was in the field of child maltreatment, we did not want to build our core family from the U.S. foster care system. Children available through the public system are typically older and frequently emotionally and physically troubled, since they have been removed—often belatedly—from birth parents for cause: abuse and neglect. We did not want to make these children's heartbreaking problems the center of our own emotional lives. I have deep respect for the people who do.

The other domestic adoption options did not look very good to us, either. With the increase in the rate of abortions and the acceptance of single motherhood from the 1970s on, the number of healthy Caucasian babies available for adoption in the U.S. has dropped far below the number of couples who want to raise them. The competition for these babies is intense, dicey, and—it felt to us—demeaning. We knew or knew of several couples who had been emotionally whipsawed, thinking they had been chosen by a birth mother, planning joyfully for the birth of "their" child, then hearing instead that the birth mother couldn't part with her baby after all—and who could blame her? We knew we could avoid much of this torment by signing up with an exclusive private agency. The crème de la crème of these agencies in Chicago reliably produced, in less than nine months, a healthy Caucasian baby for couples who paid about forty thousand dollars (in the mid-1990s). But this didn't feel very good to us. We know a number of people who have built happy families in this way. But to us it felt unsatisfying: Why compete for babies who are sure to get loving homes, when so many children in the world will go begging for any home at all?

Although our primary goal was to build a healthy family, we also wanted to do some good in the process. Adopting from Eastern Europe, where so many children were spending their childhoods in state-run orphanages, we could actually fill a need in the world as we filled the need in our lives. We could adopt a child who otherwise would very possibly grow up in an orphanage, who might—who knew?— end up a victim of the international sex trade. This is the direction in which we turned. And we turned, specifically, to Russia: the country of origin of Marc's family, the country in Eastern Europe we had visited first when the walls fell down, the country whose history and culture we knew and loved well—well enough to teach to a child.

So, we wanted a healthy young child from Russia. First, we selected one of the dozen or more local agencies that, in Chicago, handles local requirements like the home study and compliance with state laws. With their help, we selected one of the dozens of international agencies that promises to find the right child for you on the other side of the world and help you navigate the red tape generated by her country of origin. Then—once my stepmother had died—we set to work, submitting complicated agency applications, multiple sets of fingerprints, lengthy letters of reference from friends, several large checks, and dozens of documents (proving our marriage, previous divorces, health status, financial resources, educational attainments, parenting philosophy)—each of which had to be notarized *and* certified with an "apostille." (At two dollars each, apostilles are embossed seals from your Secretary of State, required by the Hague Convention on International Adoptions, to confirm that the embossed seal of the notary you have used is legitimate.) We opened our home to social workers who examined our fitness to be parents ("Have you resolved your grief over infertility?" "Are your household chemicals locked up?" "Do you have a fire safety plan?" "What is your parenting philosophy?"). We went through all this, checked everything three times at least, turned in all the forms, then waited.

In the mid-nineties as we were making these decisions, the mass media were spewing cookie-cutter stories on two topics of vital importance to us. One was the "Eastern European adoption horror story." The Romanian orphanage scandal lit this fuse: Pictures blossomed everywhere, like mold, of children crammed into cribs, sometimes chained to them, and left alone to amuse themselves and each other for hours and days and months on end. Horror story after horror story ran of children, neglected in Eastern European orphanages and given loving homes by well-meaning Americans, who couldn't attach, or who had previously unknown physical debilities or developmental delays. The parents had been ingenious in their search for competent help, often to no avail: These children could not be fixed.

Another set of stories that emerged from a completely different venue—university-based research in child development—was inextricably linked to the adoption stories for us. These were the stories on the critical importance of life experience from zero to three. Many stories, based more on parental intuition than on science, stretched claims for the importance of early experience into the uterus, where the fetus hears its mother's heartbeat and respiration, its parents' voices, their music. One such story in *People* featured a picture of a famous actor piping Mozart into his then-wife's bulging belly. Every critical factor in the child's emotional and cognitive functioning could be enhanced or not in these critical early years. Deficits in stimulation could not easily—perhaps ever—be fully rectified. Influenced in part by this research, women were quitting work in droves to stay home and devote themselves full-time to enriching their babies' lives.

Many of my colleagues in the field of child maltreatment were child psychologists and clinical social workers. To a person, they stressed the importance of getting a child as young as possible—the closer to the womb, the better. Every day, every minute of interaction with a young child counts, and tells in later development. The further from the womb, the more risky the adoption and—the conclusion was inescapable—the less desirable the child. I had two tangled reactions to this advice. One strand cried, "How heartless!" What about the older children in orphanages—the one-year-olds, the two-year-olds, the three-year-olds—the darling little children, whom these experts would abandon to their sad fate? My colleagues were obviously right in their assessment of risk; and we *didn't* want to take on a highly troubled child. But still, where was the balance with humanism, with hope?

The second strand of my tangled reaction was tinged with desperation, because there was no chance of our getting a newborn baby internationally. In Russia, the youngest child available for adoption to us would be six months of age. For six months after a child is relinquished by her birth parents, only Russians have the opportunity to adopt her. Thereafter, unclaimed by her countrymen, she is supposed to be available for international adoption. But it is quite unusual to get a six-month-old baby, because birth mothers might not take their babies to the orphanage immediately; or because, clutching for hope, birth mothers might tell the orphanage director that they're coming back, delaying the baby's ultimate release date; or because the wheels of bureaucracy stop grinding for a while. Given all of these factors and others, babies from Russia were typically eight or nine or ten months of age when they became available, or even older. We *had* to believe that babies could thrive after early deprivation.

Further complicating our assessment of the risk we were taking was the murky information available about the children's health. Because some of the Russian people object to having their children adopted by foreigners, one of the laws on the books when we were planning to adopt stated that only unhealthy children could be placed for international adoption. The outstanding children were to stay in Russia, to help restore its greatness. The well-educated mother of a Russian student of Marc's assured us that her country let out no healthy children: They retain the best genes for themselves. We were angry with her for saying this, and frightened. Was she right? The first international agency we used—I'll call it OFIA—told us that, because of this rule, all children placed for international adoption in Russia had crazy diagnoses inscribed in their medical records: things like "intercranial hypertension" and "hip dysplasia." These diagnoses were an in-joke: They were to be ignored. Easy for them to say.

There *were* other possible diagnoses, however, that had to be taken seriously: Fetal Alcohol Syndrome, congenital syphilis, attachment disorder, AIDS, hepatitis, tuberculosis, hereditary insanity. Unfortunately, terrible problems like attachment disorder and hereditary insanity would likely not be disclosed on the medical forms because they wouldn't be known with any certainty by the caregivers. And diagnoses of AIDS, hepatitis, and tuberculosis were unreliable, given the state of the medical profession in Eastern Europe. Indeed, *given* the state of the medical profession there, your prospective child would be safer if she were not even tested for these diseases, since the cleanliness of needles used to administer the tests could not be guaranteed. The children could be infected with disease in the process of being tested for it.

We took all of this in. Marc is a pediatrician. We thought he would be able to detect better than many people some of the medical problems that might arise. Indeed, Marc argued, such problems are easier to see in older children than in infants. We both had some knowledge of child development, and thought we could detect worrisome behaviors that might denote attachment problems. We determined to be extremely careful. And then what else could we do? "We want a healthy child, as young as possible," we said, and, in our agnostic fashion, prayed. And we trusted our agency—which was, in many people's experience, exactly the wrong thing to do.

## 2

# "I Have a Little Girl for You"

I was sitting at my desk on a Friday evening in April 1997. Too jittery to do anything but open mail and sort it into new piles, I was nearing the bottom of my in-box, which had not seen the light of day for several weeks. Marc was due any minute to pick me up to go home and open the FedEx pack that we knew contained the referral of an amazing child—a beautiful child, the princess of the orphanage, developmentally excellent, eleven months old. I knew that in less than half an hour I would be looking for the first time at pictures of—surely—my new daughter. My heart fluttered, my empty stomach clenched. As I mechanically cleared out my in-box, my mind's eye is flooded with vivid images from the last few momentous weeks.

\* \* \*

We had heard all about this little girl the previous weekend. We had flown to New York City for the sole purpose of meeting the two Russian women who ran the orphanage where little Nina had lived since she was a tiny baby. The orphanage's administrative director, Elena, and the medical director, Dr. Christina, were the guests of OFIA. The orphanage they directed, in Ekaterinburg, Russia, was reputed to be one of the best in Eastern Europe. The children got lots of attention, had "music therapy," "water therapy," plenty of toys, outdoor exercise. Like many other international agencies, OFIA curried favor with Elena and Dr. Christina, supporting their premier orphanage with gifts of medicine, clothing, toys, equipment, and cash, and flying them to the U.S. occasionally to meet prospective parents. Every agency wanted referrals from this orphanage. Arlene, the founder and president of OFIA, enjoyed saying that the children she referred were from "the gold coast" of Eastern European orphanages, this one in Ekaterinburg among them. A referral from this place helped ease parents' manifold fears.

We had been invited to meet Elena and Dr. Christina because we were Arlene's current favorites. Several months earlier, we had each taken a day off of work and flown to New York to spend the day with her. This seemed to us an obvious step: How could she possibly match us with a child if she didn't know us? The cost of making the trip was a drop in the bucket in the adoption process. But apparently this level of effort was somewhat unusual, and helped single us out from the dozens of other couples who had recently turned to Arlene for help.

As we sat across the conference table for that first meeting in her cluttered office, smiling nervously, photo albums of waiting children open before us, our hearts in our mouths, we listened to her at first with a little wariness. Arlene talked a great deal and quickly—about her years on Wall Street, about her frequent travels overseas with tens of thousands of dollars on her person, about the scores of orphanages she had seen, orphanages she would and would not use. Speaking of her work with the boastful quality of a legend in her own mind, she clearly relished her god-like role as matchmaker between prospective parents and children. Still, we liked her. She was warm, friendly, enthusiastic, and, in fact, a committed humanitarian. More important, she liked us. We spent the day together, and bonded.

When, therefore, the good directors of this excellent orphanage in Ekaterinburg mentioned to Arlene the imminent availability of this very special little girl, she thought of us.

"Don't be nervous when you meet them," she instructed us. Nervous? Of course not! "Bring some flowers. Shake their hands, smile. Don't ask about this particular little girl. I'll tell you what to do when."

On a beautiful April Sunday afternoon we drove with our gift of flowers through the lush suburbs of Connecticut. The necessity of attending closely to a map helped distract us from our anxiety. Several other cars were parked in front of the huge American house. Inside the impeccably appointed home we found a vast downstairs family room, crammed with toys, where the get-together was being held. The other prospective parents were a lot like us: professional, mid-thirties and up, infertile, affluent, nervous. We stood about awkwardly clutching our flowers and making the kind of small talk prospective adoptive parents make (Where are you in the process? Thinking about it? Applying? Waiting for a referral? Waiting to travel? Recently returned? Where do you want to go? Are you hoping for a boy or a girl?), sizing each other up as potential rivals. But the only thing any of us wanted to do was stare at the two odd women who might have our children, gaze into their eyes to see if we could discern the future there, divine how to demonstrate our worthiness to them.

Dr. Christina was in her late fifties, wide, plump, and low to the ground, with an open, kind face, lined with fatigue and worry, large moles dotting it here and there. She was a woman who had spent her entire life taking care of children no one else would care for and then—if all went well—saying good-bye to them. Elena was smaller, thinner, with big lopsided glasses and a terrible cut of mousy brown hair—shy, sweet, homely, late forties. On Arlene's signal, we went over to greet them. We handed Dr. Christina our flowers and bobbed, smiling. They bobbed and smiled back. How are you? Welcome to America. We're so glad you could come. The interpreter swiftly translated our mundane conversation. Such a beautiful home. How nice of them to have us. Thank you for taking such good care of these children. How long will you stay? Where will you go next? We hope to adopt soon. We live in Chicago. Yes, we love it. It's a beautiful city.

"I think I have a little girl for you."

It was Elena. My breath stopped for a moment. "Pardon?"

"I think I have a little girl for you."

We stumbled over the next few sentences—Oh, wouldn't that be wonderful? We'd love to have a little girl! Oh, that would be great. Thank you so much! We didn't dare ask, "But, is it that special little girl Arlene told us about, the princess of the orphanage? *That's* the one we want." As we nervously toppled away from them, confused and wondering, Ludmilla caught us. She was one of Arlene's Russian staff people, and had met Nina. "You are very lucky. It is Nina, yes. She is the most beautiful baby I have ever seen, and I have seen many children."

As I looked through the papers in my in-box the following Friday evening, it was Dr. Christina I saw, and Elena; I heard their words, and Arlene's throaty laugh. The referral packet for Nina—health status, pictures, video, if we were lucky—was waiting for us at home. The phone rang at a few minutes to seven. Marc would pick me up in five minutes. I plucked the last piece of paper out of my in-box. It was an odd size, slightly longer than most. It had been stamped "received" some six weeks previously. "Dear sir," I read, already rising from my chair. "I wonder can you help me set up an organization like yours in Ekaterinburg, Russia." I sat back down and stared at the letter in disbelief. The writer wanted help establishing an organization for professionals in the field of child maltreatment in Ekaterinburg, Russia. Never before had I received a letter from Ekaterinburg. I don't believe in omens. But what *was* this? My heart racing, I made a copy of the letter and flew down to meet Marc.

We drove home, gave our car to the valet, asked the doorman for our packet, rode up to the twenty-fifth floor, hurried into the dining room to turn on the light, ripped open the envelope as we walked through the door, slid out the pictures, holding our breath. Here she is! Our daughter! For the first time! Oh, my . . . *What?! No! This* is not the child we had in mind. We rifled through the photos. They did not even slightly resemble the images we had, all unawares, been nursing in our hearts. *This was the wrong one!* How could they *do* this? What were they *thinking?*

The pictures, eight or so, showed Nina from a few months of age to just recently, at around ten months. There's Elena holding her, Dr. Christina, Arlene. Without realizing it, Marc and I had each, independently, built an image of the child who would be ours. We hadn't visualized a child when we had been trying to get pregnant; we had hoarded this secret pleasure—secret even from ourselves—until we were expecting a referral. My imagined baby was a slim laughing child with big dark eyes and curly dark hair. No one in either of our families fits this description; nevertheless, that was the image I had quietly cherished of the child who would be ours. Now we were staring at pictures of a chubby, solemn child, blonde hair cropped close to her head. As I glanced through her photos, grainy images of the anonymous hordes who persecuted Europe's Jews leapt rudely into my mind's eye. Our stomachs dropped out.

We didn't know, at the time, what biological parents know: that even when a child is born to you, you might be surprised and upset— even very upset—by the divergence between your fantasied baby (who is, of course, a miraculous amalgam of the best of both of you) and the actual baby who emerges. We were no different from any other new parents who are completely unprepared for their first reactions to their baby's looks. The difference between us and biological parents was that we had a choice.

"Oh man," joked a colleague when Marc confided our anguish the next day. "If we could have given back Joey, we would have!"

That's the funny kind of thing a biological parent can say, because, in fact, he *can't* "give back" his baby. The baby is, irrevocably, *his*. When we opened Nina's referral packet we were not in the least bit prepared for the emotional implications of the astounding, the impossible fact that adoption involves *choice*. Not as in, "We choose to adopt"; not even as in, "We choose to adopt *this kind* of child"; but as in, "We choose *this particular child* as our own."

We had read, like everyone else in the adoption process, how in the bad old days when adoption was stigmatized parents used to try to help children feel good about being adopted by telling them that they had *chosen* them, their special babies. *Other* babies, biological babies, just happened; their parents didn't have any choice in the matter. This tactic, many now argue, was unwise because it made kids feel insecure: Maybe they had to be special in a particular way in order to *be* chosen and *stay* chosen. Seeking to instill security it instead highlights the gut-turning fact that becoming someone's child—or someone's parent—through adoption is not natural or inevitable, or even irrevocable, as it is when it happens through biology. There is *choice* involved. But this basic reality had not filtered down into our consciousness as a factor in *our* lives until we looked at the pictures of this lovely child and said in our hearts, "No."

Arlene had told us that we had a couple days to make our decision. That there was absolutely *no* pressure to say yes to this child. (Even though she *was* the princess of the orphanage; even though she *had* been picked especially for us.) That people say "no" for all kinds of reasons, no questions asked. One person, she told us, declined a referral because the child reminded her of a hated former roommate. *Fine.* You have to feel good about it. It's chemistry. No one can explain it. Don't worry about it. There'll be another child if this one's not for you. *Your child is out there.*

But this reassurance does not calm us in the least. Because planted in this permission to refuse a referral is the assumption that we will *know* when to refuse and when to accept—just know in our guts. Many times, at meetings and gatherings for adoptive families and prospective parents, we had heard adoptive parents tell stories about the "love at first sight" that told them they had found the right child for them. In fact, one adoptive mother, an officer on OFIA's board of directors, told us matter-of-factly that weekend, during our frantic search for the right response to Nina's referral, that if we were not experiencing love at first sight, Nina was simply the wrong child for us, and we should move on.

People love this "love at first sight" myth. It takes choice away: It means that the thing is *destined.* You're just helpless in the face of this inclination that is bigger, wiser than you. Contemplating Nina's photos, trying to make sense of our first reaction, Marc and I feared that this myth might be true. But we didn't entirely trust it. We hadn't loved each *other* at first sight. We had needed considerable experience together before we found ourselves in love. Life had taught us that guts are important; it had also taught us that guts can be wrong. But how on earth were we supposed to figure out, in seventy-two hours, from photographs, whether or not this child, born of other people, should be our own?

Our first step was to focus on the filtrum. The filtrum is that vertical indentation between your nose and your upper lip. A flat filtrum is potentially a bad sign, one of the symptoms of Fetal Alcohol Syndrome. Nina's wasn't flat. To the contrary, Nina's filtrum appeared on our first examination of her photos to be *too* prominent. We thought maybe it was her filtrum that was standing between us, making it impossible for us to love her.

We had to go to New York City again that weekend, for a professional conference for Marc and a pleasure trip for me. On Saturday morning, sick at heart, we tucked Nina's photos into my carry-on bag and headed for O'Hare. We left ourselves some extra time to critically scrutinize other people's filtrums. We were pretty sure that we would see prominent filtrums only on people who were highly unattractive to us. But we were surprised. A lot of fine-looking people had prominent filtrums. It occured to us to check our own. Come to find out, *I* have a prominent filtrum. Okay, it wasn't the filtrum; we could accept that. What *was* it, then? Was it the shape of her head, the placement of her eyes, the shape of her mouth? No, no, no.

We kept scrutinizing the pictures, searching in them for the obstacle that lay in our hearts.

Other people, looking at Nina's pictures, didn't see the flaws we saw. The night we opened the envelope we took the photos to a party and surreptitiously showed another couple, who were friends of ours. She's *cute*, they said. We didn't believe them. Their own boy was so adorable, we assumed they were being pitying. The next night, in New York, a woman friend of mine said, "Why, you guys, she's *cute!*" We didn't believe her. She was single and hungry for a family of her own. *Any* kid would look cute to her. Alternatively, maybe she was just being nice.

While Marc was in medical meetings talking with colleagues about our dilemma, I haunted the Central Park Zoo for hours, tears welling uncontrollably, scrutinizing happy parents and children. Could *that* be my child? Could *that*? Could I love *that* one? How am I supposed to *know*?

We kept examining the pictures.

Finally, my best girlfriend, an experienced mom—who confided she had needed months to love her second biological child—offered, long-distance, the truest wisdom and most important guidance we have ever received: "Use your heads now," Franny said, "not your hearts. I have no doubt that if you bring home this little girl you will love her with all your hearts, so forget about the heart part. Use your heads. What did you ask for?"

"A young, healthy girl."

"What are you being offered?"

"A young, healthy girl."

"Just say yes."

True love is not always instantaneous.

We kept looking at the photos, drinking them in, and lo and behold, she started to look . . . familiar. Like she could be ours. In fact, strangely enough, she began to look just like the baby we had been wanting for so long.

On Monday night back home in Chicago, we called Arlene and

said "yes" to Nina. With a sly smile in her voice, knowing full well how her gift would rattle us, Arlene treated us to a phrase we had never heard before: "Your daughter."

After we said yes, we couldn't stop looking at Nina's photos, which we spread out on the dining room table. We were giddy. We pulled out the list of names we had been working on, and crossed off the last few until the name we loved best was left standing: Natalie. Meaning rebirth. Birth. Accepting her, we are reborn, born as parents. Also for Nathan, Marc's beloved, Russian-born Grandpa Bob's given name. Her middle name would be Marian, after my mother. I seized the referral sheet again, eager to absorb everything I could of our new daughter off this one-page form. We had taken in and dismissed the usual dire diagnoses—in Natalie's case, perinatal central nervous system injury; intercranial hypertension; syndrome of neuro-reflex hyperexcitability; hyperbilirubinemia neonatorum; hip joint dysplasia. It was obvious from the photos and from the testimony of Arlene and Ludmilla, who had met her and held her, that this child was perfectly healthy. Birth date, birth weight, APGAR scores, placement date, father's name, mother's name. For the first time, I noticed her birth mother's name: Natalya.

We had given her, unwittingly, her birth mother's name. I thought of the letter from the lawyer in Ekaterinburg, seeking my assistance in establishing an organization like mine in their city. Perhaps this *was* meant to be.

## 3

# Are You My Baby?

The seven of us are milling about in a huge, colorful playroom, ready to jump out of our skins. We are in the orphanage, waiting to meet our children for the first time. Much of the spotless linoleum floor is covered with brightly colored area rugs. The white walls are adorned with murals in primary colors: boy and girl matryoshka dolls, a country dance, a spreading tree, its branches filled with flowers and birds. Little wooden folk-painted chairs line part of one wall; cylindrical cushioned stools line the perimeter of one rug. We gaze about, impressed. The room is littered with large plastic American-made toys—rocking elephant, huge yellow ball for rolling on, slide, seesaw, trucks. It is hot, over 80 degrees already, before ten in the morning. The room is bright. One wall is lined with screenless windows, all thrown open, looking over the driveway and front entrance. Sun pours in. Sheer white curtains stir in the slight breeze. A large plastic log-cabin playhouse dominates one end of the room. I crawl into this log cabin, and emerge at the window, waving at my fellow travelers. Marc snaps a picture. I look happy.

I am operating on pure adrenaline. Just two days earlier I had been in Miami Beach where, halfway through my organization's national conference, I had said good-bye to colleagues with whom I had worked for nearly ten years. It had been a punishing process, planning the conference, running the organization, preparing for the annual meeting I will miss for the first time, helping the board find my permanent replacement. I fly away exhausted, conflicted—the job has been my life; I have been depleted and fed by it; I can't imagine life without the job, and can't wait to get away from it. My new life begins here, in this room, with the baby we are about to meet.

Marc and I have traveled from Chicago with these other five, Tony and Brigit, Angie and Stewart, and Sylvia, who has traveled alone to pick up her second Russian child. Her husband is back at home with little Anastasia.

We seven had met as a group once before, in Sylvia's living room, to prepare for this trip. Brigit—short, pert, red-haired, freckled, a laughing Irishwoman. Lovely brogue, flashing eyes, open and warm. Tony, her husband—bald but for a band of short, black hair around his head, round all over, as Italian as Brigit is Irish, warm, open, hearty, funny. He sings opera in Chicago and teaches private students. A booming voice, booming ready laugh. His heart permanently on his sleeve. Angie—pretty face, sweet smile, thick, wavy, shoulder-length dark hair, stout. Bright woman, quiet; a reference librarian at a distinguished institution. Stewart, her husband—long, lanky, loud-mouthed. An advertising man. He seems to be all over the place at once, his long limbs flailing, his honking laugh, talk talk talk. Sylvia, an accountant with a Fortune 500 company, is a board member of OFIA, and presents herself as the experienced one, very much in control. If you have any questions, just ask her. Her superior knowledge of the process is reassuring on the one hand: It is good to have someone along who actually knows what to expect. But Sylvia's air of settled authority is a little obnoxious, too, and her bemused calm takes some of the excitement out of our experience—the sense of adventure, of newness, of being on an equal footing on our lives' greatest undertaking. Her husband, in and out of the house with Anastasia, says almost nothing to the group.

We are waiting for the call from Arlene that will initiate the formal part of our meeting. She will walk us through our upcoming trip via speakerphone. "Did you bring pictures?" Brigit asks me quietly.

"We did, actually. Did you?"

And with that, as if part of a single organism with very sensitive antennae, everyone moves swiftly with the same intent: to compare referral photos. How did we do? we all think. Does our kid measure up?

It's been about three weeks since we got Natalie's referral packet, and we're still fickle. Sometimes she looks like our dream baby. Sometimes . . . not. We haven't seen any video of her yet, haven't seen her in action—haven't, of course, gotten to touch her, hold her, play with her, drink in her presence. We did receive a more recent set of photos, just a couple of days ago. But they don't help me. In them, she looks uncannily like Boris Yeltsin. We have pretty mixed feelings about Boris Yeltsin. In a couple of other photos she looks more like Dwight Eisenhower. We feel better about Eisenhower than about Yeltsin but still, it's hard to imagine cuddling the late president. We don't yet reliably see our baby in these photos.

So we bring them out tentatively. What will the others think? Will their babies be just so much cuter it's tormenting? Will they gloat? Will they try to make us feel better? Or will Natalie shine as the princess of the orphanage she's reputed to be, and give *us* the advantage? We have no idea what to expect.

Sylvia's two-and-a-half-year-old is ordinary, and in any case of little interest to us. We're interested in kids Natalie's age. Tony and Brigit's boy is about Natalie's age, but we have the same problem with his photos as we do with Natalie's: He doesn't jump out from them and claim our hearts. We'd have to work at that one, too. Angie and Stewart's boy, though, is another story. What a beauty! There's the curly dark hair we had imagined, the huge dark eyes. There's the baby we had envisioned for ourselves before we knew we were envisioning him. I soak in his image hungrily. Why did Angie and Stewart get him, instead of us? *"Oh,"* I say, tearing my eyes away from him to look into theirs, "he's beautiful! Really." They beam and reclaim their photos. They know it. I take back Natalie's photos and stare hard at them, struggling to see past Boris Yeltsin and into the likelihood of love. The phone rings.

What Arlene tells us about Ekaterinburg we've known for three weeks from our Internet search. It's the third largest city in Russia, after Moscow and St. Petersburg. It is in the Ural mountains, in Siberia, about twenty-five miles west of the Asian border. Originally named for Catherine the Great, it was renamed Sverdlovsk after the Russian revolution, in honor of the Bolshevik who killed the czar and his family there. During the Cold War, Ekaterinburg became Russia's military-industrial capital, her primary source of military hardware and biological weapons, hermetically sealed off to Westerners. Arlene has this trip down like clockwork, and walks us through every step. A comprehensive travel-preparation notebook will arrive next week. The following week, or maybe the week after, depending on when the courts call our cases, our tickets and itinerary will arrive. On the Saturday before our court date we will fly to Frankfurt. If we can afford it, we should pay for a night at the airport Hilton in Frankfurt so we can get some sleep during a six-hour layover: We need to arrive rested, if possible. We will arrive in Ekaterinburg late on Sunday night. Monday morning, we will go to the orphanage to meet our babies. Tuesday morning we will go to court to adopt them. If all goes well, we will take custody of them and fly to Moscow on Friday morning.

"Wait, wait!" Tony shouts. "Why do we have to wait so long to take custody of the children? If we adopt them on Tuesday, why do we not get to take them until Friday?"

I am miffed at this suggestion, too. Who is going to keep us from our babies, and why? What right do they have to keep them if they're officially *ours*?

"This is just the way it's done," Arlene says firmly. "There's a lot of paperwork to do to complete the adoption, and you can't take custody until it's done. You'll be visiting, though, at least once every day, probably twice."

Her tone brooks no disagreement, so Tony pipes down.

If we get to Moscow on Friday, if all the paperwork has gone as planned, then we spend the weekend as tourists in Moscow, with our children. Monday morning, we go to the American embassy, where a doctor will clear the kids for entry into the U.S., and their visas will be issued. Tuesday morning, very early, we will head back to Frankfurt from Moscow. We will arrive home in Chicago—if all goes according to plan—on Wednesday, ten days after we left. Worst-case scenario, if paperwork glitches arise, is that we'll go to Moscow on Monday or Tuesday rather than on Friday, and will arrive home on Friday or Saturday. OFIA staff, translators, and drivers will be with us every step of the way. They are there to help us. They know the system. We are to do what they say.

Arlene stresses a couple of points. "Now, you guys, you need to take some gifts." She says this kind of off-handedly, but it's obvious from her repetition and specificity that we are not to overlook this point of etiquette. We scribble furiously. We are to take gifts for functionaries, some big (watches, perfumes, scarves, Michael Jordan paraphernalia), some small (coffees, chocolates, picture frames). Don't wrap them: Bring a bunch of gift bags and tissue paper so you can throw together the appropriate gift as needed. And, we are to take gifts for the orphanage, and the more the better: medicines, clothing, and toys, toys, toys. We should each bring, in fact, a very large box of toys for the orphanage. *Ka-ching, ka-ching.*

Another key point: We are not to tell anyone why we are in Russia. Some people do not approve of international adoption of Russian children. There could be trouble—not major trouble, but maybe a little trouble. Who needs any trouble?

"Arlene," I begin. I tell her about the incredible letter I received from the man who wanted my help setting up an organization like mine in Ekaterinburg. I have already sent him a box of material, but wouldn't it be amazing to meet him? "I would love to contact him while we're there. Would that be possible?"

"Uh, no. I don't think so. No, no, no. I mean, maybe he's a great guy, but who knows? Who knows who he is? We just don't want any, *any* curveballs. Besides, you're going to be busy. You're not going to have time to do something like that."

I think this is a little cold. What does she *think*? That this guy somehow knew when he wrote to me that I would be coming to Ekaterinburg to adopt, and he could lure me into a trap to prevent me from denuding his country of another child? *I* didn't know when he wrote to me that I'd be traveling to Ekaterinburg! I toy for a few seconds with the thought of thwarting her will and contacting him. But it is obvious that I'll never win this one, and would be stupid to try. Arlene has this process down tight as a drum.

"Listen, guys: You are there to adopt. You are not there as tourists, you are not there to sightsee: You are there to *adopt*. That's it. Got it?"

The airport in Ekaterinburg is a huge Quonset hut made of corrugated steel. We arrive from Frankfurt around ten P.M. We have said not a word to anyone about the purpose of our trip, although it has been somewhat difficult: We are bursting with the news, and find it difficult to suppress it in response to the questions that arise during the polite chitchat with fellow passengers that often punctuates international travel. It has been nerve-wracking to feel that we must travel incognito while lugging huge boxes of toys. But here we are at last, safe and sound.

We emerge from the airplane into the twilit June night, and gasp. Arching spectacularly over the entire horizon is a vivid rainbow, glowing in the setting sun. An omen, surely. A personal omen for each of us, stepping off that plane. But we cannot record it: we have been warned to take no pictures, inside or outside the airport. We amble across the tarmac through the warm liquid night under the rainbow, drinking it in, memorizing it.

Our euphoria is snuffed out the moment we step inside the airport. Inside is scary. It is eerily quiet. Hundreds of people wait in passport lines, silently. Guards and officials are thin-lipped, stern-looking, all business. The airport is barren, all concrete floors and plastic and steel chairs and benches, some of them placed at odd angles, as if they had been dropped in mid-move. The steel and plastic booths that harbor the passport inspectors are fitted with mirrors positioned overhead so the officials can see the back of you as well as the front. We seem to have entered a time warp. It's spooky. Hasn't anyone told these people that the Cold War is over? We fall into line, silent with the rest of them, sober and slightly frightened. We hope the OFIA people are waiting for us as promised on the other side.

At baggage claim, Marc is separated from us and questioned. Why are we here? He has a box full of toys. Why?

While he is being questioned, I am searching for my big suitcase, which seems to have gone missing. Airline staff are friendly and helpful, in English. *They* know what year it is. They are terribly sorry; perhaps my bag did not make it onto the plane. They will bring it on the next flight, on Tuesday night. But that suitcase contains the beautiful blue, flowered dress I was going to wear when Natalie first saw me, so she would love me faster! It contains the nice business dress I brought to wear to court, to impress the judge with my suitability as a mom. They are very sorry, but can give me only a set of toiletries and the promise of $50.00 reimbursement for the cost of a new dress.

At about the same moment, Marc and I rejoin the group, which has been joined by an OFIA driver and translator. Marc, sweating bullets, has been allowed to keep the box of toys.

An hour or so later, we arrive at our apartment. It is bad on the outside—a typical Soviet-style concrete-block tower, surrounded by weeds. The elevator is tiny, creaking. We are disoriented. We can't all fit. Is this safe for any of us? Will we be murdered, or die in an elevator wreck? We disperse onto separate floors. Inside, our apartment is brand-new, spotless, spacious. A full kitchen, a living room, a bedroom, a nice bath. We are comfortable. We get to bed around one A.M.

Seven hours later we are milling about in the dust in front of the apartment building, waiting to be picked up and ferried to the orphanage. My clothes are about thirty-six hours old. Sylvia assures me that our adoption will not be blocked by my lack of appropriate clothing in court; she will lend me a spare dress that will do just fine.

Except for experienced Sylvia, we are all so nervous we can barely speak. The usually voluble Stewart is silent, compulsively videotaping everything around him.

Just in the last week we have received a videotape of Natalie that has gone a long way toward allaying our doubts. In motion she looks less like a world leader and more like a great and interesting little kid. We have studied the two-minute tape until it's been etched in our brains and we can play it back without equipment. There she is, pointing to the video camera; there she is, reaching for the camera; there she is, rocking back and forth holding onto the little fence that surrounds her play area, as if she's revving up to attempt an escape. Kind-sounding voices murmur softly in the background, apparently giving her directions, the only word discernible to us "Nina, Nina." There she is, climbing onto the plastic rocking horse; reaching for the matryoshka doll the caregiver hands her (only the caregiver's hand visible); exploring the doll; looking for the bottom that has fallen off; reaching for a hand to steady her as she climbs off the rocking horse to get the bottom of the doll; clambering back onto the horse holding doll pieces in both hands. What intelligence! What initiative! What beautiful eyebrows! How cute, that pursing of her lips in effort!

The orphanage is a concrete, three-story, U-shaped structure that wraps around an asphalt driveway and parking area. A rutted, partially paved road distances it slightly from a potholed street lined with run-down apartment complexes. The seven of us cluster outside on the long raised stoop in the sunshine, waiting for permission to enter. It is all we can do to suppress little yelps of anxiety. The second-floor windows of the wing to our right fill with two-, three-, and four-year-old children who peer down at us until their caregivers peel them away.

"Hey, I think that's your little girl," says Stewart. He is looking through his videocamera up to the left.

Marc and I follow the angle of his camera and see her there, partially obscured in shadow behind a screen. The woman holding her smiles down at us. She knows us, from the video we have sent—a video Marc's dad filmed in his basement rec room, beret jauntily perched on his head. In it, we read to her, we sing Brahms's Lullaby. We identify ourselves as Mommy and Daddy, and say, "Bye-bye, we'll see you soon!" We sent the video along with another couple who had traveled a couple of weeks before, in a little gift bag that also contained the book we had read and a little stuffed dog that we featured in our video. The dog was wearing a tiny baby T-shirt that I had had imprinted with a photo of the two of us smiling at her. I had sat at the Goodman Theatre with the tiny T-shirt plastered against my body under my black business suit, listening to David Mamet read one night after work. I had worn the T-shirt against my skin for two full days, hoping to infuse it with my smell. Smell is so important to bonding. Perhaps she would pick up just a bit of mine this way. Peering up at her there for a moment as her caregiver points us out to her, we notice that she is holding the T-shirted dog. She looks flushed and pretty, peering down at us for that moment. Then she and her caregiver disappear, as quickly as they had emerged, into the gloom behind the curtains.

We are finally let in and ushered upstairs—the walls here, too, decorated with brightly painted murals, even the stair risers sprouting bright, painted flowers—and into the playroom. We mill about nervously, exploring the room, rolling the huge ball back and forth. I worry that Nina won't like us somehow. That, somehow, we won't like her. I dive into the plastic log cabin. Stewart's videocamera is glued to his face.

A nurse walks in with Pasha, Sylvia's two-year-old. He runs up to her and they begin playing immediately. Minutes pass.

Another nurse walks in with Bobby, Angie and Stewart's baby, and pours him into Angie's arms. Stewart stops videotaping as they bend over him and begin to coo. Minutes pass.

A nurse walks in with Frank, Tony and Brigit's baby. They take him over to a corner of the room and hunker over him.

Marc and I look at the other couples with their kids, listen to the happy little sounds they are making. We look at each other. We stare at the doorway. A nurse walks in briskly with Natalie. She is all dolled up in a dark-green velvet dress with white lace collar and cuffs. Lacy little socks pulled up to her knees, and black patent shoes. She is quiet and calm as the nurse strides toward me. When the nurse thrusts her into my arms and walks away, Natalie shatters the peace with shrieks. No one else's baby cries. Just ours. She wails at the top of her lungs. We know that this is a good thing: She is *supposed* to protest when she's separated from a trusted caregiver and thrust into a stranger's arms. This is *good*; she's *attached*. It is traumatizing nonetheless.

Instinctively I hold her close and bounce her gently, walking slowly around the room, trailed by Marc, and whispering softly into her ear, in a slow singsong, "Nina Natalie, Nina Natalie, Nina Natalie, don't be afraid, it's okay, Nina Natalie, don't be afraid, don't be afraid."

We, of course, are terrified.

It is minutes before her sobs tentatively subside. We have brought with us, in a gift bag filled with crinkly silver foil, another stuffed dog. We risk sitting down with her to introduce the gift. She is fascinated with the crinkly paper for a few minutes, and then resumes her wails. And that is how our morning goes: crying bouncing walking whispering crinkling paper crying bouncing walking whispering finding the dog crying bouncing walking whispering. Eventually she falls asleep in my arms.

The next day we go to court and adopt her, and I cry.

That afternoon, and twice a day every day thereafter, we visit the kids. If we wish to take them outside in the 90-degree heat, the caregivers swathe them in knitted caps and sweaters to protect them from drafts. The children swelter, the little red bites that dot their faces (for in their screenless wards they lie unconscious at night, feasts for bugs) disappearing into the general flush of their skin. As soon as we are a little distance away, we relieve them of layers of clothing. Every time Natalie is handed to us, she cries a little less. We joke with the others that we are bonding with her tearstained, snot-covered face. Although we had been indignant that our child would be kept from us by the authorities after they had legitimated her adoption, for the first few days the idea of taking custody makes us shudder. What on earth would we do with her? We are happy to have smiling, warm caregivers to hand her back to when our visits are over.

One day, when we are outside on the grounds, feeding her from the glass bottle of sugar water they have provided, a soft rubber nipple pulled over the top, a woman heading for the orphanage stops and peers at us. She takes a few steps closer, a tentative smile on her face. "Nina!" she affirms, nodding. Big smile. "Nina! Mama, Papa?" she asks, gesturing at us. "Da." We smile back, nodding. "Mama, Papa." She beams and bobs, apparently congratulating us in Russian, and continues toward the orphanage. A caregiver, we assume. Her fondness for Nina fills her eyes. Do I imagine the air of wistfulness?

Another caregiver haunts me. She is the one who is holding Natalie in the window the first time we see her, who hands Natalie to me several times. She is an older woman with an extremely kind, loving face, long and creased, beautiful eyes graced by crow's-feet, her long, straight, dark, gray-streaked hair pulled into a low bun on her neck, strands of hair escaping and flying around her face. A face to love. A face *I* could love. A face Natalie probably loves. She smiles at us warmly, her eyes full of kindness, when she hands us Natalie. Looking at her halfway through the week, I am struck by jealousy, and sadness, and doubt. I do not love this child yet, as she does. Is it really right to take Natalie away from this woman who loves her and whom she loves? Is it the best thing for Natalie? But yes, of course, right? The nurse probably has children of her own at home. She is too old to raise another child. She seems to be happy for Natalie and for us.

Natalie rarely smiles, but Marc finally gets grins out of her on our third morning with her. We are offered the use of strollers to take our children for walks on the grounds—strollers we have seen packed with three or four little children, all wrapped in knits, out for the air—and Marc quickly exceeds the limits of propriety by initiating a game of chicken. I stand in the middle of the path and Marc roars the stroller toward me at top speed, veering to miss me at the last possible moment. Natalie throws her head back and squeals in delight, her eyes disappearing into folds and her lips into thin lines.

By the fourth day, she looks back at us quizzically when we hand her back to the nurse. "Where are you going?" she seems to wonder. For the first time, we feel we are ready to take her with us the next time we meet.

While our children nap, we get to know the city of their birth, taking lots of pictures to show them later. Ekaterinburg is run-down, dusty, weedy. We see dirty, raggedy kids catching free rides on the coupling hitches of tram cars. Shriveled old women—called "babushkas" for their head scarves—selling dried fish and wilted flowers, cutting tall grass with scythes, sweeping sidewalks with bunches of sticks, begging around the cathedrals, refusing to let you take their picture for free. We visit the site of the czar's murder, visit the monument to Russian soldiers killed in Afghanistan, visit the border between Europe and Asia, visit a local bazaar, where we all buy small keepsakes for our children that fall apart before we get home. In a lovely restaurant one afternoon, a table full of attractive middle-aged ladies divines the purpose of our visit and applauds us, beaming. Thank you for loving our children.

* * *

While we are having this experience with Natalie, the others are having their experiences. Sylvia and Pasha are unremarkable to us. He is a pistol, but Sylvia is comfortable with him—with her relationship to him, her ability to set limits, everything. She seems to have no anxiety about the adoption. It is different with the others.

Tony and Brigit had lost their biological son at thirteen months of age to a rare brain disorder just two years before our trip together. They had told Arlene that they wanted a little girl—that they couldn't cope with trying to love another little boy. They got a referral surprisingly quickly. But, even to their untrained eyes, the signs of Fetal Alcohol Syndrome in the child's face were obvious. They sent the referral packet to one of the first pediatricians in the U.S. to specialize in evaluating children adopted from other countries. He confirmed their suspicions, and they declined the referral. Slightly miffed, it seemed to them, Arlene told them that if they wanted another referral quickly they would have to accept a boy, as healthy girls were much harder to find. They reluctantly agreed to consider boys, and shortly thereafter had accepted the referral of a child about Natalie's age.

But when little Frank-to-be was presented to them at the orphanage, they discovered that he had a large flat plane on his head. These flat planes are not uncommon among children who have been left lying in cribs for long periods of time. The head rounds out eventually once the child is up and about more. But kids weren't supposed to have been left lying around so much in *this* orphanage, the crème de la crème of Russian orphanages. And little Frank didn't have the bald spot that usually graces the flat plane produced by such neglect. Having recently lost a young son to a brain disorder, Tony and Brigit were distraught.

Arlene had warned us that the other parents we were traveling with might lean on Marc—a pediatric intensivist and pulmonologist—to allay any anxieties they might have about their children. She was right. Tony and Brigit turned to Marc, who tore himself away from Natalie to evaluate little Frank as best he could, to ask the questions he thought needed to be asked of Dr. Christina and Arlene, and to give Tony and Brigit the best advice he could generate with the information he had—which was that Frank was probably just fine. It took Tony and Brigit about twenty-four hours to resolve their concerns and determine to go forward. Arlene apologized to us over a crackling phone line for their foolishness and dependence and naivete. We were shocked. We were there with them; we could feel their fear and grief. *Their* reaction was understandable; it was Arlene's condescension that jarred.

Stewart and Angie were concerned about their little boy, too. This dark-eyed, curly-haired beauty was a little listless, and didn't make good eye contact with them. Stewart and Angie didn't demand the same kind of attention to their child as Tony and Brigit did, so we didn't pay that much attention. We were preoccupied with our own process with Natalie, and with Tony and Brigit's concerns.

On Friday morning we gather around the round conference table in Dr. Christina's cluttered office. Our babies will be delivered to us there, naked as the day they were born. We are all equipped with diapers and new clothes, thrilled and a little frightened at the prospect of dressing our babies for the first time. Stewart jokes with Marc: "Yeah, yeah, Natalie's the princess of the orphanage, *they say*. But you haven't seen her naked yet, have you? Watch: You're going to discover she's a hermaphrodite." We laugh nervously. We *haven't* seen her naked yet.

Making small talk with Dr. Christina, Tony discovers that she is an opera fan—that, in fact, her daughter is an opera singer. Tony, sweet

Tony, his heart full of love for his little Frank with the flat plane, wants to sing to her in gratitude, to serenade her in thanks. He begins singing "Climb Every Mountain" at the top of his lungs for Dr. Christina, all the way through, his thundering tenor bouncing off all the bare walls and probably waking anyone who might have been sleeping within a quarter-mile of the orphanage. We expect at any moment to hear a chorus of wails of woken children begin to surge along with his sailing voice. We sit in embarrassed silence, Dr. Christina beaming.

Just as the last reverberations die away the nurses file in—perhaps they have been waiting in the wings to make their entrance—holding our babies. Friends have told me that, cradling their babies for the first time, they are overwhelmed with wonder: I can't believe we made this baby! As Natalie is handed into my arms, I too experience awe. *I can't believe they are giving us this baby!* I look at the nurse, and back at Natalie. Do they realize that this is a real human being?

She doesn't cry when she is put into my arms. She is not a hermaphrodite.

In the bustle of diapering and dressing, we don't notice that Angie and Stewart are handed a packet of small white pills. What are these? they ask. The answer they get from Dr. Christina somehow doesn't translate. All they clearly understand is that their son is to get two a day.

As we climb into the van to go to the airport, I glance at the orphanage for one last look. There, in the window where we first glimpsed Natalie, is a small cluster of the women who had cared for our children, come to the windows to see them off. There is the special one I fancy Natalie loves, the older one with the beautiful, kind eyes, peering down, smiling, waving. I am startled, and sad for her, and jealous. I smile and wave back, but I also turn Natalie so she won't see her old nurse. I don't want Natalie to want her, don't want her to be torn, don't want her to feel sad, to start wailing to go back. She is mine now. I want her to focus on me.

Walking across the tarmac to the Ural Air jet, Marc and I pause again to consider: *Ural Air?* Ural Air is an offshoot of Aeroflot, which would have been bad enough. Aeroflot had recently suffered a public relations setback when a pilot's son, sitting on his daddy's lap learning to fly, had crashed an airplane full of people into a mountainside. As we climb the stairs into the cabin, we can see brushstrokes on the fuselage. The plane had recently been repainted—by hand. The only consolation is that if the plane goes down, we all die together.

When Marc leans back in his seat, settling in, he falls backward, his head coming perilously close to the lap of the vodka-soaked stranger seated behind him. Several seats in the plane are broken like this—unintended lounge seats. Sitting up ramrod-straight, we poke at the homemade chicken dinner served on the flight, on ceramic dishes under wrinkled aluminum foil. The engine hums reassuringly.

Saturday and Sunday we are tourists in Moscow staying at the elegant old Metropol Hotel just off Red Square. Pictures show Natalie on my lap in our room with her hand in a twelve-dollar glass of orange juice; Natalie asleep in her stroller in Red Square, the golden domes of the Kremlin surrounding her, the circus-colored domes of St. Basil's behind her; Natalie on my lap in a little bar on Red Square with stained glass windows where we have stopped to order cold drinks, both of us flushed and damp from heat. On the way to the famous Arbat Street bazaar where we buy more durable keepsakes for our babies, Natalie vomits prodigiously all over me and her new outfit. She goes easily to the other mothers, who are only too happy to hold her, while I attempt to clean up. I am annoyed with her apparent murkiness about who her mommy is.

Monday morning we are rousted at six A.M. to ensure that we are first in line at the American embassy. Inside, I size up other babies. A couple of darling six-month-old girls attract my attention. Arlene had claimed it was virtually impossible to get healthy babies so young. Marc and I initiate conversation with the parents. Where do they live? What agency did they use? Where did their babies come from? We experience a moment of envy until Natalie demands our attention again.

Tuesday morning we are up at four A.M. for the seven-thirty A.M. flight out of Moscow. In the airport in Frankfurt hours later, sitting on my lap, Natalie floods her diaper. Her clothes and mine are soaked with her urine. She turns to Brigit for help. Although I have had moments of infidelity myself, I am hurt by hers. "Your mother," I clarify a little testily as I cart her off to the bathroom, "is the one who is covered with your poop, pee, vomit, and snot."

We had been warned about all kinds of horrors our kids could inflict on us in flight—screaming and flailing because of the air pressure changes, loud noises, fear, fatigue. We had all heard, like everyone else in the world, about adoptive parents who had reached the end of their ropes and beaten their Eastern European children on the long trip home. We were counseled to avoid snapping by being prepared for great stress, to bring a myriad of toys and books and games and audiotapes to entertain the babies on the way home. Natalie's response to all the stimulation is to be amused and wide awake for eighteen of the twenty hours we are in transit. Happily wired. She will not leave my lap. When I get up to stretch and relieve myself, she hollers until I get back. By the time we get home, she is beginning to focus on me and I on her. Our journey together has begun.

## 4

# My Little Bunny

It was a beautiful fall day, warm and sunny, as I poked along a quiet street in downtown Chicago behind a toddling Natalie, completely engrossed in everything that engrossed her—grass poking out between sidewalk slabs, a squirrel scuttling up a nearby tree, a jet roaring overhead. "You *see*," a confident young voice pierced my concentration. "*That's* what you end up *doing*!" Two young women in business suits breezed by me, having been debating, apparently, the attractions of quitting work to stay home with children. The observation about my stupefying afternoon clearly carried the point.

I knew exactly what they meant. Six months earlier I could barely conceive of staying home with a child. But having made the unimaginable leap, I discovered what so many other women have discovered: that when you are *in love with* your baby, all that stupefying stuff isn't stupefying, it's fascinating. You're simply not in your right mind. It's straight out of *A Midsummer Night's Dream*. You're besotted. Even your lover's belches charm. Natalie's respiration was music to my ears. Marc and I had been amply warned by friends and family about the manifold difficulties involved in parenting, but we had had no inkling that parenthood would be the only source of unadulterated joy in our lives, that for hours on end we would revel in pure love for our daughter.

True, we did not live in a permanent state of bliss. There were afternoons at the playground that seemed like months. It emerged before too long that Natalie's will was every bit as strong as mine, and we did battle. But I was absolutely madly in love with her, and the feeling was mutual. For weeks after we got home, she would not let go of me for one moment of her waking hours. This desperate clutching—*This* one is *not* going to get away!—was both disconcerting and endearing. One afternoon, in some exasperation at my predicament, I snapped a picture of her from above with her arms wrapped around my knees, staring up into the lens, looking for my face. I called a child psychologist friend: "I know what this is, I know she needs to know I'll be here for her, I don't want to do anything to suggest to her that I *won't* be here. But how long is this going to *last*?" I just needed a sense of how long it would be before I had my body back, unencumbered by a twenty-five-pound baby. I carried her so much I developed a piercing pain in my left forearm and wrist that I thought must be a stress fracture. My knees ached from climbing all the stairs in our three-story house with an extra twenty-five pounds attached to my hip. At the first family party we attended after we got back, she would go to no one but us: not grandmas or grandpas, not aunts or uncles. She did not endear herself to others with this exclusivity, but she endeared herself to us. When Marc and I went out, leaving her with a kind, sweet young woman she knew, she screamed as if she were being murdered. She ululated, she wrapped herself around us, she clung like a monkey. She spent much of her day chanting my name in an endless chain: "Mamamamamamamamamamamamamamamama-mama." We had it at last, that precious little hand resting all unaware on a loved parent's shoulder. To me, that little touch became the most divine experience on earth. It transmitted a deeply calming electricity.

Only now, after completing our successful adoption, did more of the consequences of infertility thrust themselves upon our awareness. When we looked at our perfect child, pride—in her beauty and adorableness and strength of personality and intelligence—was immediately constrained by our awareness that we were responsible for none of that. Under the circumstances, pride wasn't appropriate; we hadn't earned it. Some more detached, less owner-oriented feeling was more fitting: something like admiration. The birth parents we had not wanted to admit elbowed their way into our awareness when we looked at this beautiful child who was ours, but made by someone else. And this realization that we could not claim her in the way biological parents can claim their children—claim authorship of her—contributed to a grief we belatedly felt about our infertility. We didn't wish we had made our "own" baby; we wished we had made *this* baby, who was ours in every other way. Sometimes, I would lie in bed with her curled up on my belly and chest, sleeping. "How could we be closer?" I'd think. "Is it really possible to be closer than this?" Emotionally, I don't think we *could* be closer; but I wanted her to have been, actually, *inside* me. Marc and I wanted there to be no glimmer of separation between us and Natalie. We wanted our lives and hers to be a seamless unity.

As time has passed, this disconcerting feeling when I look at her—that I can't claim authorship of her—has largely subsided. Now, with all my years of parenting under my belt, I see (or think I see) all too clearly my authorship of her, for good and ill: Oh, my god, there's my temper! My physicality, my willfulness. Most of the time, thoughts about our biological separateness are, now, effectively nonexistent. But certain forces bring them to the fore again. Occasionally, I am struck by her looks, and think, Whom does she look like? Her birth mother must be beautiful. I hardly ever think about Natalie's birth father. I don't think she thinks of him either. I (we) think about her birth mother. Especially on Natalie's birthday and on Mother's Day. I have always thought birthdays should be celebrated for mothers at least as much as for children. Now I have an adopted daughter, and I am helpless: I cannot *not* think about her birth mother on her birthday. I want to know what she looks like. I want to know what she is feeling. I want to swim the Atlantic and crawl across Europe to kiss her feet and thank her for her gift to me. I am in awe of her; I pity her for her terrible loss; I love her for her incomparably precious gift; and I would like to meet her—as long as there is an ocean between us. I want to study her face, I want to hear her talk and see her move, I want to bow down before her in gratitude, and I want to have total control over her effect on our lives.

Mother's Day and Natalie's birthday are, blessedly, very close together. I can experience concentrated angst about her birth mother for a couple of weeks, and then have some relief for a year. I think about her birth mother every day, intensely, for a few weeks in the Spring; she haunts me, her grief, my grief for her, my awe and gratitude. And then I move on, and this presence isn't there between me and my daughter, insinuating itself between us, like water in sandstone, exploiting gaps in our intimacy.

But as she has grown up, and gained awareness, it has been different for Natalie, and therefore different for me. "You're not my real mother!" she hurls now and then. Reading, before we adopted, that adoptive mothers invariably endure this insult as their children grow up, I reacted first with horror: Can you *imagine* how painful that would be? Then with indignation and outrage: How *could* they be so hurtful? Then with the conviction that this, like all other bad things, wouldn't happen to us.

The first time Natalie threw it at me I was overcome with shock. She was only *five*! I thought this happened much later, at more like fifteen. I said (what the books say to say, so your child feels secure), "Oh, yes, I am *too* your real mother!" then went off and cried for the rest of the morning. The second time I was prepared, emotionally and otherwise: "I *am* your real mother. I am the only mother you have, and I will be your mother forever and ever. I'm happy to talk with you about your birth mother; but I don't want to hear that I'm not your 'real' mother anymore, because it's hurtful and it's not true." This was an important message to get across, and it did get through, but it didn't stop her for long.

Natalie has asked, "Does my birth mother think about me? Does she love me?" I have said, "Your birth mother loved you enough to do the very hardest and best thing she could do for you. She loved you enough to let somebody else raise you, who could give you a much better life than she could." I have said, "I don't know if she thinks about you; I don't know if she loves you; she probably does both, but I just don't know." I have said, "I think about your birth mother a lot, too. I would like to meet her. If you want to, one day we will go see if we can find her," and with that, she actually stopped talking about her birth mother for months. I realize, now, that I must have scared her.

When she is very frustrated, or in trouble with the parents she knows, or very tired, she has occasionally cried, "I want my mommy, my real mommy, my Russian mommy!" But typically, I am more puzzled than hurt. I suspect that her longing is for a mommy whose will is an extension of her own. This mommy would immediately understand and accede to her every desire, and would envelop her in pure love untouched by conflict. This mommy would have no demands of her own, no rules or needs that impeded Natalie's will. All children have these fantasies of the perfect parents, and hurl them at their actual parents. The difference for adoptive families is that other parents are actually *out* there.

This changes the stakes completely. For adopted children, the universal childhood longing for perfect parents can be accompanied by burning curiosity about biological parents' features, grief and anger about having been abandoned, and deep anxiety about the possibility of actually being returned to real people. This anxiety about being returned—so logical to the child's mind, so beyond the pale to the parents'—is why my magnanimous offer to help my five-year-old Natalie find her birth mother someday probably frightened her severely. And adoptive parents can't just dismiss their children's longings for perfect parents as standard childhood fantasies: There are real people to whom they have an enormously complex debt, who elicit a mix of emotions that encompasses profound gratitude, respect, curiosity, pity, and fear.

I am not threatened now when she says, "I want my mommy." Nat and I know in our bones that we are indispensable to each other. We love each other with all our hearts. But sometimes I am angry. It has been on the tip of my tongue occasionally to say, "Go ask your real mommy," when, with this rejection still burning in my ears, she asks me for something. But I haven't said this yet, and I hope I never will. More often, I am sad: They were right, they were *right,* all those books we read before we adopted. There *is* no escaping adoption issues.

(One time, when she was around three, we had a conflict in which I thought I'd behaved badly—I had been too demanding, too stern. I felt awful, and apologized to her, saying, "Oh, honey, I wish I was a perfect mommy for you." She said, in her sweet baby voice, "Oh, Mommy, you *are* my perfect mommy!" What a gift! I have often, since, had the same wish—to have been more perfect for her, more understanding, less stern, less strict—but I have never dared voice it again, for fear that I will never again hear her perfect response.)

Like all parents, I want to shield my child from pain. I want to know: Are these primal wounds, which all adoptees are supposed to have as a result of irrevocable separation from the body they grew inside, separation from genetic relatives—are these real, inevitable primal wounds, or are these artifacts of the way adoption was practiced up until recently? The adoption literature is full of eloquent voices expressing the terrible pain of adoptees who were not told about their adoptions until—if at all—they were adults; whose adoptions were shrouded in secrecy and shame. These eloquent voices are filling the air with news about the pain of adoption per se. I do not want this pain for my daughter. I want her to feel always rooted, secure, stable. I want to believe that this pain is not endemic to adoption but to a type of adoption practice that, thanks to adult adoptees' protests, has changed forever.

I try to get inside their heads, inside Natalie's. I try a thought experiment. I ask myself: How important is it to me that I was inside my mother's body? If I didn't know that I had been inside her body, how would I feel? If I knew I had been inside the body of another woman who was forever unavailable to me, how would I feel? Would I want to see her?

I do not like to admit it, but sometimes when I try to imagine myself in the position of an adoptee, I feel unrooted; I feel as if I am floating free.

But then I think: Maybe I am just imagining that I would feel that way because the adoption literature says I *should* feel that way. The industry that produces reams of print predicting, describing, lamenting, and helping couples cope with grief over their failure to produce biological children made Marc and me seriously wonder if something might be wrong with us or with our relationship because we *didn't* feel this grief. I wonder if, in describing the reality of some adoptees, the adoption "search" literature helps *create* a reality for thousands of other adopted kids. Perhaps the huge literature on adoption trauma is like the literature on sexual abuse trauma, which encourages "adult survivors" to ascribe all of the pain in their lives to childhood sexual abuse. The lure of the single-factor explanation is strong.

The culture fosters this tendency to point to adoption as an easy explanation for a multitude of ills. Every tic in an adopted person's life is ascribed to adoption: Oh well, she was *adopted,* you know. *That* would explain it. Kids' bad behavior and conflict between parents and children are considered normal until the fact of adoption is made known, at which point many observers readily diagnose adoption-related difficulties.

I want to believe that the deep grief some adult adoptees feel is not adoption-specific; it is not a sign of adoption trauma. It is a confluence of many factors.

I go back to my thought experiment. If my mom were still alive, I think I would feel rooted whether I had been adopted or not. My mom was just like that: Her *love* rooted me, not my relationship to her body. If she had been my adoptive mom, I might feel curious about my birth mother, but I do not think I would feel compelled to find her. I might not even want to find her, might resent and fear the threat of her coming between me and the mommy I loved so, so much. Sometimes it feels very clear to me that many "searchers" are unhappy people who are chasing a fantasy of mythic union.

Other times I can well imagine feeling a burning desire to meet a biological family I knew existed.

I can get bogged down in this game. Here is what I know: I fear that Natalie will feel some adoption-related grief and insecurity. I do not want her to feel this grief; I wish I could just make it all go away. I will do everything I can to make Natalie feel secure and rooted.

Here is something that has haunted me, too: this question of selection, and the apparent randomness of it all. Could I love *any* child who became mine through adoption? If so, doesn't that apparent lack of selectivity seem to mock my love? It seems like I love with special intensity this particular little human being, with all her uniqueness. But if I had adopted a different child, wouldn't I love her with the same intensity? Am I not being promiscuous? Am I a robot, gyrating to the tune of "Love the one you're with"? If our coming together with Natalie was random, then how solid is the ground of our love? Knowing that I could have loved another child as I love this particular amazing, beautiful, wonderful child—*my* child—can get to me sometimes. I don't like that. I don't think about it a lot because, for me, it doesn't really matter: I love this child with all my heart; she is mine now, and that's all that matters. I think about it more for its impact on Natalie, eventually, than for its impact on me. How will she digest the fact that she could have been placed with someone else, for an entirely different life: that she could have loved someone else as she loves this mother, this father?

Some people get around this unsettling question by saying that this particular union was just "meant to be." But it becomes quickly obvious that it's only blessings that are "meant to be." Disastrous adoptions are not "meant to be"—they're actionable. The "meant to be" explanation is immensely comforting when you have questions about a blessing, and insulting when you have questions about a tragedy.

Marc says it shouldn't matter, because biological kids are entirely chancy, too—the chanciest of chances, that this particular sperm and egg should survive the sloughing process, should produce this particular child. Fine, but then add to that the chance that this particular miracle child—rather than another one—should be bestowed on you—rather than on somebody else.

During our very attenuated process of adopting a second child, Natalie paused on the stairs one day and asked, in her dear little four-year-old voice, all bravery, "Mommy, when you get my little sister, will you give me to somebody else?"

Just rip my heart out.

Another time, on the same stairs (magic stairs), "Mommy, will you love my little sister as much as me?" Unprepared for this question, not wanting to scare her, I hemmed and hawed a bit. "Mommy," she said with urgency, "you *have* to love her just as much!" My answer, eventually, was that I would love her little sister just as much, but not the same, because she wasn't the same little girl. And I realized that perhaps that is the right answer to this whole problem. Children are not interchangeable: You can love lots of little children, but you will love each one differently, because each one is different, and elicits a different relationship from you, and makes of you a different parent.

Sometimes I would worry that, while I was writing my dissertation, the child who was meant for us would be given to somebody else. But then I stopped worrying, because it's like a river: When you step in is when *your* journey begins. There's lots coming before and after you that has nothing to do with you. The child we catch when we step in is, by definition—somehow—the child who is meant for us, the child we will love.

*The Runaway Bunny* became *our* book. When I first read it, I didn't get it at all, and I was vaguely insulted. Why did that darn little bunny want to run away in the first place? His mommy was perfectly nice!

I wonder if Margaret Wise Brown was thinking about adoptive families when she wrote it. Probably not. But it is perfect for us. The little bunny wants the mommy bunny to be as tenacious in her determination to claim him as he is in his determination to put distance between them. And she is. And I am. "You are *my* little bunny," I say to Natalie, and she understands me perfectly.

## 5

# A Sister for Natalie

We were sitting in the spacious living room of an old Victorian house that had been converted into adoption agency offices. The room—the agency's waiting room—-was comfortably furnished with overstuffed chairs and sofas. Reading material included, of course, the glossy magazine *Adoption Today,* as well as back copies of the agency's own newsletter, filled with pictures of kids adopted and adoptable. We were dressed up, as was Natalie, who, a couple months' shy of her third birthday, was climbing all over the furniture, ignoring the toys that dominated one corner of the room.

We were there, for the second time in four days, to meet the director of the agency's international program. We planned to get to know her, just as we had gotten to know Arlene, so she could find the right child for us, as Arlene had.

Marc was wondering aloud, again, why we were there, instead of with Arlene. But it was obvious to me. True, Arlene had done more for us than any other human on Earth besides our parents and Natalie's biological parents—she had put us together with Natalie. And she had done it quickly, smoothly, and with good humor. But she wasn't such a godsend to others. Our discomfort with the way she had treated the couples we traveled with had grown rather than diminished in the years that had elapsed. Brigit and Tony's boy, who had had the troubling flat plane on his head, turned out to be just fine, as Arlene had insisted he was. But her original referral to them of an alcohol-affected child when they had said they wanted a healthy child, and her callous manner toward them during the process—especially given their heart-breaking history of loss—angered us more as we became better friends with them.

Then there was also a little dirty business that clung to Sylvia's trip, which we'd learned about long after. Russian law states that both adoptive parents have to make the trip to adopt, unless they have both met the child previously. Presumably, this is to protect the child against possible rejection by an adoptive parent who first lays eyes on the child after the deed is done. Sylvia was able to travel alone because, she and Arlene told the Russians, her husband had seen little Pasha when they'd gone to get their daughter the previous year. But that wasn't true; he had never seen Pasha. So somebody was breaking the law, and it was for the benefit of a member of the OFIA board of directors. That Sylvia should be an officer of the board while she was a waiting parent—with her dearest heart's desire to gain from the organization—was itself a surprisingly glaring ethical lapse. That the organization would then quietly break Russian law to suit the board member's present needs was, though it did no clear harm, definitely smarmy.

But our gravest objection to Arlene was what she had allowed to happen to Angie and Stewart. They didn't push their concerns about their little boy, Bobby, while we were at the orphanage together, like Tony and Brigit had. But they should have. The extent of the damage to Angie and Stewart's boy had become appallingly clear as the months passed. He was profoundly delayed in every way: motor, language, cognitive, and emotional development. It had taken them six months with intensive professional assistance before he would make eye contact with them. When we four families got together for what should have been happy reunions, it was difficult to talk freely. Bobby was the elephant in the room. While the other children chattered happily away and had begun to play together, Bobby made grunting noises and whined, he flapped his hands, he flailed at his parents, he shrieked, he had to go home. "The other kids aren't as delayed as Bobby," his father noted at one of these reunions. The rest of us were startled by this graphic evidence of Stewart's cloudy perceptions in relation to his little boy. The other kids weren't delayed at all, and Bobby was much more than delayed. Something was terribly wrong.

It turned out that Bobby had suffered a catastrophic history of prenatal violence, premature delivery, abandonment, and severe institutional neglect. It is hard to blame the orphanage staff for their neglect of this extremely needy and difficult child: They had all they could do to care rather well for the healthy, easier children in their charge. But the effects of this neglect, on top of everything else, were devastating. Arlene, who was close to Dr. Christina, almost certainly knew more about this child's history and difficulties than she revealed to the adoptive parents.

The last time we saw Bobby, we were stunned at the scope of the tragedy that has befallen this loving couple. Their six-year-old boy had self-inflicted bruises and scratches on his face. He pounded himself with his fists, and raked himself with his fingernails. He would erupt in anger when frustrated—or sometimes just because—and lash out at others and at things in his environment. He often needed physical restraints. He barely spoke. He engaged in virtually no sustained, positive social interactions. He slept just sporadically during the night, and required twenty-four-hour assistance. Barring a miracle, he will never be normal.

Marc and I reflected: We got the princess of the orphanage, and Stewart and Angie got heartbreak. Why should this happen? Did Arlene make some kind of deal with the director: You get the princess, but you also have to take this troublesome one off our hands? The fact that Arlene had visited upon Stewart and Angie this irreversible tragedy was deeply troubling to both of us.

Still, Marc said, "But she did well by *us*. Look what she did for *us*!"

"Yes, fine—but would she do it *again*? She's so capricious. Maybe this time she would treat us the same way she treats others! You can't *trust* her. Her practice is awful!"

So here we were, in another agency waiting room, hoping to initiate a close relationship with another woman who had the power to find us a child as wonderful as Natalie.

Our hearts were so full with Natalie that we did not have a burning desire for a second child for ourselves. As Natalie's face and fingers started to lose their chubbiness, as she started to be more grown-up, I thought with anguish, many times, "One is not enough! I must have another baby!" But as Natalie grew she became more independent and more interesting, and we found that having one child was wonderfully manageable. But we wanted Natalie to have a sister. We were older— we wouldn't be around for her as long as we would like to be. All of her (biological) cousins had biological siblings: as siblings, they would be closer to each other than to her. According to the psychology literature, only children do just fine, even extremely well. But we wanted Natalie—as an adoptive child of older parents in an extended family full of biological children—to have a sister who was also adopted; someone with whom she could share the "issues" as they arose; a sister with whom to dissect her parents; someone for her to love forever, someone to love her forever. So we went in search of a sister.

But it couldn't be just any sister. She had to be as fabulous as Natalie. Most loving parents contemplate a second child with some trepidation: We all want our second child to be as wonderful as our first, and generally doubt that such an amazing feat is possible. How could any other child be as glorious as our first one? How could we possibly love another as we love her?

And in our case, this besotted skepticism was infused with fear. Adopting a second child brought all the risks adopting a first child brought, and then some. The dire warnings from experts about the impact on a child's development of prenatal care and early life experiences—all of these warnings, which had scared us during our first adoption, were even more frightening as we approached our second. Now we were risking not just our own emotional well-being, but that of our daughter, of our whole little family unit. We had been so extraordinarily lucky with Natalie. Our little family was such a happy one. What were the chances that the universe would smile upon our grasping for yet another immeasurable gift? "Oh, you guys," Marc's mother would fret. "Look at what you *have*! You'll *never* get another child like Natalie! Why not just be happy?"

Surely, what we *should* have been thinking was something like this: "There is another child out there who needs us—a sweet, helpless child who needs a family's love. We want to share our love and home and all of our resources with this child, whom we now must find." But what we *should* have wanted is not what we *did* want; what should have motivated us is not what did. We embarked on our quest for a second child not primarily to do good in the world, not primarily to rescue an unknown-but-already-loved child, but primarily to complete our family as we saw fit. And our sense of "fit" required that the new child fit our current image of ourselves, which was pretty darn high. I am embarrassed to say it, but it's true.

As I've thought it through, I have realized that parental narcissism is an unlovely, universal, and double-edged fact. On the one hand, the parents' narcissism can largely account for the baby's creation and survival: The narcissistically gratifying baby is happily fed, clothed, and cooed to. From birth through college and beyond, the child who makes her parents proud is likely to be swathed in the most expensive designer apparel and lifestyle accoutrements doting parents can afford. But narcissism has its dark side, too, and narcissism's dark side contributes to the emotional and physical abuse or neglect of children who do not sufficiently flatter their parents. The child who fails to meet the demands of highly narcissistic parents can suffer terribly from her parents' disappointment. Some people, as we know, are narcissistic enough to create a market for genetically modified "designer babies" with the genes for height, hair color, eye color, and other features parents desire. And some people won't consider adoption because the result is not narcissistically gratifying enough for them: Their own special genes did not combine to make this child, who fails to reflect them to themselves.

Marc and I learned, through painful experience, that the realm of parental narcissism is another in which adoption emerges as different, less private, more exposed than biological parenthood. All parents want perfectly healthy babies, but only adoptive parents are forced to express this desire, as a first step in their search for a baby, as a series of

"No's." All parents are influenced by narcissism, but only adoptive parents, who have to tell strangers what they want, who make so many unnatural choices in the process of becoming parents, are so exposed in their narcissistic demands. Marc and I were not so narcissistic that we would not even consider adoption; but we were narcissistic enough to want our children to confirm our high opinion of ourselves. The referral of Natalie, the princess of the orphanage, was highly gratifying narcissistically. We wanted that kind of flattery again.

Throughout our search for a second child, this subterranean want was at work in us. It was not admirable, but it was there, subconsciously influencing our decisions right alongside our more rational, predictable, defensible demands. We knew that there were children whose needs could swamp us, children like Bobby, whom we would not choose to parent. We knew as well that there were healthier babies out there, other abandoned children, who needed us; but would they fit our image of ourselves? We embarked on our quest for a second child planning to do some good in the world, and intent on preserving our familial self-image; bristling with determination to protect our family and expand it at the same time. We went out searching for the impossible: a child like Natalie, but not Natalie; a child we could imagine loving as we loved Natalie; an unknown child who would not threaten our happy equilibrium.

I had chosen Our New International Agency (ONIA) because of their outstanding reputation and long experience. They—in fact, Lynn, the very woman we were waiting to meet, the director of international programs—had been among the first to facilitate the American adoption of Russian children more than ten years earlier. They had a long track record and an excellent reputation.

We were therefore taken aback when Lynn failed to show up for our first meeting. I had made an appointment through our caseworker to meet Lynn; she knew that we were coming from Chicago specifically for this purpose. We flew into the nearest large city, about two and a half hours from the agency's headquarters, and stayed that Thursday night with friends. On Friday morning we drove to meet Lynn, all dressed up, with Natalie squirming in her dress in her car seat. There we wait, for the first time, in nervous anticipation, in the Victorian living room, waiting room, and in pops a perky young woman on her way back from lunch.

"Oh, *hi,*" she bubbles, standing in the doorway. "I'm Alison." Our caseworker. "It's so nice to meet you! Just give me a second, and I'll be right back."

We are momentarily confused. We are not here to meet *her*; we're here to meet her boss.

"You know, we're expecting to meet Lynn," I say, before she can slip away. I'm the one who arranged all this; I'm in the family hot seat.

"Lynn?" She turns back. "Oh, well, she's not here today. She works up north most of the time. She's usually only in here on Tuesdays."

I don't immediately believe my ears. Marc shoots me a look and moves to the edge of his chair.

"Alison, didn't you tell her we were coming? I thought we had this all set up. We've come all the way from Chicago to meet Lynn."

"Oh! Well, I can meet with you. She's not here."

"But, Alison—we have come specifically to meet Lynn. *From Chicago*. I understood from our e-mails that this had been arranged. I thought you'd said this was a good time for us to come and meet with her."

She seems to be drawing a complete blank. Why would we want to meet with Lynn instead of her?

Seeing that Alison is going to be of little service, we ask to speak to a program manager, but none is there on this Friday afternoon. Even I am upset. Marc, and the male half of the couple we are staying with, takes this lapse as perhaps a sign that we shouldn't work with this agency. But I think that is going too far. Maybe I hadn't been clear in my communication with Alison. Maybe it had been my fault. The agency receptionist, who has seen our dismay, kindly exerts herself over the weekend to reach Lynn, who agrees to see us on Monday. So we extend our trip, and again drive the two and a half hours to meet with her.

Natalie is behind the sofa when Lynn walks in. Attractive, in her late fifties, well-dressed, good short haircut, erect. Frosty. She warms up, though, as the meeting goes on. She is very well-spoken. She and her husband, a businessman, seem to have had an interesting life, with lots of international travel. They have adopted children themselves. Lynn asks why we don't want to go back to OFIA, and I explain our (my) ethical concerns. She seems to appreciate our (my) position. I can see that we understand each other. She is impressive—a real professional, a class act.

"Well," she says smiling, as we stand to leave after our hour's talk, "Natalie's a hard act to follow, but I'll do my best!"

I smile back at her, pleased and uncomfortable. She has recognized Natalie's specialness, exactly as planned. We had brought Natalie to show her: See, like *this*. She has seen. And she has promised: *I'll do my best*. She will give personal attention to the task. But there is also the warning: *Hard act to follow*. I will do my best, *but it might not be that good*. She might have said, "Natalie's a real gem, that's for sure. I will make sure I find you a good match for her, the just-right child for your family." But she didn't say that. She said "hard."

I choose to focus on the positive. "Wow," I say, as the door closes behind us. "She makes Arlene look *tacky*."

"I don't know. Look what Arlene *did* for us!"

"Honey, Lynn's going to do the *same* thing, only she's going to do it in a more professional way, without all the cult of personality Arlene requires."

"I don't know."

The problem with ONIA was size. Lynn delegated appropriately. We didn't get to talk with Lynn unless we made special efforts to do so; our regular contacts were with Alison and a string of other twentysomething caseworkers—sweet, idealistic, competent, perky girls who had almost no emotional resonance and (one hoped) virtually no power in the process. One of the problems with Arlene was that she couldn't delegate—trying to do everything herself, she often bollixed up the works. But we didn't *want* to be delegated; this was about our *child*! We wanted other adults—people who had parented, who understood firsthand our pain and fear and desires—to be in charge. At OFIA, we had gotten that; at ONIA, we didn't. To maintain our relationship with Lynn, we would trek out to the distant suburbs of Chicago once a summer to a picnic of families with children adopted from Eastern Europe. There, in (inevitably) sweltering heat or pouring rain, we would chat and smile with her for five or ten minutes, show her Natalie, growing, try to reimpress our image on her mind.

It was taking so long because—after we had gotten our dossier together and were moving up the waiting list—Marc and I decided to put our application on hold until I finished the dissertation I was writing for my Ph.D. We thought if I didn't finish it now, before I had primary responsibility for two small children, I'd never finish it. So we interrupted the adoption process as I toiled on the dissertation. And as I wrote my dissertation, the Russians rewrote their adoption laws.

There has always been nationalist sentiment in Russia opposing the international adoption of their children. I can understand this sentiment. It's not hard to see those of us adopting internationally as rich, greedy Americans plundering the single greatest asset of poor, struggling countries. A few years after we adopted Natalie, a dear friend of mine was preparing to adopt as a single mom from Southeast Asia. Doing her emotional due diligence, she attended an adoption conference at which an angry young woman who had been adopted from Southeast Asia confronted the would-be adoptive parents who were learning how to keep their children connected to their countries of origin.

"If you all are so wonderful," she spat, "if you all care so much about the people of Southeast Asia, if you care so much about the *moms* who have to give up their *babies,* why don't you take all the money you're going to spend adopting and just *give* it to the birth mothers? That way they could keep their *own* babies!"

My good friend was stricken with guilt. She didn't *want* to give her money away so another woman could keep her baby. She wanted a baby herself. For her—for all of us—the adoption process is selfish that way. We don't spend all that time and money so somebody *else* can parent: We spend it so *we* can parent.

Is this selfishness inconsistent with sympathy for the birth mothers who can't afford to raise their babies? To some extent, it is. Are we hypocrites for professing empathy with bereaved birth mothers but not giving them the means (which we seem to have at our disposal) to raise their children? To some extent, we are. Empathy has its limits. There's no way in the world Marc and I would have spent that much money to keep a family on the other side of the world together. I empathize with Natalie's birth mother, but my determination to parent is stronger than my empathy. I grieve for her loss, and I revere her for her gift to me. But I am thankful to the depths of my being that *I* am raising Natalie, and not she. The reality—that her loss is as great as my gain—is flat-out brutal. But that's life this time, and I thank all the powers in the universe that I am the lucky one.

Some people who adopt (and maybe the angry young woman at the conference heard these notes in someone's voice) think of themselves as orphan-rescuers, noble souls altruistically taking in abandoned children. Other people, non-adopters, sometimes endorse this vision. I see the image of this orphan-rescuer in the eyes of people who say to me earnestly, "It's so wonderful of you to have given your girls a home." I saw it in the eyes of the medical technician who assisted in Natalie's and Lana's eye exams on a day when they were at their shrieking sibling worst. As I dragged them out of the doctor's office, she said to me, shaking her head in sympathy, "You're a saint." On the part of adopters, this image is a gratifying self-delusion; on the part of others, it's a failure to understand. There is a huge payoff for us adopters: *We Get To Be Parents.* I am at least as blessed by their adoption as my girls are.

Sometimes when I look at Natalie I think of the loss, not just to her birth mother, but to Russia of such a child. And there are thousands more like her—healthy, smart, Russian-born children in this country who could have helped rebuild their homeland. Theoretically. But in real life, in actual fact, no Russians had stepped forward to adopt Natalie before she was thirteen months old. Surely she would not have emerged from the orphanage in her mid-teens a great asset to her country. It is in fact probable that she would have been exploited, at worst in the international sex trade. Have we plundered Russia by removing her to America? Maybe, in a way. Would we have done a better thing if we had taken her from the orphanage and given her back to her birth mother, with the thirty-five thousand dollars or so we spent in the adoption process? Well, *maybe*. But (a) we're not that noble; (b) that one-time gift would not have altered the crushing cultural conditions that had so harmed her birth parents and would harm their children; and (c) even with such a gift, her birth parents could never have given her the opportunities to fulfill her potential that we have given her. We did, almost certainly, the best thing for *Natalie,* even as we satisfied our own deepest heart's desire. The right response to the problem of Russia's loss (and that of other poor countries) is to improve the conditions future children will be born into so they can fulfill their potential in their own countries. Until that's done, Russians who really love children will secure the best for those who are already born by facilitating international adoptions.

But that's not what the Russians were doing while I was finishing my dissertation. The revision of the Russian adoption laws in the late 1990s tilted the process in favor of the nationalists, making it harder than ever for non-Russians to adopt from Russia. Two of the changes had huge ramifications for us.

When we adopted Natalie, the procedure was for orphanage directors to "batch" referrals—put together the dossiers of several children at once—and send the whole batch to a U.S. agency. This allowed professionals who best knew the waiting families to make the individual placements they thought most appropriate.

Under the new laws, referrals were made to U.S. families directly from the Russian orphanage. The orphanage director would have bare-bones information about a family and its preferences, and would make a referral directly. The U.S. agency with whom the waiting family was working had no choice but to pass the Russian referral on to the family, no matter how inappropriate (in age, sex, health status, etc.) the U.S. professionals thought the referral might be.

The second major change in Russian law was a retroactive one, making all Russian-born children Russian citizens until the age of eighteen. Russian-born children adopted internationally could be citizens of their adoptive countries as well, but would be dual citizens, according to Russian law, until they were eighteen years of age. With this change in the law, Natalie, a U.S. citizen, became a Russian citizen again.

With these legal changes, and perhaps because of other, unrelated, interagency changes, ONIA effectively lost the ability to place kids from Russia. Unfortunately, they never advised us of this handicap.

It is December 28, 1999, my father's eighty-first birthday. My dear new stepmother and I are bustling around the kitchen of their modest home, cleaning up the dinner dishes, putting the finishing touches on the cake. Marc and my dad are helping Natalie with a puzzle in the adjoining room.

In Railyanka Village, Ukraine, a young woman staggers into a hospital. Her labor pains are intense and quickening. The next morning, after stopping to talk with the hospital's psychiatrist, she leaves. Her child, a small baby with huge brown eyes and improbably long lashes, blinks in the gray light of the hospital's dismal nursery. Hungry, chilly, she begins, appropriately, to cry.

As I was finishing my dissertation, we told ONIA we were ready to reopen our dossier and receive referrals. Among the new paperwork we had to complete—twice, because of an unexplained glitch either in Russia or at ONIA—were thirteen sets (one for each of the Russian regions where ONIA was doing business) of three different documents, each of which required separate notarizations and apostilles.

Having submitted all the new paperwork, we waited. We were at the top of the list, so we expected a fairly rapid turnaround. But there were delays. Every time I called to check, our caseworker assured me that they expected referrals the following week. But none came. Week after week after week, we got no referral, no phone calls with suggestions about how to speed it up, no explanations.

We knew other people, working with other agencies, who were getting referrals of healthy children and traveling. But for us, from ONIA, nothing, for months and months. I defended my dissertation. I studied French. I passed my language exam. I graduated. No baby.

"I *knew* we shouldn't have changed agencies! I *knew* we should've stuck with Arlene!" Marc would say, seething with rage.

I was defensive and alienated. "We left Arlene for very good reasons. Remember Angie and Stewart? *Remember?* Arlene is *careless,* she *hurts* people!" Obviously, ONIA was a bad choice. But it was the best available by the lights we had at the time. Or, by the lights *I* had. Marc would have gone with Arlene again. If I wanted another agency, I had to find it.

"We should *never* have left her. I *knew* it! Look what she *did* for us."

"She was *unethical.*" I disdained him for not taking this small point into consideration. "ONIA has a fabulous reputation. *Everybody* says so. They're supposed to be the *best!*"

"It was stupid! *Stupid!*" *I* was stupid. He purported to take responsibility, but he hadn't, and he wouldn't. It was me on the hot seat.

"We are *screwed.* I should *never* have let this happen! We can *never* go back to Arlene now!" It was true: By going to another agency we had effectively burned our bridges with Arlene. The international adoption community is a relatively small one, and word gets around; she would know that we had strayed. Marc's message, in couple-speak, was that he should never have been swayed by me.

Five dollars for every time Marc and I had this lacerating exchange would have gone a long way toward defraying adoption expenses.

Desperate, sad, angry, I called a couple of other agencies to see what their process in Russia was like, how long we might have to wait with them if we started over again right now. I heard that ONIA worked only in a few regions of Russia; that we would have better chances with an agency that worked in all the available regions.

In a moment of calmer despair, Marc and I discussed changing agencies. But we already had several thousand dollars and years of interaction tied up with ONIA. We didn't want to go to the back of the line as a brand-new couple with another agency that might or might not perform for us. It was getting late.


"You guys," Shelley begins quietly. It is an unexpectedly quiet moment in the midst of a gathering with Marc's family. Grandparents are in the kitchen, refreshing their drinks. Shelley and her husband, Marc's brother, are listening with sympathy as Marc and I bemoan the adoption morass. Our five-year-olds, compatible cousins, are occupied in the basement playroom. Shelley's ten-month-old baby is cruising around the coffee table, scattering crackers and carrot sticks, ricocheting off our shins occasionally as we talk. She clears her throat, pauses, looks at her husband and back at us. "If you want," Shelley says, "I'll surrogate for you. I mean, if that's something you want."

This offer whizzes at me from out of the blue and hits me like a body slam. I catch my breath and glance at Marc, whose look is clear. I force a grateful smile. "Oh, my god, Shelley. Wow. That's an incredible offer. Thank you so much! But . . . I don't think so. *Thanks*, though!"

How incredibly rude of me, to turn down so vast a gift. But in one sharp instant, Shelley's offer has clarified for both Marc and me how *little* biology matters to us. The point is not to reproduce. The point is to find a baby to love. The thought of spending a small fortune to make our "own" baby seems shockingly off the point. We want to love a baby who already exists. We have to find that baby, that's all.

Marc's brother scoops up his cruising daughter, tosses her above his head, and catches her, laughing, ending the awkward silence.



I am home playing Barbie with Natalie after nursery school one day when the phone rings. It is our perky caseworker.

"Hi! Listen! We have a referral for you!"

The automatic surge of joy all waiting parents experience at the word "referral" is checked in my case by the sound of strain in the girl's voice.

"What's the matter?"

"Lynn wants to talk with you before we send it."

A few hours later, Marc and I are both on the phone with Lynn. "I want you to know that this is not a referral I would have made myself. You know the new rules—the Russians make the referrals directly. *I* would not have made this referral to you because of your stated preference for a healthy little girl."

"What's wrong with this child?"

"Her mother had syphilis." Lynn continues in her businesslike fashion. "Now, the medical form says the mother was treated while she was pregnant, and the baby was treated immediately after birth. She actually *looks* fine, and she might well *be* fine. But there's a certain amount of risk, and you were very clear about wanting a healthy child. I would never make this referral to you myself."

"Okay. Well . . . I guess you should go ahead and send it." Marc's voice sounds a little dead.

"Okay. We'll FedEx it tomorrow. I just wanted you to know ahead of time." Click.

Marc heads for the study to research congenital syphilis. If it is treated quickly after birth, complications could be well-contained, virtually nonexistent.

In the video, a little girl with dark curling hair and huge, dark, wide-set eyes sits in a pool of small colored balls, looking at the camera, smiling. She is pretty, and has a sweet smile. But even I can see that she seems to be very passive. She doesn't play with the balls, doesn't react to sounds around her, just stares at the video camera.

Marc watches the video, moaning softly. "Ohhhhhhh. Mmmmmm. Nnnnnn."

*"What?"* I snap.

"Those facial anomalies."

*"What* facial anomalies?"

Marc rewinds the tape, stops it. "See there? See how wide-set her eyes are? See the flat nasal bridge?"

"Maybe."

"See the bony prominence of her forehead?"

*"Maybe."*

"Those are all sequelae of congenital syphilis. If she was treated, it wasn't right after birth. Syphilis took a foothold in her."

"She looks like Jacqueline Onassis! This is probably just what Jackie Onassis looked like as a baby!"

Marc looks at me, shaking his head. He will be gentle, but firm.

"Look, honey, look how passive she is. She just *sits* there, staring at the camera!"

I study the video again.

"Well, maybe she's never seen one before! Maybe that's the most interesting thing in her environment for this two or three minutes. It probably *is*. Anyway, *any* child can be passive for a couple of minutes!"

He doesn't want to give me pain, but we will not be accepting this child.

"Let's see what Nick and Kevie think," I suggest. Nick and Kevie are dear friends of longstanding, who had thrilled to Natalie's first photos and followed every step of our current plight.


They are quiet when they see the video.

"Well, what do you think?" I ask.

They hesitate. "Well . . . she seems awfully passive, Theresa," Kevie says quietly.

The conversation continues but the question is settled. I want a baby very much, but I do not want to bring home a sick baby. Marc and Nick and Kevie are not cold people. They are admitting something that is there. I have to accept it.

Stonily, I check the "No" box on the referral form, and mail the packet back to ONIA. For quite some time, at odd moments, the image of the little girl sitting in the pool of balls, smiling at the camera, floats before my eyes.

Weeks and weeks and weeks pass. The only contact we have with ONIA are the ones I initiate by calling for a status report. All I hear from the increasingly testy caseworker are variations on "soon" and "I don't know." Finally, I snap: "Well, where on earth *can* you get us a healthy little girl?"

"Oh!" she chirps. "Kazakhstan! There are *lots* of kids waiting in

Kazakhstan! I could get you a little girl in Kazakhstan, oh, maybe, next *week!*"

Kazakhstan. Let's Google that. Very big country. Very far away. Former Soviet colony. Lots of Asians, Euro-Asians. Thirty-seven percent Muslim. Very kind and welcoming people, hospitable. A favorite national pastime is a form of hockey played with the headless carcass of a goat. We read it again. Not the *head* of a goat, the headless *carcass* of a goat, which men on horseback somehow swat around with paddles.

Will we be able to imbue a child from Kazakhstan with a robust sense of pride in her culture?

We call the caseworker back the next day. "If you can find us a healthy little ethnic Russian girl in Kazakhstan, we'll consider her." We'll just forget about the Kazakhstan part and focus on the Russian.

We are informed that in order to enter the Kazakhstan program we must withdraw from the Russia program and complete more paperwork.

The chances of getting a referral from Russia?

Don't know.

Kazakhstan?

Next week, probably. Two weeks, tops.

A pause to take this in.

Just a quick question. Why didn't you tell us about this option before?

You didn't ask. You said you wanted Russia.

We move to the Kazakhstan program. Sure enough, about a week after we have completed the new paperwork, our caseworker calls.

"I have a referral for you!" She pauses, shuffles papers, peers at a picture, pauses. "She's kind of cute!" She sounds surprised and a little tentative.

"Kind of cute." How careless of her. "Can you tell me any more?" I ask.

"Well, let's see. Her name's Vera. She's two and a half. It says here her mother? Is Kazakh, and her father is Russian. What I like about this video? Is that she seems to be attached to her caregiver. She seems to be comforted by the caregiver when she's frightened, you know? *That's* a good thing. And the caregiver? She looks really, really nice."

The next evening, after Natalie is asleep, we pop in the video. We have glanced through the photos, unmoved. But we know that means nothing. Suddenly, the image of a frightened little girl fills our television screen. About eighteen months old, she stands unmoving, looking at someone off camera, her eyes brimming with fear. She is wearing a little jumpsuit and, pinned to her head, a large decorative poof ball. These common adornments look like the bunchy net exfoliators we use in the shower, and are about half the size of the child's head. Voice-over narration in English tells us what's happening as we watch. On the verge of tears, the child is joined momentarily by a plump Asian woman in a white coat, frosted streaks in her short dark hair, loving smile on her bright red lips. This woman gives Vera a dolly, which she clutches for dear life. Off camera again, the caregiver tells the child to make the doll dance. Vera jiggles the doll around momentarily, then clutches it again as if it's the edge of a building she's nearly fallen off. "Vera learns tunes very quickly and dances rather well," says the voice-over. After a moment of blackness, she's a year older. Her pale brown hair is longer and starting to curl. She's wearing a pretty little polka-dot jumpsuit. She's cute and shy and plump. The same caregiver rolls a truck away from them, and tells Vera to go get it. She does, and returns it with a big smile, proud of herself, one hand behind her back, like a maître d' delivering a prized dish. The loving caregiver gently turns Vera to face the camera, which she glances at shyly before looking down.

The child looks fine—better than fine. She looks decidedly lovable. But our reaction is muted. Something is missing. Puzzled by our response to the video, we arrange a call with Lynn.

"So, Lynn, we have a referral."

"I know."

"What do you think of this little girl?"

"I think she's fine."

"Is this a really good little girl?"

"This child would fly out of our office."

We're not getting what we need, and we're not sure what it is. We grope a little. "Lynn, see, when we adopted Natalie, it was very different. Natalie came with a *story*. The story was that this was a great little girl, who was specially matched with us."

Lynn listens politely, but doesn't respond when we pause.

"We're not getting any *story* with Vera, you see? It's just, 'Here's a child, she's kind of cute.' Do you understand? We're just . . . It just doesn't feel very special."

"Mmmmm."

We wait in vain for more. "So, you see, this might be a good child for us, but it just doesn't *feel* very good."

Lynn remains silent. We become uncomfortable. I begin to feel stupid, demanding, dense. Marc becomes frustrated.

"So, what do *you* think? Is this the right little girl for us?"

"As I said, this child would fly out of our office."

We end the conversation quickly.

What was Lynn thinking during her silences? Was she thinking that we were too demanding? That we needed special handling? That we couldn't think for ourselves? Perhaps she was managing her contempt. All of these possibilities seem real to me. But she should have been critiquing her agency's slapdash referral process and making mental notes for improvement. Looking back can I see what we needed: We needed, from another responsible adult, a flourish that said, "Here! I think this child could be wonderful for your family!" We didn't want someone else to make the decision for us, but we wanted to know that some other wise, dispassionate adult had given this some thought, considered our needs, and identified a child who, in *her* best judgment, would be a good fit for our family. It was for just this kind of help that we had tried to form a relationship with Lynn. We wanted to hear from her *anything* specific about this little girl that made her seem right for us—any little tidbit about her laughing eyes, or her sweet personality, or her ability to attach that would give *us* something to attach to at this critical juncture.

Asking for such support does not seem ridiculous or too demanding to me even now. The moment of choice in adoption—whether it is over with early, as for couples adopting from China or Southeast Asia, or persists through the referral of one or more babies from Eastern Europe—is profoundly rattling. Providing compassionate, knowledgeable, emotional support—even just helping couples understand their need for it—seems legitimately part of the job description for people in this line of work. This is what we blindly—and vainly—sought from Lynn.

We are baffled and disappointed when we hang up the phone. We sign the paper accepting the referral of Vera and send it back to Lynn's office with a check for the thirteen-thousand-dollar "foreign program fee." We are not elated. There is none of the joy that surged the first time. We feel uncertain, unsettled. This is what we get, we figure, for having abandoned Arlene.


In an orphanage in Ukraine, a tiny seventeen-month-old child with huge dark eyes tries to pull herself up. She manages to stand, weaving against the edge of the little table, but she can't walk. She looks around for someone to hold on to. A nice lady comes smiling toward her, gives her a hand for a moment. The child knows this round, creased face; this lady was here a few days ago. She will not be here tomorrow, but she will probably come back sometime. The nice lady strokes the child's head and speaks a few kind words in Russian. The child smiles up at the lady, takes strength from her interest. The child takes a step. Across the room, another child screams. The nice lady dashes away, and the staggering child, empty-handed, falters and falls.

# 6

## Kazakhstan

My mother-in-law sits silently watching Vera's video, lips clenched. When it is over there is a brief pause.

"Well!" she says brightly, brows furrowed in worry. "Okay! So when do you kids go?"

It is Mother's Day 2001, a couple of days after we accepted the referral of Vera. Marc had wanted to keep the referral a secret until we had a travel date. What if something happens? What if it falls through? he argued. This isn't a done deal yet; we shouldn't announce it to the world.

"What can happen? Nothing is going to happen! We're going to go get her!"

"You don't *know* that, Theresa!"

"*What is going to happen?*"

"*I* don't know! *Anything* could happen!"

"People are going to Kazakhstan to get babies all the time!" I whine like an incoming missile. "Nothing is going to happen! You just want to take the joy out of this. You just won't embrace the *joy!*"

Marc's refusal to be excited about Vera's referral is an obstacle to my own wavering enthusiasm. I fight it tooth and nail.

"It is *inconceivable* to me that, after all these months of telling everybody day by day and week by week that, no, we don't have a referral yet, no, we don't have a referral yet, no, we don't have a referral yet, that now when we *get* a referral of a healthy darling little girl we don't *tell* them! Why can't we *celebrate* this?"

"Theresa, we just don't *know. Anything* could happen."

I win. Marc is right, theoretically and intellectually: Anything *can* happen. That's life. But he's all wrong emotionally, and he sort of knows it: We *should* celebrate this event. We cannot let Lynn's refusal to give us a story we want—to kindle our enthusiasm for this child—cloud our perceptions. Vera is a cute, sweet, healthy little girl. We need to embrace her entry into our lives. Still, Marc is uncomfortable. He only reluctantly agrees to introduce Vera to the local grandmothers (his mother and stepmother) on our Mother's Day visits.

The false enthusiasm from his mother is unsettling. It is *exactly* what we don't need—exactly, precisely, specifically cut-to-measure wrong for the occasion. I suppress my anger for the time being, but I have no control over my anxiety.

Our next stop is much more comforting. Marc's father and step-mother coo and exclaim during the video. Oh, how cute! Oh, look at that! Oh, what a sweetie. Oh, sweet, sweet thing. Let's watch it again! We go out to dinner and talk about Vera, talk with Natalie about being a big sister. We talk about the anticipated trip and the timing.

On the way back into the city, I fume about Marc's mother. I cannot shake her reaction; it is plaguing me. When we get home, I reach into the bag for the photos. I need a quick fix, reassurance that we have done the right thing. I will stick the pictures on the fridge, a reminder of the rightness of our decision, an assertion of the reality of our upcoming trip.

But the pictures are not there. They are not anywhere. They are not at Marc's father's house, at the restaurant, in the car, under the mat, stuck in folds of wrapping paper in the bag. Vera's pictures have disappeared.

This is *ridiculous*! They *must* be here!

But they are not.

My heart pounds. My scalp crawls. I do not believe in omens unless they confirm what I've already decided to do. I try to joke, but my voice quavers. I am scared. This is like the omens associated with Natalie's referral, but in reverse. That letter from the man in Ekaterinburg was amazing—as inexplicable as vanished photos that have been carefully placed. I fight my fear with stern, rational words.

The following Wednesday I pick Marc up at work so we can go to the far north side of Chicago to get our fingerprints taken—*again*—for the INS. This is the fifth time we have had to be fingerprinted in the adoption process. (Ten days later, we discover that they find this set of prints unreadable, so we must both take hours off from work to be fingerprinted yet again.) I have with me the travel packet for Kazakhstan, which arrived from ONIA yesterday. It will be my reading material for the afternoon.

After a few minutes I hunker over the pages, my heart thudding, intent. I do not read aloud to Marc. He cannot know this yet. Surely it is not this bad. Surely there is a way to escape from the badness of it. I must find the way to change it, to make it even approximately acceptable, before I talk to Marc.

Vera is in an orphanage in Kostanai, Kazakhstan. If you have wondered where the end of the earth is, this is it. It takes some forty hours to get to Kostanai via commercial travel from Chicago. We should plan to be *in Kostanai* for at least two weeks and up to four. This is to allow the wheels of Kazakh bureaucracy to turn, and to give Vera time to get to know us before we take custody. We should plan on being gone for at least four weeks and perhaps for six. We will go through Moscow coming and going, and will spend several days on the way home in the former Kazakh capital of Almaty. At the Almaty airport we might encounter a nasty bit of business (so sorry!): Local warlords have been known to separate men from their families and demand a payment of five hundred dollars or more to board the plane home. To avoid this difficulty we are advised to stash all our cash on the wife, and pay a fifty-dollar per person "VIP" fee ahead of time. We will have a week to ten days' notice—any time in the next several months—before being required to travel. You cannot drink the water in Kazakhstan. There is no air conditioning, and inadequate heat. The phones are unreliable. If you are invited into someone's home you will be served fermented mare's milk, which you will be expected to drink as a show of respect.

If we were traveling to Paradise on the Concorde, the prospect of leaving work for four to six weeks on ten days' notice would send Marc into orbit. He has patients, and students! He has a lab, with people in it, doing experiments! He has papers to write and grants to review and courses to teach. What are they *thinking*? (This was *our* reaction at the time. For people in less secure positions than Marc's—people who can actually get *fired* from their jobs, and would, if they took off for so long on such short notice—these ridiculous demands are actually impossible to meet. Why should *they* be denied the possibility of adopting from Kazakhstan—or the many other countries with long waits and unpredictable travel schedules—and not us more privileged souls?)

My stomach twists as I take all this in. . . . I don't dare tell him yet. I have to make it better.

I must be casting my eyes about like a caged animal being randomly shocked.

"So?" he asks, looking at me quizzically as we settle back into the car. My fingers are tingling a little from the cleaner they use to remove the ink. "What's it say?"

"Um, well," I say weakly. "It sounds a little challenging."

I have told him pretty much everything, ameliorating it as best I can ("Maybe it'll only be *four* weeks") and endured the crashing and sucking waves of his distress by the time we reach the hospital again. We sit there at the curb, the car idling, awash in anguish. I do not know how to make this better. Finally, he says, "Theresa, what if Natalie gets sick? What if she gets *sick* while we're there? What if she gets appendicitis?"

The idea of Natalie in danger catapults me over the edge. What if we hurt our one beloved baby trying to get another one? I begin to sob, my face in my hands. "I'm sorry. I'm so sorry. I am so, so sorry," I wail.

I am sorry, not about infertility—Marc has never let infertility be an issue between us. I am desperately sorry that I have forced him to make a public commitment to Vera, to tell Natalie about her new little sister, before we understood how awful it would be to go get her. Maybe—probably—before saying yes to Vera, we should have asked some crucial questions. Where is she? How long does it take to get there? How long do we have to stay? Is it safe for our older child? But we didn't ask these questions. We only asked, "How old is she? Is she healthy? Can she attach?" We had been waiting so long; we got the right answers to our three critical questions—the other questions didn't occur to us until it was too late. Finally finding a child who met our criteria, I had been certain that, whatever the obstacles, we could overcome them to get to this little girl. How could we know that there was a healthy little girl in the world for us and then let ourselves be deterred in our pursuit of her by some inconvenience? But that bravado melted in the face of towering obstacles like a forty-hour trip, a four- to six-week stay at the end of the earth, and potential danger for Natalie.

It was a very, very difficult journey between us there, in the idling car, to the decision that now in fact we could not go back on our commitment to Vera; that, having told especially Natalie that she had a baby sister at last, having shown her Vera's video several times, we could not turn around and tell her we had changed our minds. Now we had to go forward.

Marc did not abandon me. He forgave me—about ninety-two percent. It was now my job to make this trip safe and bearable.

I began in the obvious place—with the professionals at ONIA. Surely they would be able to help. They knew that we had always planned to take Natalie with us when we traveled. We had discussed this with Lynn the first time we met her, years ago, in the comfy Victorian waiting room of her agency. One of the reasons I especially liked her was that she had said that taking Natalie was our decision, not hers. Arlene had said that we could absolutely not take Natalie on a trip to adopt a sister, and that was that. She wouldn't *let* us. Lynn said that it could be difficult, true, but with proper support we could do it. It was up to us.

Now Lynn said that maybe we should leave Natalie at home.

The adoption literature is full of bad news about the adopted child's potential psychic traumas. Now, at the other end of the phone line, an adoption professional was advising me to leave my five-year-old adopted child at home? For four to six weeks? While we go to get a baby sister? This is the child who has asked me, "Mommy, when you get my baby sister, will you give me to somebody else?" They wanted us to leave her behind? Astounding. We could not survive without her for that long, and we didn't think she would survive very well without us, either. She had been away from us once for two nights, staying with her cousins when we went to New York City, and had cried inconsolably for hours the first night. How would she cope with a four-week trip to get a baby sister? It was out of the question.

No? Well, then, how about leaving her home for *part* of the time, and having someone else bring her later on?

Right, right. Have someone *else* bring her over—some amazing person with unlimited uncommitted time, deep reserves of stamina, and intimacy and trust with Natalie almost as great as our own. Have *that* person travel with her for forty hours through multiple airports to the other side of the world, after she hasn't seen us for a couple of weeks. *That'll* work.

The impediments to this ludicrous suggestion are insurmountable without even considering the little problem of getting Natalie safely through Moscow.

Since Russia declared all children born there to be citizens until they are eighteen years of age, they have refused to issue visas for Russian-born children traveling on American passports. Russian-born children, as Russian citizens, must travel in Russia on Russian passports.

We think, of course, we will cheat on this. We just won't tell them where she was born. But there it is, right on her U.S. passport—place of birth: Russia.

When we were in ONIA's Russia program, waiting indefinitely for a referral we could accept, so we could travel *with Natalie* to pick up her baby sister, no one said anything to us about rethinking our plans in light of the new requirements. When I asked one of our case-workers, just to make sure, if it was still safe to travel to Russia with Natalie, she had said, "Yes, it's fine. It's *hard* to travel with a young child, but it should be fine."

Now, from another caseworker, now that we have accepted a referral that requires travel with Natalie through Russia, I get a different answer: "*I* wouldn't do it."

Lynn demurs. "Oh, well—you know, of course, people get nervous about it. But we've never had any problem, and I don't think there *will* be any problem."

I try to picture how it's going to work: Marc and I going through U.S. passport control, and five-year-old Natalie going through Russian passport control. They won't let us go with her. We get separated. She gets lost in the throngs.

I startle awake in the middle of the night in a cold sweat, my heart hammering in my chest.

Another version of my nightmare is that I am with her in the passport line and they decide to keep her. Our Russian-born girl, whose excellent genes are immediately obvious. They won't let her back out. I will never leave her. I am torn away from her, screaming, as she is hauled away from me.

The suggestion that someone *else* bring her through passport control is too absurd even to discuss.

I fight my panic. This won't happen! They couldn't take care of these children in the first place! Russia and America are friends! It would cause a huge international incident!

On the other hand, the Russians are squirrelly. She *is* a Russian citizen. There's only so much the U.S. government could do. All it takes is one petty bureaucrat to cause a nightmare. Our story could get buried, never see the light of day. Our baby could be gone.

I call our senators' offices. I explain our situation. I need a letter, I say. Could the senator please write a letter, something like this:

*Dear Russian Authority: We know the people who are carrying this letter. They are valued American citizens. We know their travel itinerary. We trust that you will expedite their travel through your country.*

Could the senator provide such a letter?

"Are you sure you have to take her?" asks one aide. "I don't think I would risk it."

I swallow the vomit that threatens to rise in my throat and say yes, we do have to take her. Can I please get such a letter?

I get such a letter from each of our senators. Svetlana, a technician in Marc's lab, translates them into Russian for us, types them in Cyrillic. She does not think that they will help. A paper shield.

I resolutely ignore this doom and gloom and copy the letters, put them in plastic sleeves, add them to my notebook.

Another day: I have lost my composure and am blubbering to the very kind woman on the phone. "But can you get a five-year-old out of Kostanai, Kazakhstan?" The woman listening is with an agency that provides emergency medical evacuation insurance. I had asked her in a shaky voice what it was exactly that they did. She has just explained to me that they operate a fleet of planes and helicopters that swoop down out of the heavens to airlift sick people out of remote places and get them to safety fast.

"Yes," she replies, sounding moved. "We can reach Kostanai quickly. We *can*. You'll be *fine*."

I apologize and struggle for enough composure to ask my questions. How do we activate the service if we need it? You just call, and we're there in no more than three hours. But the travel packet has said the phone lines are unreliable. What if we can't get through? People going to remote places usually take satellite phones. They almost always work.

Almost always. Do any satellites pay attention to Kostanai, Kazakhstan?

Even if we get a cell phone that works from Kostanai, Kazakhstan, and successfully contact the insurance company, what would they do?

They'd take her to the nearest decent hospital.

Where would that be? Somewhere in Russia? Where Natalie is a citizen? Where half the hospitals still don't have running water?

No, no, we would be taken to a good place.

I thank her for her information and compassion and hang up. I will call her back when the time comes.

I make some phone calls to learn about satellite phones, and decide where to get ours. The satellite phone salesmen assure me the phones work reliably. In a grocery store line a couple weeks later, somehow the fact of our approaching trip to Kazakhstan comes up between me and the stranger behind me. He's been there, on business.

"Taking a satellite phone?" he asks me.

I nod.

"Don't bother. They never work."

I will have to talk with the salesman about this.

One Sunday we go to REI to stock up on things that will save us. We spend $500 on bug spray and a water purification system, filters, bladders, a portable shower.

All this time I am in the process of finding someone to go with us to care for Natalie while we are in the orphanage and taking care of official business. The caseworker at ONIA has suggested that we might be able to get someone in Kostanai to care for Natalie in our absence. But the idea of dragging Natalie halfway around the world to a completely alien place and then leaving her with a stranger unsettles me. What if we don't like the person? What if we don't trust him? What if the person lets Natalie drink water or eat something contaminated and she gets sick?

But finding someone to go with us on this trip is not easy. The family yields no takers: brothers and sisters have children, spouses, jobs; older nieces and nephews have love interests, college, jobs; grandparents lack the stamina. Everyone has a healthy trepidation about the prospect of such a trip.

It is very hard to find someone who can drop her life on ten days' notice for a six-week trip to Central Asia. Only nuts want to do this. Young, adventuresome, independently wealthy or, conversely, matter-of-factly impoverished nuts. Unemployed. Just try to find a person who actually wants to and is able to go on a trip of this description, with whom you could tolerate traveling, with whom you would also leave your young child for large parts of days.

I solicit applicants through local universities' list servs for students interested in the region. I solicit through a list serv of returned Peace Corps volunteers, folks who love exotic travel. I talk with every friend and colleague I have. I develop an interview process and an application packet with a questionnaire (What's your prior experience with international travel? What's your prior experience with child care? How would you entertain a spirited five-year-old in a room for four hours? How have you disciplined children?) and a list of joint responsibilities (ours include providing emergency medical evacuation insurance, a satellite-based cell phone, all expenses, and a salary). I follow up on every lead. Marc and I interview several people.

We would have taken Harold, in a pinch. Harold was studying Central Asia at the University of Chicago. He was studying Arabic this summer, but would take the time off for this trip, which was a chance in a lifetime. He had taught high school for years, had returned to the university for his Ph.D. He was very strong, intelligent, self-assured. He was a little familiar with Natalie, though—in our presence, on his first visit to our home, he had the temerity to correct her behavior. We did not like this, and neither did she. Also, how smart was it to take a young man, a stranger, to leave your daughter with on the other side of the world? Still—Harold was a possibility, a second choice.

Our first choice was Amy, a darling, bubbly, sweet young woman who had just finished her master's degree at the University of Chicago's School of Social Service Administration. She'd had extensive professional experience with children, and was instantly at ease with Natalie, who was instantly at ease with her. Amy saw a trip to Kazakhstan with us as a grand adventure to enjoy before taking her job in the fall in Washington, D.C. The start of this job was flexible, but she didn't want to start any later than Labor Day. Would we be home by Labor Day? Oh, *surely.* In late June, we booked her.

The young women at ONIA had told us, correctly, that we could get a referral of a healthy little girl from Kazakhstan immediately. What they hadn't told us—besides that the trip to get her would be absurdly long and harrowing, and that taking Natalie through Russia might not be so safe anymore—was that we would wait an indefinite period of time before traveling to get this little girl. So tangled and inefficient are the bureaucracies in these countries (almost as bad as our own INS) that children and prospective parents can grow old and die—or at least go half-mad—waiting for the wheels to turn. The first snag for us came the week after we accepted Vera, in the form of a two-week hiatus in all paperwork processing while the Kazakh government decided whether to use DSL or FedEx for its official business. Thereafter, snafus and bottlenecks caused by missing or overwhelmed or indecisive bureaucrats were the order of the day. Week after week after week, we were advised of problems and given revised estimates of a possible travel date. Occasionally we were asked to send more money (for ancillary expenses such as messenger deliveries, yet more apostilles, photocopying, document preparation). Marc, never sure when we would be called away for six weeks, could never be sure what professional commitments he could make and keep. He took this uncertainty like a scoop of sand in his lunch.

I found the president of Kazakhstan's forty-five-page vision for his country—published on Kazakhstan's website—a source of some comfort during this difficult time. Although I couldn't force myself to read the whole thing, it seemed to me strong evidence that the country was on the right path. Although they did play with headless goat carcasses, a country with a website and a visionary president (so he was a crook, too—at least he had vision) clearly wasn't populated entirely by warlords. I printed it off and added it to my notebook as a security blanket.

All the possible dates for travel in June passed; then all the possible dates in July; then half the possible dates in August. In mid-August, Amy regretfully took her leave of us and moved to Washington, D.C., to start her new job. We would be traveling with Harold, then, despite our reservations—*if* the trip occurred in time for his return to full-time studies in mid-September.

In mid-August, Natalie served as the flower girl in my niece's wedding in Oregon. We had thought we would be bringing Vera to meet the family at that wedding. Instead, we showed her video to an assembled throng of aunts and uncles, grandparents and cousins. "How could you not love that little girl?" breathed my brother's wife, Sarah, when the video stopped.

A week later, Sarah called me and said, "I'll go with you to get Vera."

My valiant sister-in-law was taking a huge leap. Her four home-schooled kids were now off on their own, and her work was all volunteer: She *could* go. But she had never been away from my brother for any length of time, or from her children for more than a few days. She was not an intrepid traveler or a fan of the third world. But she would go because she had lost a bet with my mother nearly thirty years earlier.

My mother had loved babies—she was "baby-batty," my dad liked to say—and had committed herself to children all over the world, all her life. She was a public school teacher, a Sunday school teacher, a Girl Scout leader, and the chairperson for our small Indiana town's annual UNICEF fund drive. Every year at Halloween-time, she sent us forth—four little reluctant do-gooders jingling our black-and-orange cartons as we fanned out over the neighborhood, trick-or-treating for UNICEF. I had been, probably, her most difficult child. "Spirited" is the favored parlance today for the child who is passionate, persistent, and headstrong, as I was. ("Impossible" is the word their mothers use when no one else is listening.) Looking at me, though, my mom could see that someday, when I finally settled down, I would want to be a mom. Sarah bet my mom that that day would never come. This was a bet Sarah was happy to lose. She would do everything she could to help me become a mother, in loving memory of *my* mother.

Once Sarah signed on, my relief was deep. Marc's intense dismay had been a heavy burden for me to carry alone. I had had to fight Marc's terror and anger as well as my own. Sarah and I agreed that, although this trip was daunting to us soft, spoiled Westerners, it was nothing to what our pioneer foremothers faced crossing the prairie, or the ocean in a wooden ship. We chastised ourselves for our quailing.

We bolstered each other's strength. Sarah was my partner in optimism, my partner in "We can do this. It will be quite a tale to tell!"

We accepted Vera's referral the week before Mother's Day 2001. On September 11, 2001, Natalie clutches my hand as we walk into her kindergarten class for the first time. It is about eight-fifty A.M. Central time. We have been listening to Mr. Rogers's *You're Growing Up* audio-tape on the way in to school, and are still humming his perky tune, "Everything Grows Together," as we walk through the door. As I glance about expectantly, looking for other parents I might know, the atmosphere seems odd. Some parents are going around happily with their kids, exploring different play stations. But a surprising number are looking stricken, talking into cell phones. When one of these fathers drops his arm to his side for a moment and looks up, I catch his eye.

"How are you doing?" I ask brightly, trusting that my sense of something amiss is all wrong.

He looks at me, failing in his attempt to return my smile. "Haven't you heard?" he replies.

"There's no way we can go to Kazakhstan now," Marc says on the phone to me later that day. I am reeling in my initial shock.

"*What?* What's this have to do with *Kazakhstan*?"

"Theresa, it's *right there*. It's in the same region of the world. There's no way we can go there now."

"Can't go? Of course we can go! We have to go get Vera!"

"Theresa."

"*You* don't know we can't go. You *never* wanted to go. You're just using this as an excuse."

*"Theresa, are you insane? Of course we can't go."*

"We don't know that. Let's wait and see what happens."

"If Sarah won't go, we can't go."

"Sarah will go. Let's just wait and see."

Quick, get out the map. Where's Kazakhstan in relation to Afghanistan? Past it, on the other side, far away. It's a huge country.

A day or two after September 11, Sarah calls and says she can't go anymore.

I think, "We'll have to find somebody else."

Marc says, "That's it then. We can't go."

I call the U.S. State Department. I explain our plight to the Central Asia expert: We have a little girl there, in Kazakhstan. We are supposed to go get her soon. What does he think? Would we be safe?

He is a very nice man. He wants us to be able to go adopt our little girl. There is no warning about traveling to Kazakhstan, he tells me. You can go, as far as the U.S. government is concerned. The problem is, you just don't know how long you might be held up. If there is military action, it could affect the airports. But fundamentally, it would in all likelihood be safe to go.

We could go, but there's no telling when we might get back, if a war started.

Marc and I hold anguished talks at all hours. Are we just wimping out? Are we just using this as an excuse not to go? We never wanted to go in the first place. We had not been concerned, before, that a plurality of the Kazakh people are Muslim. The Lonely Planet website says that the Kazakh people are very kind and hospitable. The gentle, loving face of the nurse in Vera's video has been a beacon of hope, a promise of what to expect in the people. But now, this Muslim plurality is more concerning. Might some tiny fraction of that plurality be radical? What if we become targets for just one or two extremists? We are obviously American; Marc is obviously Jewish; we are traveling with a tall, blonde child. We would be conspicuous. The odds of being hurt are very, very small, but still . . . they are greater now than they were on September 10. It would be different if we were traveling alone, if we didn't already have a child. If it was just the two of us, childless, going to collect our first child, we would not have been deterred. But to expose Natalie to the increased danger changes the equation completely. Taking her in peacetime would already mean exposing her to absolutely the highest risk we would consider; an iota more risk for her tips the scale.

Vera's image floats before my eyes. The scared, darting eyes, the hands clutching the dolly. The big smile, the little fist clenched behind her back as she returns the truck to the nurse. We had not watched her video over and over and over again in the months since we had first received it. Studying it would only have caused pain. Why nudge ourselves into love with a child we can't yet reach? But Natalie has not been so well-protected. She has incorporated Vera into her doll play from the moment she first saw her video. For months now, virtually every time she has played with her dolls—more than once a day—the story has involved Vera: going to get Vera, or being home with Vera. Vera, her long-awaited sister.

It takes me about a week to accept that we cannot go get Vera. It feels like I am aborting a live little girl. I cry and cry. Finally, in bed one night, I break it to Natalie. "Natalie, honey, I have some bad news." She stops moving and looks at me closely. She is dimly aware that bad men have crashed planes into buildings in New York. "We can't go get Vera anymore, honey."

*"What? Why?"* she wails.

"Honey, those bad men are in between us and Vera. We're safe where we are, and Vera's safe where she is, but it's not safe for us to go get her anymore." I clutch her as she starts to cry. "I'm sorry, baby. There's a war going on between us and Vera. We can't go anymore."

For months we have been going to get Vera. And now we aren't. Natalie arches her back and wails, tears streaming through tight-shut eyes, "No, no, no, no, nooooooo!"

Marc, seeing his baby get hurt, is in anguish. His anguish becomes fury directed at me, because I am the cause of Natalie's pain. I insisted that we tell her about Vera, despite his reservations. I can feel his seething dismay on the other side of Natalie's wracked little body.

"Well, when *can* I get a baby sister?" she cries after a while.

"I don't know, baby, but we'll keep trying. I just don't know."

I have been worried that Natalie will be troubled by the vagaries of adoption, the apparent randomness with which certain children become *your* children, *your* brother or sister, and others don't. How will it feel to her, knowing that we could have been Vera's family, and now we won't be? That Vera would have been happy with us, but we trust she will also be happy with another family?

I say, "God, or the forces that be in the world, meant for us—for you and me and Daddy—to be a family. They didn't mean for Vera to be part of our family. We don't know why. But Vera is supposed to be with someone else, and she will be. The little girl who is meant to be part of our family will be part of our family. We will find her."

Those lost pictures on Mother's Day. It *was* an omen.

Vera drops out of Natalie's play forever.


For the week and more after September 11 while we are going through this wrenching decision-making process we hear not one word from ONIA. Finally, I call, and our little caseworker answers the phone as chirpily as ever.

"I can't *believe* I haven't heard from you," I spit.

"Why?"

"*Why? Why?* Hasn't this little problem in Afghanistan had some impact on the Kazakhstan program?"

"Not particularly, actually. People are still going."

*"People are still going?"* For a moment I think it again: We are wimping out. We lack guts. We don't care enough about that little girl.

"Yes."

"Well, we're not."

"Okay."

"We have to relinquish the referral of Vera."

"Well, I'm sorry to hear that. Are you sure?"

I explain our thinking.

"I can understand that. But we were just about to get a court date for you."

"We *can't go*. Please send me the paperwork we need to relinquish this referral, and send us a refund. And would you please have Lynn call me? I want to talk with her about our next steps."

"Actually, Lynn retired."

"Retired. Lynn *retired*? *When?*"

"Mmmmm, about two months ago?"

Lynn, the woman we had devoted so much effort to courting, had retired without so much as a form letter fare-thee-well. She was as cold as she had appeared the first time we met her. I had just willfully blinded myself to it.

By this time we despised ONIA, but at least they *knew* us. Indeed, as one of the caseworkers had let slip, the sheer bulk of our file was something of a rueful in-joke around the office. Also, they held thousands of our dollars. And, if we wanted to go back into the Russia program, we would return to the top of their waiting list. For a few days, we thought about that possibility: Maybe just staying with the devil we knew would be better than starting from scratch with an unknown entity. But then the caseworker called to inform me that, in fact, we *can't* re-enter the Russia program because we are too old. During the years we had waited for them to do the job for us—either to get us a referral or to refer us to an agency that could—we had aged out of their program, apparently without their realizing it.

Of the thirteen-thousand-dollar foreign program fee, they refunded four thousand dollars. They had spent the rest, they said, getting us to the point of near-travel in the Kazakhstan program.

I have a magnet on my fridge, a quote from Winston Churchill during World War II: "Never, never, never give up." Well, okay, but what about just recognizing when you're bashing your head against a brick wall, and changing your strategy? Maybe we should just be happy with the family we have.

The problem was, we *were* happy, for ourselves. But we wanted Natalie to have that sister. The fact that we had promised it to her was important: We couldn't honestly tell her that it was *impossible* for us to get her a sister. Babies were always available, for enough money. But we felt we could have explained that it just wasn't worth the costs, that we were happy just with her. She'd've gotten over it, I think. But it was our concern that she have an adopted sibling to share her life with after we were gone—*that's* what kept us going back to that blasted brick wall where we'd already left so many of our brains and so much cash.

## 7

# More Dead Ends

Arlene's voice at the other end of the phone is cold. She has waited days to return my phone calls. I am in full grovel mode. I have nothing to lose by baring my throat. Our only alternative to returning to OFIA is starting over with another international agency. The week before, Our Stalwart Local Agency had hooked me up with the good people at their favorite international agency. The staff people at the international agency are friendly, businesslike. They inform me that we will wait twelve to sixteen weeks for a referral after we get all our paperwork done—another three to four months. This feels like an eternity after all we have been through. Desperate, I place a sheepish, exploratory call to OFIA.

"Are you guys placing kids from Russia?" I ask the man who answers the phone.

"Sure, we're placing kids from Russia."

"About how long does it take?"

"Oh, not long at all. Arlene has a whole stack of referrals sitting on her desk right now."

My heart leaps, but then I realize I must have misheard, or he must be mistaken. How could she have a stack of referrals sitting on her desk, when the system doesn't work that way anymore? "She has a stack of referrals? From *Russia*?"

"Well, I *think* they're from Russia. Let me check." I knew it. They're from Brazil or somewhere. Click, click, click. I wait on hold. "Yes, they're from Russia."

"Arlene has a stack of referrals on her desk, from Russia."

"Yes."

I envision this stack of documents and photos and videotapes. We are back in the days of Natalie's referral. Arlene is the rainmaker. I do not care any longer how she is getting around the rules. We will do anything to get one of those referrals.

"Would you have Arlene call me? Please?"

Several days later, she finally calls.

"Why the hell did you go over to ONIA? I thought I did pretty well by you guys."

"Oh, you *did*. You did great by us! Natalie's just wonderful."

"Well, so?"

"I don't *know*! I don't *know* why we switched!"

She's not buying this helpless act. "Come on," she urges. "I mean, what was *one thing* you were thinking?"

"Well, you know, Arlene, we were going to use you, but you're so expensive. And when I called Maryanne"—the director of placement, whom I had loved—"to ask how to get the costs down, she was so cold! She said, 'Stay in a cheaper hotel'!"

"No, no. Maryanne's not like that."

"Well"—this was exactly what Maryanne had said—". . . right. Maryanne's not like that, I know, I love Maryanne. She must have been having a bad day."

"Come on. There must be something else."

My back is against the wall. I can see no alternative to telling her some part of the truth. I begin slowly. "Well, you know, Arlene, we were kind of disturbed about what happened to Angie and Stewart."

There is a moment of silence. "What do you mean?" I can see her narrowed eyes. I gain a tiny bit of courage. I'm not crazy. I didn't just make up all this stuff. Marc might dismiss it. Marc might think I'm too scrupulous. But I think he's too cynical. He's willing to ignore Arlene's unethical practice. Maybe we made a mistake going with ONIA, but I wasn't stupid to criticize Arlene.

"*Bobby,* Arlene! Bobby's a wreck. He'll never be normal. They didn't want a child like that!"

She shoots right back. "*You* don't know what they wanted."

I freeze. Is she right? Had Angie and Stewart told her they would consider a disabled child, and just gotten, through no fault of hers, a child more disabled than she or they had reckoned for? I am momentarily confused, and then I fold.

"Well, that's true. You're right. I *don't* know what they wanted." I take a deep breath before plunging into full confessional mode. "I'm sorry, Arlene. I was wrong to leave you, I was just all screwed up. But believe me, I've been *royally* punished for it already. Marc is furious with me, for one thing. He *never* wanted to leave you! He's been mad at me for *years*."

As I detail some of our suffering at the hands of ONIA, Arlene begins to soften. She asks questions to flesh out details. The sound of her competitors being trashed is music to her ears. When I finish my recitation, I am fully prostrate.

"Please, can you please, please take us back again? *Please?* I swear, I would crawl over hot coals if you could get us a referral soon."

She laughs. I exhale. I have accomplished what Marc has been furiously certain is impossible. I have wormed our way back into Arlene's fold.

"Yeah, okay. I might be able to work with you again."

"You can find us a healthy little girl in Russia?"

"Of course. There are lots of them."

"Soon?"

"Yeah, soon. I have a lot to do right now, though. I'm sending forty families to Russia next week." She pauses for effect. All those other people, loyal to her, traveling next week. We could have been among them.

"Wow," I say. The memory of our trip to get Natalie is sharp and painful. "You must be really busy."

"I am, yeah. But once this is all taken care of, I'll get back to you."

Ten days later, Arlene calls us at home in the evening. This is the kind of thing she would do if you were favorites: She'd call you at home, off-hours, sometimes late, and begin an intimate, exciting conversation about your hopes and dreams. She had gotten those forty couples off to Russia. Now it is our turn. She wants to send us to Russia in a couple of weeks. If we can get our dossier done in forty-eight hours, she can do that for us.

"Two weeks? You can send us in two weeks?"

"Well, yeah, if you can get your dossier together, I mean, like *right now*. I wouldn't ask just anybody to do this, but I know how efficient you can be, Theresa. I know *you* can get it done."

My heart is thudding away. Marc and I are walking around our bedroom, holding separate phones, practically jumping up and down.

"Now," she says, "let me get this straight, so I know what I'm looking for. You know this thing I do, right? The rank-ordering?"

Oh yes, oh yes, we remember. There are three factors to consider: age, sex, health status. What are our preferences? Which is most important to us? She loves this talk, and so do we. It's part of the dream: What do you want in a child? Let me get this straight, so I can pick just the right child for you. What do you want? We talk it through with her. We want a girl, one to three years old, emotionally and physically healthy. Health is the most important factor; age is last. Is this possible?

"Yeah!" she says brightly. "Yeah, sure. I have lots of healthy kids on my desk. Now, let me think a minute, there's . . . well, for that one, hmmm . . . You know, you guys, you might have to travel twice. Are you willing to travel twice?"

"Of course! Can Natalie go?"

"No, no, no. Natalie can't go. It's just, you guys, it's just too much. You're so busy when you're over there. She can't go."

"Oooohh." We envision being away from Natalie for so long. "That would be bad. How long would the trips be?"

"I'm not saying for sure that you'd *have* to travel twice, but you might. Depends on the region. If you have to travel twice, the trips would be about ten days each."

It seemed possible that we and Natalie would survive two ten-day stints apart. If this is what we had to do, we'd do it. Leaving her at home did have the huge benefit of relieving us of tremendous anxiety about her well-being in Russia.

"Of course we don't want to. Leaving Natalie for that long would be very difficult—"

"Oh, she'll be fine."

"Well, yeah—she'd probably be fine. If we have to travel twice, we just will."

"Hmmm. Well, that's good. I'm sort of thinking about a couple kids right now—"

We stop breathing. The rainmaker is at work.

She continues offhandedly, as if she is talking to herself. "They're in Astrakhan, a two-trip region." We don't *care*, we don't *care*! We'll *go*! "But, no, no—they might go to somebody else."

To Somebody Else. She is in her element now. She is God.

The next morning, a Friday, I drop everything else I am doing and tear all over Chicago ordering and collecting documents—police clearance letters, birth and marriage certificates, an updated home study, passport copies, a letter from the bank vouching for us—all of which have to be notarized and apostilled. Monday afternoon I FedEx the complete dossier to Arlene in New York with a check for nine thousand dollars. Two weeks! We would have a referral in two weeks! I would crawl over hot coals.

And we hear . . . nothing. No response. On Thursday it strikes us that we have been complete and total idiots. We should have *carried* the documents to her office! What were we *thinking*? How could we have *been* so careless?

Friday morning I call to find out when she can receive us on a visit. We will go there, and make the magic work all over again, just like before. But the person I speak to could give me no dates, and we hear nothing for days, then weeks.

Maybe she's looking for kids for us. She must be really busy.

She's *punishing* us, Theresa, for *abandoning* her.

She was *always* like this. This sort of thing is why we abandoned her! We were her favorites!

This is outrageous.

*We* were outrageous. We *never* should have left her. I *knew* it!

Finally, one night, she calls us back.

"So, Arlene! We expected to hear from you a few weeks ago!"

"I'm sorry, you guys. I've been so busy."

Must have been Somebody Else who got the last batch of kids who were on her desk.

"Now, remind me. What is it you're looking for again?"

In an orphanage in Ukraine the child with huge dark eyes is nearly two years old. Her impish spirit is both a delight and bane to the harried ladies who rotate through her life. Only occasionally do they have the time or patience to pursue her when she dashes off, flirting, hoping for pursuit. At times it seems she can neither give nor get enough hugs. The little food she takes in drops, useless, through the deep well of loneliness at her core.

About a week after her last call we meet Arlene in a sumptuous lawfirm conference room high above Chicago's Loop, where the president of OFIA's board works. The air bristles with our anxiety as she strides into the room. But we quickly locate in each other's eyes what we liked so much there before. We hug, joke, know that we understand each other. There is some healing to be done here, but it is in progress.

Ludmilla—remember Ludmilla? Arlene reminds us: Ludmilla had congratulated us in Connecticut on our capture of Natalie. Well, Ludmilla is in Russia right now, meeting children. She will be back in ten days, two weeks. When she gets back, Arlene will have a referral for us.

Three weeks pass. When I call OFIA, I am told that Arlene is in Chicago. We have not heard from her, and do not get return phone calls.

Weeks later, my cell phone rings. "Hey!" It's Arlene. "Listen! I'm in Chicago! Are you guys free tomorrow morning around ten? I think I have a referral for you. I *think*."

"You *think*?"

"Yeah, yeah. I'm pretty sure. I have to make sure that this kid's available now. But I'm pretty sure. I'll call you back in the morning with an answer."

Marc cancels his morning meetings. At nine-thirty A.M., Arlene hasn't called. I call New York to get her cell phone number, and dial it.

"Oh! Hi! I was just looking for your number! Meet me at the main library at ten."

This is barely possible. But she has a baby for us, and we will break our necks.


The Harold Washington Library does not make videocassette players available to patrons. "But, see," Arlene explains breathlessly to the man behind the video library desk, "I have a referral of a kid from Russia for them. I need to have a videotape player to show it to them! It'll only be a couple of minutes. Really!"

This trumps everything, right? I have a baby for them. You've *gotta* let us in!

We get settled, she finds the videotape, and she fast forwards through waiting kids. Flip, flip, flip. Not that one, not that one, not that one. Here! She stops on a six-month-old baby whose unfocused eyes blink dully. The child doesn't track to sound, despite valiant efforts of someone near the camera; her head bobs about on a shaky neck, mouth hanging open. Marc and I are stunned. We have written and spoken, several times: "A healthy little girl from one to three."

"Well, what do you think?" Arlene grins when the video is over. She's excited, she's in sales.

"Well, Arlene," Marc begins. He's the only one who can say this, since he never wanted to leave her and she trusts him more. "Actually, we are looking for an older child."

Arlene is surprised. "Everyone wants a baby! I thought I was doing you guys a favor!"

"Well, actually, *we* don't want a baby. We're too old, Natalie's too old, we don't want the hassle. We want an older child," Marc says calmly. "From one to three years old."

Arlene studies us for a moment. We appear to be serious. She jumps up and seizes a notebook. "Okay, okay, let me check something." She flips through the book. "Here! Wait a minute!" She whips out her cell phone and ducks behind a shelf full of videotapes. We sit uncomfortably, miserable. The librarian comes back to ask us if we're done yet. We'd said it would only be a minute. We beg for a little more time.

"Okay!" Arlene strides out from behind the bookcase. "I have another one for you." She pops another videotape into the player. Babies meant for Somebody Else whir by in a blur; she stops occasionally on a face just long enough to see it, then whirs onward. Here. A beautiful little girl, about two-and-a-half, dark hair, pixie cut, huge black eyes, dimples. Eagerly tossing a ball to her caregiver, thrilled with the game. Given a doll, she is lost—what is she to do with this? Where's my ball? Where's my daddy to play ball with? Very personable. Active. Gorgeous, expressive eyes, beautifully arched eyebrows. Responsive to caregivers. Our hearts leap.

"Wow," we say, when Arlene stops the video. "She looks great. What about attachment?"

Arlene hasn't met her, but Ludmilla has. In a moment we are talking with Ludmilla via cell phone. Ludmilla says, "Oh, yes, I noticed this child right away. She's really special. Beautiful eyes. Intelligent, full of personality." Appropriate interaction with adults—doesn't come running for attention, like some of the children; but neither does she stay away, isolated. She responds appropriately to kind attention. A lovely child.

We hang up and turn to Arlene. She has done it again. A little sloppily this time, to be sure, but still: She has found the perfect child for us. I can't speak, and when I hold Arlene in a long hug, tears fill my eyes. "Thank you," I finally whisper. "Thank you so much." When I pull away, I see that she is weeping too.

Later that afternoon, Marc calls me. Her head is way off the charts. What? The child—Daria—is macrocephalic. Marc had taken the medical information provided on Daria back to work, and plotted her growth points. Her head is more than twenty-five percent above normal size. And her height is at the bottom of the charts.

I had commented while we watched the video that her head was beautifully shaped. That roundness in back, though—apparently there is too much of it. A lot too much.

"Well *so*?" I am *not* letting this one get away.

"There are a number of very severe neurological problems associated with macrocephaly."

"There is obviously nothing wrong with this child. If she had a terrible brain disorder, wouldn't it have shown up in her behavior by now? Wouldn't she be stumbling, or lolling, or something?"

"Not necessarily. Sometimes symptoms are not evident until the third or fourth year."

"Honey, *no*!"

Our reaction to this child was different than it had been with Natalie. This time we actually *had* fallen in love at first sight. Marc a little less than me, but still. This is difficult for him, too.

"Let me talk to some people."

For days, Marc consults with neurological experts across the country. He asks Ludmilla for new measurements on Daria, and gets them quickly. Her head is growing rapidly, at a much greater rate than normal, and her height is slipping further.

"Well, maybe she had short parents with huge heads!" I think of people I know with big heads, very bright people. Look at Robert Reich! He's short, and has a very large head. Maybe she's brilliant.

Maybe she is. But macrocephaly by itself is risky—it reflects something like a twenty-five percent chance of serious neurological problems. Macrocephaly and short stature combined present a very clear risk for neurofibromatosis. We hear absolute unanimity from our medical advisors, a chorus of "No's." The risk of severe neurological problems in this child is extremely high.

I cannot accept this. I talk with my older sister, a minister. Surely she will counsel me to go with my heart. To take the risk. To love this child.

She listens quietly while I tearfully explain our situation. "Honey," she says gently, when she has taken it in. "I'm really sorry. But you need to listen to the doctors. I had a family a few years ago who brought home a child with macrocephaly, because they had fallen in love with her. And she did have severe neurological problems. Now she can't walk or feed herself—their lives have been taken over by caring for her. I don't think this is what you want. I know you don't want it for Natalie."

The best advice now is the same as it was when we were considering Natalie's referral: Trust your head, not your heart. It is wildly counterintuitive, in a matter with such vast implications for your heart, to give your head the reins first. But it is right. Our hearts were not immediately able to see what a precious bundle Natalie would become for us. This time, our hearts are saying yes and our heads are saying no. It is infinitely more difficult to say no to Daria than it was to say yes to Natalie.

I need days to let go of Daria. Just when I think I have numbed myself to my loss, I think of hers, and am thrown into fresh paroxysms of grief. To the best of my knowledge, her fate will be terrible, and I am intentionally abandoning her to it. Whatever awaits her, she will have to face it without us.

The reels of the little girls we have left behind replay in my head. The little syphilitic girl smiling up from the pool of colorful balls. Vera, clutching her dolly for dear life. Daria, gleefully rolling the ball back to her nurse. How strange and disturbing, to have such a hand in someone else's fate.

We write a lovely note to Arlene refusing Daria's referral with deep regret. We don't mention that we think her staff should have vetted the referral in advance, that we think the referral was inappropriate, that we are angry to have been inflicted with this sharp and unnecessary pain. How long does it take to chart a child's head circumference? We don't ask what our nine thousand dollars is paying for, if not for this minimal amount of due diligence. We say that we are deeply grieved at having to turn down this beautiful little girl, and that we hope to hear from her again soon.

We hear nothing at all.

For weeks.

When we finally write to tell her we are emotionally exhausted and wish to withdraw from the program, we hear nothing. Many weeks later, after several written requests for a refund of our nine-thousand-dollar fee, she returns four thousand five hundred. She has spent the rest, she claims, through her accountant, servicing us. At the rate, we figure, of about eighteen thousand dollars per hour.

We never talk to OFIA again.

\* \* \*

By the time we decline to parent Daria, it is nearly Christmas. If we had started work with a new agency in late September, we would be nearing the time expected for an appropriate, aboveboard referral. Instead, we had fallen again for Arlene, with her seductive promises, her mysterious capacity to produce babies.

At dinner one night, just before Christmas, we talk about Vera. The military action in Afghanistan is over for the time being. We think: We can go get her now. She has haunted us, that darling little girl in her polka-dot jumpsuit. What will happen to her? We decide that I will call ONIA on the next appropriate business day and see if Vera is still available.

On December 23, I don't call. On December 26, I do. But it is hard to pick up the phone. Talking about going to Kostanai, Kazakhstan, for six weeks in the middle of winter while we are sitting in a nice warm restaurant in Chicago is one thing. Making the phone call that could entail our taking that dangerous trip is another. An echo of the old terror surges. Are we crazy? No. This is something we have to do, for Vera, and for Natalie. We have promised to be Vera's parents. She needs us. And what would it say to Natalie about our commitment to *her* if we decided not to go get Vera now that we *could* go? I pick up the phone. When our former caseworker answers, I say, "If Vera is still available, we are ready to go get her now."

There is a shocked pause. "Oh. Oh, I'm sorry. Her new parents left this morning to go get her. I'm sorry."

She is ready to comfort me on our loss. But I feel only relief. Thank God, we have done what we needed to do to discharge our responsibility to Vera, and we did not have to make that harrowing trip after all. She has a home, in America, and parents who are willing to make that trip to bring her to it. More power to them. Wherever they are, I hope they are as happy as we are.

## ❧ 8 ❧

# The Perfect Place for Us

"You guys are the perfect candidates for our new Ukraine program."

If it had been anyone but Susan, I'd have laughed and hung up. But Susan was the home-study worker from Our Stalwart Local Agency. OSLA had never made a promise they couldn't keep, had always found answers to our questions, had given us all the support we could reasonably expect, and more. Now, just as we were admitting defeat, OSLA was opening a new door. For years, OSLA had taken delighted couples directly to China to adopt, eliminating the need for an international agency. Now, they were planning to do the same thing in Ukraine. I couldn't believe my ears. I peppered Susan with questions.

Could we take Natalie?

Sure. That's a parenting decision.

Do we go through Russia?

No—Warsaw.

How long do we wait for a referral?

Usually two to six weeks after your dossier is completed.

I hung up and paged Marc. We had found our solution at last.

Three weeks later Marc and I ring the bell on a cold gray morning at OSLA's shabby, low-rent offices. OSLA wastes no money on pretension: Its exclusive focus is creating families. We are there to meet with OSLA's executive director, Abe, who wants to take us step-by-step through the Ukraine program process. We are to be his first family in Ukraine. We carry our completed dossier and our checkbook. We just want to get going. It is early February. We have figured it all out: Six weeks from now is late March. Add a month for hitches. We plan to have our new child by spring. I will spend the summer at home with my two girls, all of us bonding into a happy new unit.

We are sitting on plastic chairs in the large, cheaply appointed conference room when Abe rushes in clutching a box of slides and a sheaf of papers. In our few brief encounters with Abe he has struck us as a little goofy, but nice. Tall, gangly, with wide-open eyes behind round tortoise-shell glasses, thinning curly hair sticking out over his ears, clown-style, Abe always looks surprised, amused, and game. Abe has just returned from Ukraine, where he was a guest of the Child Rights Alliance (CRA), a group of attorneys who help prospective parents navigate the web of laws governing foreign adoptions from Ukraine. He has spent the last few weeks tagging along with a couple from another agency whose adoption search CRA facilitated. He wanted to understand the process and to vet CRA. Now he burbles with enthusiasm.

"Hey, guys, it's great to see you," he says breathlessly as he rushes into the room. "Gee, I'm sorry I'm late." Cold air flows off his coat as he sheds it onto a chair and starts looking around for a slide projector. "You know, you guys, Ukraine is great. But I've got to tell you—this process is not for the faint of heart. I'd say that, maybe five, ten percent of people who are initially interested in the program will decide to go through with it once they understand how it works."

We are hardy. We have stamina. We will not be deterred. This is our last shot. And if the process is grueling, if people drop out, good for us—that means there are plenty of children there. He explains what we're in for.

Ukraine is one of the few countries that will not refer a specific child ahead of time. Instead, two to six weeks after your dossier is received in Kiev, the Central Adoption Authority sends you a letter inviting you to come to the country. When you meet with the director of the Central Adoption Authority—a large, imposing woman—she says to you, "Why are you here? There are no babies here."

We look at Abe in disbelief. *Really?* After they've invited you to come, they tell you there are no babies?

Yes, yes. Not everyone knows to expects this, and so they're put off, confused. You have to be prepared. You say, "It was just in our hearts to come at this time." Then the dragon, appeased, grudgingly assigns you to one of a handful of psychologists who inhabit offices down the hall from hers. These are the people who make referrals to children. In the best circumstances, CRA will have informed the psychologists about what you want in a child—age, sex, ethnicity, health status—and the psychologist makes an appropriate referral to one or two children residing in an orphanage somewhere in the country. You go to them via taxi, bus, train, private car, or plane. You spend a day or two, as long as you need, deciding which if either of these kids is a good fit for you. If you decide one of them is a good fit, the process continues and in a couple of weeks you go home with the child (*un-*

*less* the child resides in one of the regions that requires a thirty-day wait before the child can be released, in which case most people go home and come back). If neither child is a good fit for your family, you simply say so, and go back to Kiev to the Central Adoption Authority, and they refer you to another one or two kids. This goes on until you find your child.

One of the hitches in this process, Abe discloses, is that the psychologists in Kiev often know very little about the children. You might not know until you get to the orphanage the child's true age, ethnicity, health status—even sex! However, once you *get* to the orphanage, all this is cleared up. The orphanages are extensions of the hospital system, and are run by doctors (like Dr. Christina, the head of Natalie's orphanage, we think). These doctors are proud of their orphanages, proud of the good care they take of the children, and eager to share with you every jot of information they have on each child.

We are comforted, thinking of an orphanage network run by benevolent Dr. Christinas. If women like that are looking after the children, everything will be fine in the end. But the apparent near-randomness of the referrals troubles us. It feeds Abe's sense of wonder that the people he had traveled with had gone to find a baby girl and came home instead with a beautiful half-Roma young boy. Abe asks us to allow ourselves to be surprised by love of a child who doesn't fit our criteria. But we have no inclination to open ourselves to such wonderful life surprises. We want a little ethnic Russian or Ukrainian girl to go with our existing family. What if no one listens to us, and we have to go back to Kiev over and over and over again before they refer us to a healthy little girl? How long are we going to have to stay in this country?

Abe says that, according to CRA, only a very few people have to go back to the adoption center in Kiev more than twice. So think, at most, three or four weeks in the country. It's hard to say. And nobody goes home without a child, unless they're just not ready for some reason.

What if, visiting an orphanage, we fall in love with more than one child? After September 11, I had thought, for a time, "Love is the answer. Love as many children as you can." But falling in love spontaneously with a child is not an option in Ukraine. Many of the children in the orphanage are there only temporarily. Their parents can't feed them, so they board them at the orphanage for a while. Don't even look at children not referred to you. They're other people's kids.

Finally, Abe says, "I want to go with you guys. Because you'll be the first couple to go through our Ukraine program, I want to go and make sure your experience is good." He'd be as inconspicuous as possible, just accompanying us as a shadow, snapping pictures at key beautiful moments to show to other prospective families (with our permission) so they'd know what to expect.

We are ecstatic. Although we envision some awkward moments involving bodily functions and normal bad behavior that we don't particularly want to share with a stranger, the relief of having Abe there to hold our hands dwarfs our concerns about privacy. We gleefully hand over our completed dossier, write a large check, exchange bear hugs with Abe, and head out the door counting the days.


Of course there are delays. Lots of delays. Some caused by OSLA's foul-ups, some by whimsical rule changes in Ukraine. I begin to fear that I actually *am* Sisyphus: For the rest of my life, I will push paper up a slippery mountain of—what else?—paper, believing that a child is just over the top, almost within reach, only to go sliding back down to the bottom when a bored bureaucrat in some godforsaken place teeming with orphans tips the toe of his raggedy boot.

We receive the draft agreement for OSLA's Ukraine program in late May. It stipulates that we will be referred one child per visit to Kiev, that we can go back for a referral no more than three times, and that we have no legitimate claim against anyone on Earth if we come home without a child.

What if the nationalists are in control of the whole process? we ask Abe. What if they make a point of referring only sick children, because they don't want us to take any healthy ones? Why are *we* the only ones with exposure here?

Abe promises to pay us back all eleven thousand dollars of OSLA's foreign-program fee less direct expenses if we come home without a child. We would still be out our airfare, hotel—all our expenses, plus heartbreak, including Natalie's—but at least he wouldn't rake in the foreign-program fee, too. We sign a revised agreement guaranteeing our money back if we can't find a child. It is our last chance.

It is Sunday, June 23, 2002, and we are settling in to bed. Nattie, for once, is asleep at a reasonable hour, and in her own bed. Her summer school reading class starts at eight-forty-five the next morning. We had given up on traveling in April, then May, then June, then July, then most of August. The best estimate we have been able, with repeated hounding, to get out of OSLA is that we will travel in mid- to late August or early September. Marc has clustered all his responsibilities in the first half of the summer quarter, and cleared his calendar after July 30.

Marc picks up the phone and listens for a moment, then starts spluttering. "What? No! *What? No!* But you said . . . I don't think so! Oh, God, I just don't know!" He hangs up and whirls on me. "They want us to be in Kiev on *Thursday!*"

There are a couple of anomalies that Abe cannot explain. Like, if there isn't a specific child we are going to meet, why is it so urgent that we go this instant?

Well, apparently there *is* a specific child.

There *is* a specific child? Well, what's she like?

They can't tell us that, because there's not supposed to be a specific child. No one is supposed to know anything about her until she's officially available for adoption, on Friday, July 5.

Well, if she's not officially available until July 5, why are we being asked to drop everything and go to Kiev right now?

Alexi—the nominal head of the Child Rights Alliance—says we need to be the first ones on the ground, ready to claim her.

You mean, a *lot* of people want this child? We're actually in *competition* for this child? We thought there were tons of kids in Ukraine who need homes.

Well, yes, I think there are.

But then why are we in competition for this particular child, about whom we know nothing?

Look, guys—I don't have all the answers. I think we need to do what CRA says and take it on faith that they know what they're doing.

Because it might be months before we are invited to Kiev again; because Marc is in contract negotiations with another university and our house is on the market and we might move to another state— where OSLA is not licensed—before another referral comes; because

OSLA's Ukraine program is our absolute last chance to adopt again; because, at base, we trust Abe, we decide to go. With rapid pleading, Abe buys us a couple of extra days. We can leave on Friday for a Monday morning appointment at the Central Adoption Authority in Kiev.

My sister-in-law, Sarah, is a straightlaced person with no pretensions. She eschewed her liberal religious background and embraced conservative Christianity, with my scientist brother as her willing partner. She bore four children and schooled them at home, never leaving them for so much as one night. Because we love each other well, we never discuss politics and religion, about which we passionately hold diametrically opposed positions. After our Kazakhstan plans fell through, Sarah put herself on hold until we needed her again. When I call her on a Monday night to tell her we need to leave for an indefinite stay in Kiev on Friday, she is silent for a few moments. Probably praying. Then she says, "Well, what do I need to do?"

At eleven A.M. on Friday all of our suitcases are in the limo, and Sarah, Marc, Nattie, and I are taking pictures of each other waving and grinning in the sun next to the gleaming white car. The limo to the airport is a special treat for Natalie, and an assertion: We are off on a big adventure, a happy turning point in our lives! We are going to find a sister!

Moments after we alight at O'Hare, Abe strides up behind us. "Hey!" he says, full of cheer. "Let's go to Kiev!"

At Schiphol Airport in Amsterdam, Abe leads us out of the terminal and into a luxury grocery store in the shopping center attached. There, on his advice, we buy small treats for our hosts in Ukraine:

Dutch coffee and chocolates, stroopwafel, small items that will show we care.

On this trip, we learn everything about Abe, and like all of it. He has habits of speech. "Crikeys!" "It's a bell curve" (his explanation for everything). "Let's rock and roll." "I don't do sick." He is a sweet, sweet man. He said on our trip—his eyes bright and wide—that his mother's consumption of alcohol while pregnant probably shaved ten to fifteen points off his IQ; but, the implication is, he's doing okay, he had a few to spare. He doesn't begrudge her (or anyone else) anything. He has an amazing facility for languages. He learns languages very quickly, he said, by thinking of them as music—and by not being afraid to try. If people laugh at him, he doesn't care; he has such a generous nature, always giving everyone the benefit of the doubt, that he is shielded from too much hurt from others. He gives them and himself the benefit of the doubt of his generous nature. Yes, he can be laughable, they can be laughable, we all can be laughable in this amazing experience of life. Let's keep laughing together so we can get through it. He has traveled all over the world for the last twenty years, usually in very trying conditions, bringing children and parents together.

Some twenty sleepless hours after we have left home, we stagger into the terminal in Kiev. Natalie is doing her level best to be a great traveler, but sleeping at a time like this—when she is about, finally, to get a baby sister, maybe—is too much to ask. It is four P.M. Saturday afternoon. We groggily follow Abe through the crowds who throng the area looking for arriving family and friends. As we emerge from the airport into the parking lot, Abe stops short and throws his arms around Alexi.

Alexi is chubby and rumpled, with a wide, open face, kind smile, wide mouth, hooded eyes, dark straight hair falling over his forehead. He looks tired. He and his wife, in addition to their sixteen-year-old daughter, have a six-week-old baby, who is keeping him up at night. He and Ivan—short, trim, thirtyish, with an elfin face ready at every moment to burst into a grin—lead us through the open parking lot outside Kiev's airport. We are comforted by the kindness and good humor in these faces. "Ah," Abe says with relief while they load our bags into their cars, "I love these guys."

Alexi and Ivan drive like maniacs, like everyone else coursing through Kiev. We careen through city traffic for a good fifteen minutes before pulling up in front of an apartment. As we step out of the cars and look up, Natalie says, "*Oh,* no. *Nooooo.* This is not what I had in mind at *all.*" It is a typical Eastern bloc apartment building— concrete and steel, dirty, ugly, surrounded by weeds, overflowing trash containers nearby, shrivelled grandmas wearing babushkas sitting out front. There is a small, ratty playground across the drive, shared by a few neighboring apartment buildings. We are afraid our hosts have heard her. We hurry to explain to her, quietly, how much nicer it is inside than outside—how it was the same when we went to get her. *Remember the pictures of the apartment we stayed in in Ekaterinburg? Yes. Well, this is like that. It's very nice on the inside, it just looks really crummy on the outside.*

She is warily mollified for the moment. She will withhold judgment until she sees for herself.

We crowd into an elevator that, like the one in Ekaterinburg, is terrifying and small. It is very dark, like the hallways, and noisy, creaking ominously, and lurching. Every time it stops, there is first a loud crack and a violent lurch. Then, slowly, the door creaks open, yawns a moment, then closes again. We must ride in this dim box all the way to the twelfth floor. With clenched teeth and white knuckles, we reassure Natalie that we are perfectly safe, and pray that we will be spared. Clearly, we are in the greatest danger by far on this trip when we are driving or in elevators. The Ukrainians ride silently, unmoved; this is what elevators are like.

When we step off the elevator we are turned toward an open cage. In the cage are two smiling ladies standing at doorways, through which light flows into little squares in the dark hallway. Natalie bounds to the far end of the cage, toward plump, sweetly smiling, ruddy-faced Irina, and disappears. "This is my room!" we hear her say from afar, and, nodding our way past a proud Irina, find Natalie in a pretty bedroom flooded with daylight from the long row of open windows, the double bed graced with a ruffly flowered spread. A fan stirs the hot air, and city sounds float through the window: traffic, airplanes, trains. This is the apartment that Natalie, Marc, and I will inhabit in Kiev. Sarah and Abe will share Christina's apartment. Both of the apartments—the landladies' homes—are clean as a whistle, carefully and proudly kept. Irina and Christina vacate as often as they can to accommodate adopting families. The eighty dollars per night we give them for each apartment and all meals is more than their month's rent.

Shortly after we arrive, all five of us crowd around the tiny enamel-topped table in Irina's spotless kitchen while Irina and Christina hover, smiling and bobbing, serving us the food they have prepared: toasted ham-and-cheese open-faced sandwiches, a peeled vegetable salad, hot cabbage soup, parsley buttered potatoes, and ground chicken patties sauteed in butter, chocolates for dessert. It is the first of many similar meals: tasty, heavy, fatty, and hot.

Natalie wishes to sleep with daddy tonight, for safety. Poor daddy. She crashes for a few hours, then wakes. I sleep soundly on the living room sofa with earplugs in while Marc tries to calm and entertain Natalie through much of the night.

Sunday, Alexi and beautiful young Anna, our interpreter, take us for a tour of downtown Kiev. Some of what has been restored is quite beautiful. Parts could be Paris. We take in the ancient city gate; the old "cathedral way," a long stretch of boulevard with beautiful cathedrals at either end; the ancient cobbled street that winds down the hills behind cathedral way, lined with dozens of booths selling beautiful folk art, and good little restaurants tucked away in the courtyards of two-hundred-year-old buildings; a vast central city promenade, which features a McDonald's, a large fountain like a spurting disco ball, and a high-end underground shopping center covered with a long, domed skylight that runs down the center of the square.

The central streets have been closed to traffic on this beautiful Sunday. People stroll through the streets, arm in arm, enjoying the day. It is impossible not to notice women's dress. A very high proportion of women here are strolling about nearly naked. Marc attributes this to the heat; but the men are fully dressed. One of the favorite tops for women this summer is a handkerchief held against the front of the torso by shoestrings that crisscross the naked back. Heels are very high, skirts are very short and very tight.

"Have you noticed," Abe asks at one point, "that almost no young women are wearing bras?" I have noticed. So has Natalie, who has been carefully trained to believe that only your family should ever see your belly button. She is a little confused. Later, I joke with Abe about his wandering eye. Good man, he says to me, "My Bible says, 'He who honors himself honors his wife.' But crikeys!"

Rock music blares from loudspeakers in the central square. A public service. There is no escape from it. Huge screens in an amphitheater along one side display rock videos. Sarah imagines the voice of some party appartchik coming over the loudspeakers instead of music, his face looming over us from the screens. Either way, it is ear hegemony, and strange. What if we wanted to hear Mozart?

Sarah stumbles upon another tourist wearing a cross pin in his lapel. They strike up a conversation. As she happily discusses our trip with this stranger, Alexi becomes agitated. He pulls Abe aside. We are not to tell people why we are here. We are not to make friends here with strangers. Later, in the bazaar, American missionaries hear our English and ask what we are doing in Kiev. "Vacationing," we say. "How unusual!" they reply, pleased.

We go home to another full, heavy, delicious meal, and try to recoup lost sleep for a second night. Alexi and Anna will pick us up at eight A.M. to go to the Central Adoption Authority. We picture the large lady who will tell us there are no children. We are ready for her.


Marc has been told not to wear a tie. Men don't wear ties. It would be odd. He wears a sport coat and chinos, and I wear a beautiful casual dress that cost three times our landlady's rent, but doesn't look it. Abe is perky, ready, as he says, to "rock and roll." As Sarah pins me in a long good-luck hug, Natalie sleeps on.

From the back of Alexi's car, we watch people going to work in Kiev on Monday morning. A woman in a slinky red satin evening gown with spaghetti straps stands out to us, but apparently not to anyone else. Women in filmy black tops, short tight skirts, and stiletto heels are common. I might as well be wearing a bedsheet.

Alexi pulls up next to a dirty old building on a tree-lined street. Like so many places of official business in the former Soviet Union, the Central Adoption Authority is housed in a dingy old unofficial-looking building, with blackened stucco walls. The entrance is inside a shaded courtyard, which we enter through an arching stone gate. Alexi deposits us along the wall, and goes off with Abe. We stand there, looking at other small clumps of people, talking.

Alexi returns after ten minutes or so, with Anna. They walk us over to one of the little clumps of people we've been eyeing and introduce us to Nina, the woman who has made all these arrangements for us, who has worked the system on our behalf so we can meet this particular little girl. Nina is plump, with a broad, open, sunny face, permanently flushed, big laughing blue eyes surrounded by creases, shaggy blonde hair. Immediately she and I are intimate, on the same side, friends.

With Alexi's and Anna's help, Nina briefs us on what to expect, what to say and do. Expect to spend hours. Friday was a holiday; the caseload is backed up. You may wait a couple of hours just to see the director. Then you have to wait again to see the psychologists. You must just be patient. When you do see the director, don't make a point of wanting a girl. Don't make a point of *having* a girl. These instructions are infused with urgency. Girls are harder to get than boys, she continues; if she knows you already have a girl, it might be harder to get a referral of a girl. On the other hand, the referral to this girl is pretty secure. We think we have this locked up. It dawns on us that the director won't be able to understand us anyway. Won't Anna, who has served as the interpreter for couples in this process many times before, translate appropriately to protect us from ourselves? Well, yes, they concede. She will take care of you. We basically *can't* make a mistake. We feel like very large and awkward puppets. It is a little unsettling, though, that our *handlers* are nervous.

We get the signal—some invisible signal—to go in. Nina nods to us. Anna says, "Come," and in we go up a dark staircase, and down a long, unlit hallway lined with dozens of people. I wonder when they will turn on the lights. We squeeze past all of the other supplicants and into the director's office. We sit at a small rectangular table that abuts the director's desk to form a T. Across from us sits a French couple who, I fancy, look more their age than we do. No makeup, very plain clothes, no hair coloring here. Birkenstocks. Quiet, very intelligent-looking. They have their entourage, too, their seconds: translator, facilitator. We smile small nervous smiles at each other, and wait for the dragon lady to appear.

In sweeps an official, a secretary in her wake. She settles into the director's chair and eyes us with a wry smile on her face. She is not large, or particularly forbidding-looking. She speaks in Russian to those in the room who can understand her. They look at us, comment to each other. We smile, sit on the edge of our seats, raise our eyebrows so we look innocent and earnest, scrubbed and wealthy, young enough. Look from face to face, smiling.

She starts official business, asking to see the translators' passports, the facilitators' passports, finally our passports. Nina and the official talk. They sign papers. Occasionally a question is directed at us.

"Where do you live?"

"Chicago."

"Al Capone, no? Michael Jordan. Do you like it?"

"Very much. It is a beautiful city."

"Do you have other children?" This is a trick question. If we have other children, we have less of a claim than childless couples. But we can't lie.

"Yes."

"Boy or girl?" Another trick question. If we say "girl," we're less likely to get another girl. But we can't lie.

"A little girl, six."

"What sex child do you want?"

"A girl." We blurt it out despite Nina's instructions. Then we try to patch up. "Our daughter wants a baby sister very much. But, of course, we will love any child referred to us." What has Anna translated?

The official looks amused. They talk about us openly, untranslated. Papers are being signed.

The walls are adorned with pictures of beautiful children, many of them in families. Pictures are signed with greetings like, "With love from the Hershey family in Orono, Maine." Marc attempts a little banter. "What beautiful children," he says to the translator, pointing at the pictures. She translates to the official.

"They are not beautiful until you take them home," the official says back, graciously, meaning, they are not beautiful in the orphanage.

Encouraged, Marc sympathizes with her workload: "This is like a vacation for us," he says. "For you—so much work!" The director laughs at this, as do I. A *vacation*? She's charmed.

More papers are signed. As in Ekaterinburg, all the momentous transferring of parental authority is recorded on paper, in gigantic old ledgers.

Ten or fifteen minutes after we were led in, we are led out, back through the waiting throngs, down the dark staircase, out into the shadowy courtyard. It is shortly after nine A.M. We will wait now, in the bar around the corner that sells coffee. It is very narrow and dark. We sit with the French couple and our translators. Our translator does not speak French, and neither do we. The coffee is the worst anyone has ever tasted, anywhere. We load it with sugar in an effort to make it drinkable. After a while, we stop trying to converse, and just talk among ourselves. Alexi does not know how long we will wait. We will go see the psychologist next, yes. It seems to be going well, yes.

While we sit, a television hanging over the bar plays a bizarre sur-realist drama. People emerge unpredictably in barren moonscapes, which turn into apartment courtyards of the type we have seen—dirty, trash-strewn, with broken-down cars in them, stray dogs; people walk through walls, dematerialize and rematerialize, have violent mis-understandings, are dressed in costumes, walking down the street. We do not know as we watch it, puzzled and amused, that it will become an emblem of our experience in Ukraine.

Nina comes after an hour or so and releases us. The fix is in. We are done in Kiev. The psychologists do not need to see us.

We are delighted. Here we are, again, in the best hands.

Now we can know: The child is in Odessa, in the far south of the country. Odessa! Home of the Jews, brilliant, funny, tragic, beautiful Odessa. Marc's paternal great-grandfather was born there. Perfect. All of the omens are good.

We will go there on Wednesday.

## 9

# Do Not Pass Go

At ten o'clock Wednesday morning we are hurtling toward Odessa. Alexi is driving his own van, bearing Abe, Marc, Sarah, Natalie, me, Svieta, and all of our luggage. Svieta is a slim, pretty, blonde young woman, very proper-looking. When we climbed into the van that morning, I asked her if she was Alexi's wife. She blushed. Oh no, no. I am Svieta (for Svetlana). The translator. I had expected Anna, who had already entered our comfort zone. But here is Svieta, sweet and quiet. A little disconcerted, shy again, we settle in around her.

There is one unbroken road between Kiev and Odessa, which turns from a potholed two-lane road to a fairly smooth four-lane highway and back again with some regularity, with every gradation in between. People like Alexi, who want to drive their late-model vans at eighty miles per hour whenever they can, share this road with much older and less reliable vehicles: ancient Ladas, lumbering military vehicles, hay wagons, tractors. Some of the drivers obviously feel that they have nothing to lose.

Happily, Sarah and I are both wrapped in the settled conviction that we are not going to die in the attempt to reach this child. Without this conviction, we would be terrified. Nevertheless, we try not to look at the road, and instead attempt to sleep, entertain Natalie, and take in the scenery.

Trees line the road on either side for much of the way, which makes it prettier than it would otherwise be. At some railroad crossings, little whitewashed keepers' huts have lace curtains billowing out the windows and flowers planted alongside. Along much of the route, sometimes on both sides of the road, ripe sunflowers stretch as far as the eye can see, creating a scene of great beauty—gold fields underneath blazing blue skies. The Ukrainian flag. Apparently, the blue and gold have been reversed at times, but now they've decided on blue on the top, like the sky, and gold on the bottom, like the fields of sunflowers and wheat. All along the way, hundreds of small farmers line the road selling produce from upturned boxes—everyone selling the same thing, side by side by side by side, all along the road. Goats and sheep wander among the wares.

Alexi's phone rings often. He talks quickly, in Russian. Sometimes he is obviously agitated. He has a hard job. Again he has left his family to be with us. He will be in Odessa with us until the adoption is complete. He is playing tapes of soulful Ukrainian ballads, loudly, which he turns down to yell into his phone.

About halfway to Odessa we stop at a Soviet-style hotel that Alexi says is the best we can do for a pit stop. There is a cavernous dining room, gas station, and vile bathroom, a stinking hole in the floor, wet, splattered. Revolting.

In Odessa, seven hours after leaving Kiev, we roll slowly down a wide, dusty, tree-lined street. Small concrete-walled shops line the street on either side, shaded by the drooping trees. It is hot, still. Alexi pulls into a parking space in front of a shop, and walks away. While we wait for him, we buy water and sodas and chips and ice creams, with Svieta's help. Nothing costs anything. An ice cream is one or two grivna, less than forty cents.

After about ten minutes Alexi returns with Anastasia, the woman who will make everything happen as it should in Odessa. Abe has told us that Alexi has told him that Anastasia is brilliant, meticulous, dogged, a superb facilitator. She is beautiful, but severe-looking. She is in her forties, probably, very slim, tall—elegant. Short hair, good but severe cut, dyed dark brown. Large eyes, large lips, good nose, excellent makeup. It is very hard to get her to smile. She makes only furtive eye contact. Her Russian sounds clipped. She sniffs, or seems to. She directs Alexi to the hotel.

We are disappointed that it is not in the center of town. We wanted to stay in the downtown area. But we say nothing. It is new, and looks good and clean from the outside. It is on a busy thoroughfare, facing a complex intersection like Boston's turnarounds but bigger. Alexi asks us politely: Would we like to look at the rooms first? Do we wish to approve?

Anastasia turns on him. He is to understand that she desires us to stay at this hotel, like it or not, because it is convenient to the orphanage—not many are. Svieta translates shyly, with an apologetic smile.

Alexi does understand, but in his gentlemanly fashion insists on our prerogative to refuse the rooms. We don't really care about the rooms; if this is close to the orphanage, that's all that matters. We please them both by looking at the rooms and approving them instantly. They are large, modern, well-appointed, very clean, cool. European. We just want to go to the orphanage.

We sit waiting for Alexi on the hotel's side patio, on bright orange plastic chairs at a bright orange table under a bright orange umbrella in the blazing late-afternoon sun. We have freshened up a bit and gone down to wait for him to take us for our first meeting with the little girl. Natalie knows that she cannot go to the orphanage with us, and has wisely stayed in the air-conditioned room with Aunt Sarah. Abe is with us, perky and enthusiastic.

Alexi trudges up to us, a tragic look on his face. It is a look we get to know well in the next several days. "I am sorry. We cannot go today." His English is not great. "The orphanage director says no. She says it is too late."

We are sharply disappointed. "It is too late?"

"Yes, the children, they are getting ready for supper."

"So we go in the morning?"

"I think so, yes. I think so."

"You *think* so? Maybe we won't?"

"No, I think we go in the morning to meet this girl."

We suck it up. What else can we do? Alexi and Anastasia, feeling terrible, wish to make it up to us by showing us Odessa tonight. In an hour they will come back to take us out.

They drive us over cobbled streets to the city center, where we get out and walk. The waterfront is defaced by industry, blighted by old rusting hulks of ships and machinery. The once-beautiful plaza facing it boasts a majestically colonnaded walkway, the soaring white arch pocked, cracked, defaced, worn away. Art students dot the plaza, facing the colonnade with the sun setting behind it, painting other things: dogs, horses, field scenes. Behind them is a street lined with beautiful buildings fallen into disrepair, splashed with graffiti.

From the plaza we walk up a long, tree-lined walkway. On our right is the waterfront; on our left is a boulevard lined with beautiful old buildings, most of them faded and crumbling but some recently restored to old glory. The walkway is dotted with vendors: Several sell pony rides or rides on kiddie-sized electric cars, others a chance to pet a monkey or a lizard, others a chance to have your portrait drawn, or to be photographed with someone in costume. We stroll up the lane and into the main shopping district, where the vendors are thick and the open-air bazaar is buzzing. Attractive couples walk around arm–in–arm, the women a little more reliably covered than in Kiev, but only a little. Street musicians play, and recorded music spills from other kiosks and restaurants and sidewalk cafes. The entire long street feels like a bustling carnival, and right in the middle of it, on one side of the street, is an actual carnival, with a dozen different rides and amusements for children.

Anastasia leads us to an open-air steakhouse in the midst of the goings-on. It could have been anywhere in America, a T.G.I. Friday's. We expect that this will be a time for us to get to know our Ukrainian hosts—Anastasia, Alexi, and Svieta—to have a glass of wine or two (or ten) and chat. But they order sodas and so, of course, do we, and when we try to make conversation with them, we can't. They look at us as little as possible. When we ask questions, brightly at first, they seem not to understand, or they respond with one word, a short phrase, and then lapse into silence again, look down at their plates or out into the street. They do not ask follow-up questions. Have we offended them in some way? Unwittingly trespassed some sacred social code? Do they regard us as chatterboxes? Hysterically sociable? We squirm, confused, extremely uncomfortable.

And then, Natalie blows. She has maintained heroic good behavior throughout the trip, which we have amply warned her might be very difficult at times. She will do anything to get a baby sister, including restrain herself. But this awkwardness that is smothering us all like an elephant lowering itself into the middle of our table is too much for her to bear. She begins to wrestle with her daddy, one of their favorite pastimes. But *not here*. Ignoring our efforts to constrain her, she pummels his arms, leaves her chair and hangs from his neck, pulls his hair and puts her fingers in his ears, and then, in a final affront, wheels around to kneel on his lap and lick his nose.

Anastasia's plucked eyebrows shoot up, her full lips purse in a frown, and she looks away.

Anxiety nails me to my seat. She disapproves of us. She's going to decide we shouldn't have this little girl.

Abe, too, sees Anastasia's reaction.

As we stand to leave, I am brimming with embarrassment and anxiety. We are chronically lax with Natalie. She never listens to us. Marc never controls her effectively. Now, because we are bad parents and she is uncontrollable, she will be deprived of a sister by these people, the keepers of all sisters in Ukraine.

Abe takes Alexi aside for a chat.

"Are we okay?" I pounce on Abe the moment he is free.

"Yeah," he says. There is reservation in his voice. "But they're not used to that kind of thing. It's just not what they do. It would probably be good to rein her in a bit when we're around them."

Easy for him to say.

While Abe walks ahead with the Ukrainians, I quietly lash into

Marc. "Why'd you let her *do* that? Why don't you control her? Now Anastasia thinks we're bad parents."

Marc is quickly furious. "Who is she to pass judgment on us? What does she know about raising kids—she doesn't even have any! How dare she judge us? How dare she disapprove of Natalie!"

He is right. If she is judging us, she is doing so with too little data. But—there is no escaping it—she is the keeper of the keys. Anxiety and anger are both reasonable responses to her displeasure.

What we don't know, because the Ukrainians don't want us to know, is how worried they are about what's happening at the orphanage.


Dropped back at the hotel, we go across the street with Abe to the little grocery store, stock up on vodka and cherry juice, and bring it home and start sipping. Marc and Abe begin a game of chess with the large wooden set Sarah bought for my brother, her husband, at the street market in Kiev. Sarah is writing in her diary. Once Nattie's settled into bed, I pick up a well-known book on toddler adoption. I had read this book all the way through when we were waiting to go to Kazakhstan. It strongly affirms that the families it discusses were greatly enriched by their adoption of toddlers. But the experiences related in the book look to be "enriching" in the same way that what doesn't kill you makes you stronger. In those leisurely months while we waited to travel to Kazakhstan, I could read the book cover to cover and absorb its lessons calmly. Now, however, I am looking for a quick fix. I just want the good parts—the parts that reassure you that what you're doing is not insane—and I can't find them. All I can find are the sections—which indeed comprise most of the book—about what can go wrong. Here's the chapter on the children who sit bolt upright in bed screaming in the middle of the night for months on end and can't be woken up. The chapter on the children who won't bond with you, no matter what you do. The chapter on the children who are inconsolable for the first year—who stand at doors and windows sobbing and crying out in a foreign tongue for lost loved ones. The chapter on aggressive toddlers who may assault your other children. I can't find the part that says, "It's going to be just fine."

When I have spoken with Abe before about some of my anxieties about toddler adoption—worried that any of the terrible problems enumerated in this book could happen to us—he has said, "Nawww, I don't think so. In my experience, it's always worked out." Abe is always looking on the bright side. He's one of those people who believe that "everything happens for a reason." Several people I love very much take great comfort in this happy platitude, this agnostic's version of faith. I want to believe it, too, but it's too softheaded. I don't buy it.

Now, as I rifle through the book, looking in vain for reassurance, my hair starts to stand on end. Finally, I throw it out. I don't need this stupid book. This isn't going to happen to us.


The next morning, Thursday, we are happy. Today, finally, we get to meet the little girl. We tell ourselves we will not love her at first sight. We prepare ourselves for ambivalence, uncertainty, initial disappointment. We expect that, as we did with Natalie, we will spend the morning with her at the orphanage, then break for lunch and nap, then go back for a couple of hours in the afternoon. We will fall in love with her gradually, and she with us, as we pass a few days of this routine while the wheels of Ukrainian bureaucracy do their grinding. We'll be our charming best. We dress up for our first meeting with her, with the orphanage director. We look cheery and loving. Aunt Sarah has brought a new baby doll, with homemade clothes and a homemade blanket to match. This doll is perched at the top of our little bag of toys. We wait in our cool rooms, sipping strong coffee, with Abe.

Shortly after the appointed time, Alexi calls up from the tiny lobby. We rush down. He looks tragic again. We need to talk.

We go into the mod dining room, bright orange like the patio chairs. "Guys," Alexi sighs as we sit down, "we have a problem. The orphanage director, she says there is another couple who wants this child. A Ukrainian couple."

"What?"

"She says a Ukrainian couple might want this child. I don't believe this, I don't. But if a Ukrainian couple wants a child, they get first pick."

"Well—why are we here if the child is not available to us?"

"You see, this couple has not been registered with the Central Adoption Authority in Kiev. Nobody there knows anything about this couple. The orphanage director is supposed to notify Kiev in such situations. She has not done this."

"So what do we do now?"

"We will wait."

"For what?"

"For her to produce this other couple."

Alexi thinks that she is really holding this child for an Israeli couple who is working through an agency that has given the orphanage a lot of money. Right now adoptions to Israel are on hold, because of the violence there. So the orphanage director has pulled this trump out of her hat: a Ukrainian couple. Even if a Ukrainian couple just *might* want to adopt the child, she is taken out of the pool for international adoption.

But it is illegal to hold a child for a couple without notifying Kiev.

Another orphanage director in Odessa just got in a lot of trouble for doing this. All the authorities involved in adoption in Kiev, Alexi tells us—the director of education, the director of children's services, the prosecutor—know about our situation and are pressuring the orphanage director to obey the law.

Well, so maybe there *is* no other couple. If Alexi's right about this, and the law's on our side, we should prevail. But what if there actually *is* a Ukrainian couple?

If they want the child, they get the child.

How long do they have to make up their minds?

Oh, awhile.

Days?

Yes.

Weeks?

Maybe. Awhile.

Does a vacillating Ukrainian couple always trump a firmly decided foreign couple?

Yes.

And what happens to the child if this desultory Ukrainian couple ultimately decides not to adopt her?

Then she will become available for international adoption again. (At least, until another Ukrainian couple takes an interest.)

And what do we do in the meantime?

Wait.

For what? We're not going to wait around here for some indefinite period of time while this Ukrainian couple, if they exist, go through their languid decision-making process.

No, no—not for this. We will wait for the orphanage director to respond to the pressure she is receiving. "Remember," Alexi stresses, "this child"—we still do not know her name or age, or anything else about her—"she is not officially available until the end of the day tomorrow. The orphanage director does not *have* to show us her until tomorrow anyway."

This is not turning out too well. We came to Ukraine days before this mystery child was available so we could be the first people on the ground to claim her. And CRA thought that was okay, because they expected that the orphanage director would do the humane thing and let us spend as much time with the child as possible. Nothing is working out as planned.

A little complication, Alexi tells us, is that the orphanage director leaves tomorrow on vacation. She will be gone for two weeks.

Marc and I look at each other, trying to figure this out. "Why didn't somebody call the orphanage director before we came down here to make sure we could see this child?"

"There was no need to check, see, because it is against the law, what she is doing."

Abe thinks that if this director just meets us all the barriers will fall.

We pin our hopes on credibility and charm. Alexi will return for us at two P.M. to take us to the orphanage.

We fill the time by taking in some local color. It is blazing hot, and very dusty. The only landscaping in the city is on the plot surrounding McDonald's, which is planted in sod and bushes that keep the dirt in place. But elsewhere there are only trees and weeds, no sod, few bushes, so the dirt dries to dust and swirls around in the slightest breeze. We want to keep the sliding doors onto our small balconies closed to keep out the dirt. But the rooms are sweltering much of the time. The air-conditioning units in our rooms, though they look like new, work only intermittently, even when the power is on. Both electricity and water are turned on and off unpredictably throughout the day, to save resources. Usually we are safely out of the shower before the water is shut off in the morning, but not always. The first day, Abe is sudsy when the water stops flowing, and has to rinse with bottled water. Now we need more bottled water, and a few other items: sun hats if we want to go out at all, fruit juice, instant coffee and a hot pot, a sharp knife for cutting the bread and cheese we will buy for dinner. We will search for these items in the open-air market that lies between our hotel and the McDonald's a quarter-mile away.

A great deal of commerce in Ukraine takes place in these flea markets, where you can find almost anything you need in life. By night it is a nearly empty lot, scattered with the occasional rickety wooden display a merchant has decided to leave for morning, empty wooden crates, scraps of trash, and fruit and vegetable remains. Very early in the morning, the merchants drive up, back their battered cars in, and unload their wares into makeshift storefronts and onto crates. You can buy Right Guard deodorant and raw chicken, Maybelline eye shadow and ten different kinds of cookies in bulk, lightbulbs, eggs, and roughly hewn slabs of raw pork and beef sitting out there on a tray in the sun, under greasy plastic wrap. Electric appliances, embroidered handkerchiefs from Taiwan, shoestrings, shoes, hats, underwear, bread, cheese, utensils, berries, plums, peaches, nuts, dish detergent, bras, sparkly dresses, diapers—everything. It is a department store served up out of the trunks of broken-down cars. We wander through, agape, looking like rich Americans no matter what we wear: It is the health of our skin and hair, the way we carry ourselves, our air, perhaps, of confidence, which emanates from us even though we are bewildered and angered by their authorities, who tell us that one of Ukraine's children can be ours, then arbitrarily keep her from us, dandling her cruelly behind a curtain we cannot penetrate.

We amble through the open-air market and into the more permanent market, where the wooden stalls are sheltered by semi-permanent pale-green corrugated fiberglass, which forms a ceiling about seven feet off the ground. It is like being underwater, wading through narrow aisles bathed in green-filtered light.

We emerge with our purchases across the street from our lunch destination. McDonald's is a lush, cool, dust-free oasis. We enter it gratefully, sink into hard plastic seats. People stare at us everywhere we go. Very few Americans in Odessa.

On the way back to the hotel, walking down the other side of the busy thoroughfare, we pass a water station—it is like a communal well from some third world country where villagers gather to fill their earthen jugs. Here, the jugs are plastic. The station is not an open well but a series of faucets around a central source, covered with a bright blue plastic canopy, so everyone getting their water moves around in cornflower-colored light. This, they are told, is clean water, taken from deep underground, not like the poison that flows from their taps. People come and go at all hours, carrying their water.

We are back at the hotel and all dolled up again—as dolled-up as we can get without running water—by two P.M. Now at least we will be able to meet the director, we will have the opportunity to impress her. We picture Dr. Christina, from Natalie's orphanage. We can make friends with her. She will like us.

Sergei arrives, a little late, a little downcast. The director is remaining adamant that this other couple exists, that they have first choice. "But I think, I think that if we go there, she will see us. So—let us go there now, and show her that we are here, we are serious."

The orphanage is a cluster of three low buildings in a dusty, weed-filled lot behind a concrete and wrought-iron fence. There are rusty remnants of a playground anchored in dust in front. We can hear small voices coming from one of the one-story buildings, which is clad in dirty, chipping stucco. One of the buildings is new and clean-looking.

This is the administration building, where the director has her office. Marc, Abe, Svieta, and I go in with Sergei, who tells a woman in the first office that we are here to see the director. We wait while she walks down the hall to deliver the message. The offices are built around a central, one-and-a-half-story atrium, the roof of which is an octagonal skylight. The skylight focuses the sun like a magnifying glass onto the hardwood floor of what seems to be meant as a playroom, for there are a few toys on a shelf along one wall. The rest of the room is empty—of furniture and of people. It is blistering.

The receptionist comes back and tells us curtly that the director is still at lunch. We may wait outside until she returns.

We sit on a bench in some nominal shade in the weed-choked lot, looking at each other. "Crikeys!" says Abe, looking from one to the other of us, his eyes wide. "I'm sorry, guys. This isn't what I expected." Marc and I start to feel numb. We are not used to being this passive, this powerless. *Just tell us what to do.*

Small voices drift from the old low buildings, but no one comes out into the yard.

Across the street from the orphanage is some kind of religious order, hidden behind high stuccoed walls. Women cover their heads when they walk through the double wooden doors that face the street. Bells toll every fifteen minutes. No breeze stirs the weeds.

After two tollings of the bells, Alexi goes back inside. He is gone for a while. Abe is reading *Stalingrad*. Marc and I haven't brought anything to read. Alexi comes back out, and penetrates our gathering stupor. "She will see us now. Come. We can meet the director."

We are expecting Dr. Christina. She will like us, we know. We love Dr. Christina. She will be impressed with our education, our resources, our earnestness, our life's work. She will recognize us as kindred spirits. She will give us this child.

The woman who steps out from behind the desk in her large, comfortable office is no Dr. Christina. She is in her late forties, curvaceous but trim, dressed in a clingy flowered black-and-white chiffon dress, sleeveless, V-necked, with a kicky ruffled skirt. A party dress. Her mid-length hair is dyed jet black and teased into a nouveau bouffant. Her large dark eyes are rimmed heavily with black mascara and liner, frosty white shadow on the lids. Her lips—caked with orange lipstick that exceeds their natural boundaries all around—are set in what looks like a permanent sneer. She flicks her eyes in our direction once, then homes in on Alexi. Svieta translates for us.

"These people"—the Ukrainian couple—"really exist," she insists coldly.

She is furious with him. He has let it be known that he thinks she has invented this couple.

"They have been visiting this child regularly for about six months. They are about to make a decision."

"Who are they?" Alexi demands. "You must prove that they exist."

"I do not have to prove anything to you!" she snarls. "I have to prove only to Kiev, and they know."

"They don't know anything about this couple."

"They know now."

Alexi tries another tack. "Can we just see this child now, so that, if the Ukrainian couple decides no, this couple will have met the child?"

"No. She is not available."

This woman is like dry ice. I have never seen anything colder.

"I do have some other little girls who will be available in a few months. Perhaps your couple would like to meet one of them."

We are dismayed. A few months? We dropped everything to come here to adopt a child who is available *now*. In a few months we will have moved, everything will have changed!

"I have one little girl who is not bad. Some eye problems. Perhaps they would like to meet her. She is available in September, I think. She is not bad."

We will meet this little girl. First, Alexi wants to nail down the process with the director. She is going on vacation for two weeks to-morrow. Who will make decisions in her place? How long will we wait for the Ukrainian couple to make up their mind? They are hag-gling over these questions as we are ushered out of the office and back into the dusty yard.

We wait for a few minutes until Alexi joins us. "Let us meet this little girl. This is not going to be your child, but let us meet her. It is part of the game."

We walk into the long, low building that has been emitting child sounds. Two young women meet us with polite smiles. A doctor and a social worker. Please sit here in this office. We will bring in the child.

We perch on the edge of our seats.

In a few minutes, the doctor returns, bent over double to hold the hand of a little mite who can barely walk, and whose eyes go every which way. She is twenty-six months old. "She was blind from birth," the doctor explains, "but the eyes are repairing themselves naturally. She can see light now. We think that, with surgery in the United States, she will be fine."

Marc picks her up gently and looks into her face. She doesn't seem to notice. She is turning her head sideways and up and down indis-criminately. We say her name. "Hello, Sasha. Sasha, Sasha? Hi, Sasha." She seems to be deaf as well as blind. She does not orient to sound. She has a little befuddled smile frozen on her face. Marc puts her down, tries to get her to walk to him. She does not hear him. She staggers sideways.

"Would you like to take her outside?" asks the doctor. "To get to know her better?"

Abe says, "Yes, of course."

We go outside with her for a few minutes. We cannot elicit her engagement. There are holes where our stomachs used to be. This is a little human being. A pathetic little human being. Why not choose to love her? Could we not choose to love her? I think of the disabled activists in the U.S. who have named their group Not Dead Yet. This child is alive, as needy of love as anyone else. And capable of . . . who knows what? What is wrong with us that we refuse to let her into our hearts? But no, no. This is not a child we want to parent. This is not the sister we are going to bring home for Natalie. We go through the motions of examining her, then return her to the doctor. "We will think about it," we say through Svieta.

Marc and I walk like automatons through the weeds to Alexi's car.

Alexi and Abe are stricken. "Guys, I am very sorry for this," Alexi says. "I am so sorry. Nothing like this has ever happened to us before, never. I am very sorry for this." He assures us that he, and Anastasia, and Nina in Kiev will do everything they can possibly do to make this work for us.

"Crikeys!" adds Abe. "Well, it's a bell curve. Some processes are very easy, the majority are somewhat difficult, with predictable difficulties, and some are extremely complicated, like yours. Your experience is an outlier, that's what I'm thinking. Crikeys! I'm really sorry!"

"It's not your fault, Abe."

"I know it's not my fault. But I'm in charge, and you didn't sign on for this. I'm just really sorry."

Alexi drops us back at our hotel. We release him from any dinner obligation. We have no desire to spend another tense evening with

Alexi and Anastasia. We want to be alone with our family and Abe. Sarah and Natalie, who have been reading and playing in the room, are eager to hear about the child, and have some news of their own.

Natalie has been sick. They went to McDonald's for lunch, and Natalie was sick to her stomach on the way. She still feels a little woozy, and looks it.

All of a sudden, we are terrified. We don't have medical evacuation insurance. We didn't think we'd need it for Ukraine. After the threat of Kazakhstan, Ukraine seemed like Europe. Now everything here seems so primitive, so threatening. What if Natalie gets very ill? What if any of us does? For a moment we are overcome by panic. Should we try to buy insurance over the Internet? The connection to the Internet in Odessa is tenuous. Should we e-mail my brother, Sarah's husband, and see if he can get it for us? We thrash through our options for a while, and as we do, our panic subsides. Natalie was only sick once. We all feel fine, physically. Heat, dust, anxiety, strange diet. We'll keep a close watch on her.

Sarah is appalled at our story. "My God!" she fumes. "Do you guys think you're supposed to pay someone? Is this just an elaborate scheme to get more of your money? That *must* be it!" We are entirely confident that that's not it. No one has mentioned money at any point. Money—our money, at least—is not what the orphanage director is after. This is a different game, more baffling.

"You know, Theresa," Sarah says to me quietly when we're alone. "Good things come to those who pray."

I look at her. So this is what happens to people like me, who are not sufficiently religious. Everything in me rebels at the suggestion. If God is just, that is not how the world would work. We would get this child because we are *good* people, moral, thinking, loving people who have worked very hard to get the child, and would give the child a loving home with every advantage in life. Withholding the child because we neglected to pray would be like blackmail. Where would be the justice in that? The suggestion that we are not getting our child because we have not paid dues to God seems like a slander on God to me, a facile view of faith.

I say none of this to Sarah. I love Sarah. She is doing us an immense favor by being here. She is being wonderfully inventive and patient with Natalie. She is a very bright and loving woman. Surely I have misunderstood her; but I don't dare get into it. I smile slightly and remind her, "We were agnostic when we got Natalie, Sarah."

We are all awash in bafflement and wonder: We have been shoved through the looking glass. Suppose we *do* meet this child, and decide she is not a good fit for our family? It is almost unthinkable that we would decline to become her parents. We are in a pitched battle with obscure forces for a child we have never seen, a child we know absolutely nothing about.

That night, downtown, we indulge Natalie shamefully. Pony ride? Sure. Merry-go-round? Of course. Every ride in the amusement park? Why not? Want to get your picture taken in an elaborate stage costume? Of course, honey. We would have walked down the street on our hands if we could. What amusement could we conjure that might distract her from our failure to find a sister?

The next morning around nine, Alexi calls. He will pick us up at eleven. We will go back to the orphanage. If we are there, if she sees us there, then she knows we are serious. We need to be there. Perhaps she will have a change of heart. She will see that we mean business, that we will not be turned away. Also, we have to tell her we have decided not to adopt the other little girl.

Arriving at the orphanage at eleven-thirty, all dressed up, we are told that the director has gone out to lunch. We should return in the afternoon.

We go back to the hotel. Rest, eat.

Two hours later, we return to the orphanage. We are told that the director has gone. She is on vacation now. She will be gone for two weeks.

Marc and I look at each other, astounded. We are lead characters in an absurdist drama and have never seen the script.

Alexi talks briefly with the assistant director, the stern young doctor who showed us the blind girl the day before. She will be making decisions in the absence of the director. But she cannot do anything until Monday. The child is not officially available until five P.M. today, after the orphanage is closed to visitors. We have no right under any circumstances to see her before that time. Just go home. Come back Monday.

Back at the hotel, we head straight for the bright orange bar— Alexi, Marc, Abe, Svieta, and I. Abe will be leaving on Tuesday morning to attend to pressing business back home. Our plan is to nail Alexi down to a specific, step-by-step time frame, a Plan A, and a Plan B. "Now we will wait" won't cut it anymore.

"Alexi," we begin, "this just doesn't seem to be working. We don't think we're going to get to see this little girl. Can't we go back to Kiev and get another referral?"

"Well, yes, yes, I have been talking to Nina, in Kiev. You see, you see, there are not very many girls who are available right now."

"This is the only little girl in Ukraine who needs parents?"

"Well, no, not like that, but she is the only one we know of right now who is available for adoption. Other children, they need parents too, but they are not available for one month, two months, three months maybe, or maybe more."

We try to take this in. So the picture that had been painted for us, of a cache of needy kids ready for adoption, was misleading. Actually, there are *no* little girls in Ukraine right now who need to be adopted.

We look at Abe, architect of our fate. He seems to be as confused as we are.

"You see, you see, these little girls who are available now, they have already been promised to other people."

We try to penetrate what Alexi has said. But—we understood that we had to drop everything to come here so we were the *first ones on the ground* to get in line for this little girl when she became available. Now you're telling us that *other* little girls who are available now—and maybe this one, too, under the table—have already been *spoken* for? Were spoken for weeks or months ago? Isn't that against the rules? If everyone else is ignoring the rules, why aren't *we*? We're like chumps here, playing by the rules and coming up empty-handed, while everyone else is wheeling and dealing in back alleys and under the table!

We are getting worked up.

Alexi shrugs, hangdog. "No, no. It is not really like this. It is hard to explain."

"Why don't they *fix* this system?"

"Oh! This *is* fixed. It is much better than it used to be, *much* better."

"Alexi," I blurt, desperate, "have you told her about us? Have you told her that we're doctors, that we have plenty of money, that we have a house full of toys, that we've devoted our professional lives to children? Have you told her we'll give the child everything, the best education, love, everything?" Abe sits back. Marc puts a hand on my arm.

Alexi shrugs. "This, all this, it doesn't matter. If the other couple were, say, Italian, or were another American couple, all this might make a difference, see? But this is a Ukrainian couple. None of this matters. All that matters is they are Ukrainian, and you are not!"

"Alexi, what are our plans now?"

"Well, I think we will wait. Today, you see, today is really the first day of our process. That is because only today was this little girl available. So, really, Monday is the day we can really demand to see her."

"But Alexi, the director is gone for two weeks! What if the assistant director says she can't do anything in the director's absence?"

"No, I don't think she will say this."

"But Alexi, what if she won't let us see the child?"

"I think, I think we will wait. The other people, who are in charge of adoption here, all these other people, they know what is going on. They are working to make this all right."

"Okay, that's good. We're glad they're all on our side. But what's our Plan B? We need a Plan B."

"Plan B? What is this, 'Plan B'?"

"Plan B is your backup plan. You know—your plan for what to do if your first plan doesn't work out. We need a plan for what to do if we don't get to see this child. We can't wait around forever. This is very expensive for us!"

"Yes, I know this. This is expensive for me, too. I do not like this, either."

I think of his wife and two kids back in Kiev.

"So, we all want to get out of here," Marc affirms. "We need to have definite action by, say, Tuesday. Wednesday at the very latest. By Wednesday, if we have not seen this child, we have to have a referral to another child."

"Okay. I will work on this. I will talk with Nina. We will see if we can find another girl."

"This needs to start *right now,* not next week," Marc clarifies.

"Okay, yes."

Marc and I look at each other. They are going to scour the country for a little girl who is still available for adoption—some little girl who has somehow escaped detection by the ravening hordes of parental hopefuls who have descended on their country. We think back to Natalie's referral. "I have a little girl for you." A delightful girl—healthy, robust, the darling of one of the best orphanages in Russia. Here in Ukraine, they will see if they can find *any* child for us.

"What if we would consider a boy?" I ask. "Are there any healthy little boys available now, whom we could take home on this trip?" We strongly prefer a girl, for a thousand reasons (beginning with existing toys, clothes, rooms, and interspousal agreement on how to raise girls). But bringing home a boy would surely be preferable to bringing home no child at all.

Alexi raises his eyebrows, shrugs. "Maybe."

We solidify our understanding: Nina will start right away looking for another child for us. If we have not been allowed to see the little girl here in Odessa by Tuesday, the day Abe will begin his long return to the States, Nina will fax us another referral from Kiev. If we have not met an available child by Wednesday, eleven days after our arrival in Ukraine, we will go home empty-handed.

As Marc and I trudge upstairs toward our room, Abe hangs back to talk to Alexi privately. In the hallway on the second floor is a little alcove lounge. I sink onto the couch, and start to cry. Marc sheds his tears in the chair opposite. All of this because we couldn't conceive. I said once to a woman friend, a biological mom, that adoption was much harder than childbirth. She became all huffy and hotly denied it. But however hard labor is, it never lasts more than a day or two. Pregnancy lasts no more than nine months. We had been being tortured now for years. This was just baffling. Why was this being so hard for us? After a few minutes we walk toward our room, wiping our faces, knowing that Sarah and Natalie are waiting there eagerly to hear what the little mystery girl is like.

Having heard the disappointing news again, Natalie follows me into the other room, where I will get ready to go out that night. I am so worried for her. She needs to be prepared for failure. "Honey," I say, taking her on my lap, "we might not get a baby sister in Ukraine."

"I know, Mom," Natalie chirps. "That's all right."

I look at her. What's she thinking? She wants a baby sister with all her heart, and has for years. Then I get it. She thinks I mean *in Odessa.* We have thoroughly briefed her about the process, told her there *might* be a sister for her in Odessa, but there might not. We'd just go see, and if her sister wasn't there, we'd go somewhere else to find her.

"Honey, I mean we might not find a baby sister *at all.*"

She replies without missing a beat, but in a very different tone: "That's *not* all right."

I look at her, my darling girl, whom I will leave alone on Earth before I want to. In this instant, it becomes crystal clear to me: Failure is not an option. It is impossible that there is not a little girl in Ukraine who needs our love and whom we are willing to parent. We will not leave here empty-handed. We *will* find a little sister on this trip.

## 10

# A Little Snowflake

It is Saturday morning, a week to the day since we arrived in Ukraine. Our hosts want to entertain us while we kill more time. Southeast of Odessa about 150 kilometers, on a large bay of the Black Sea, is a very old town, first settled 2,500 years ago, that boasts the remains of a medieval fortress. They will take us there, to tour the fortress. The town is Bilgorod-Dnistrovsky.

We have been driving over rutted highway for about two hours when Alexi and Anastasia drop us off at the fortress, with Svieta, around noon. They are going to visit the region's director of education, who lives here. She should be able to help us to get to this little girl. They will be back to pick us up at three.

It is July 6. The temperature is 103 degrees Fahrenheit. The fortress is huge, fascinating. It is surrounded by a deep, wide, weed-filled moat. Just inside the gate, in a dark little room next to the wall, a wizened old lady sells the guides to the fortress, in Ukrainian: two and a half grivna, about fifty cents. The inside walls are crisscrossed with ancient staircases worn nearly to ruin. Through slits in the fortress walls, we can see blue water sparkling in the blazing sun. There are many rooms along the exterior walls, a few of them dark and spooky. What vermin might lurk down there? Insects thrum in the tall grasses that cover the ground inside the fortress walls. Swatting our legs and arms, we follow the dirt paths that have been worn from one point of interest to another. Maybe twenty other people are touring the fort. We take pictures of each other perched perilously on steps and walls. Natalie fumes when Marc won't let her climb railless crumbling stairs to the tops of parapets.

In two hours we have exhausted our interest in the place. Scorching hot, we make for the only shade there is, around a refreshment stand. Eat ice cream as fast as we can, before it melts. Drink cool bottled water. Sarah refuses to take much in; she does not want to have to use the facilities—reeking outhouses—before we return to Odessa.

As we head back to the parking lot to meet Alexi and Anastasia, we notice a red-and-white striped tent that has gone up since we entered the fortress. Abe, ever-eager, ever-resourceful, discovers that a traveling circus has set up. The show will begin at three. It is two-fifty-five. When Anastasia and Alexi drive up, Abe asks, "Can we go to the circus? Do we have time for this?" "Sure, sure—we will come back." We insert ourselves into the bustle around the entrance to the tent. Natalie gets cotton candy spun onto the cone right before her eyes into a ball three times the size of her head. Delight. We pay three grivna apiece to enter—less than seventy-five cents. Inside, in the gloom, it must be 120 degrees. We find seats on the loosely packed wooden bleachers, and wait. We are fifteen feet from the ring.

While we wait for the circus to begin, I look at the children in attendance. They look good, by and large. Healthy, well-cared-for. Well-loved. Who is in the orphanages? Directly across from us sit two little ravishing blonde girls, their long, white-yellow hair aglow under the tent. Plump rosy cheeks, rosebud lips. Three or four years old, all dressed up for the circus, bows in their gleaming hair, shiny little shoes. I want a child like *that*. Are there children like that in the orphanages?

The lightbulbs that have been strung overhead go out. The spotlights go on, the emcee's voice blares, the show begins. The circus is amazing! Beautiful girls ride two ponies at once, one foot on each back as they gallop around the small ring. A man who is all muscle wears a firebird suit and performs astounding acrobatic feats atop a stick in the air. A pretty young boy and girl, a brother-sister team, do an expertly coordinated tumbling routine with horses, ramps, and rings that seems fit for the Olympics. The clowns somersault and leap under and over each other, pulling feathers, balls, and springs out of every orifice of their bodies. We laugh and gape and shriek and clap along with everyone else, sweat pouring off our faces. Abe turns to me, his face aglow. "This is Kismet, isn't it? Isn't it just amazing that this would be here, just now?" It *is,* I must admit, a happy coincidence.

We pour out of the tent after the show, past the performers who cluster near the exit selling souvenirs and sweets. We say to the acrobat in the firebird suit, as if he could understand us, "Amazing work!" He is handsome, and small, and older than he looks in the ring.

He asks us, in English, "Where are you from?"

"Chicago!"

"Oh, Chicago! I have been to Chicago! Welcome to Ukraine." Then we are past him, blinking in the sun. Anastasia and Alexi find us, and steer us toward the van.

Their work has gone well, they say. They think everything will be fine for us. The director of education for the region would like us to come back tomorrow, to her house, for a home-cooked dinner. She will make her famous fish soup for us. We would like to come, yes?

How interesting. How hopeful. Of course. Perhaps a turning point arrived with the magic of the circus.

That night, Alexi and Svieta accompany us to downtown Odessa again, where again we indulge Natalie in every distraction on offer. At eight-thirty P.M. we sit down for dinner at the sidewalk cafe of a high-end restaurant just off the main carnival street. There we sit for hours, waiting for food. Alexi's phone rings at ten P.M. It is Saturday night, and a business call. He talks for a long time.

Odessa is, among other things, a resort town, and our hotel is about a half-mile walk from a vast sandy beach. Sunday morning we walk the narrow road along the beach, which is lined with vendors selling plastic buckets and shovels, water wings, iced bottled water, ice cream, and other comforts. At ten A.M. it is already nearing 100 degrees. Sarah and I wait under a canopied balcony while Marc, Nat, and Abe head for the shore. Women sunbathe with their tops undone, carelessly sit up. Marc and Abe are delighted. Natalie is scandalized. "Mommy! Did you see?!" Marc will not let Natalie go in the water. He is safeguarding her health. They play in the scorching sand while Abe frolics in the waves.

Back at the hotel that afternoon, we get a call from Alexi. We cannot go back to Bilgorod for dinner after all. The director of education is sick. She is very sorry. Instead, for a lark, we board the rusted, creaking trolley that rumbles past our hotel several times a day and head out of town. Abe has been trying out Russian on everyone around him since the moment we set foot in the country. Occasionally people laugh outright at him. Mostly, they try to be helpful. Here on the trolley, people stare at us as if we were giraffes. Some look amused, a few annoyed. A small middle-aged lady, the conductor, comes by and asks for our tickets, punches them, hands them back with a grin. A drunken man lurches around, and is booted out by the conductor at the next stop. We rumble past some large homes, surrounded by weeds. A lumberyard. Shacks. A dirt parking lot where goats and sheep intermingle with the old cars. After three stops, we get off. We don't want to get stranded in the Ukrainian countryside. We buy ice cream at the little fly-ridden store by the track, and wait for the return trolley.

Strangely, we are beginning to dislike the little girl we have never seen. Our resentment and anger at the people who are keeping her from us are seeping into our thoughts of her. Who does she think she is? Is this child another princess of the orphanage? What if she's a prima donna? She can never hold a candle to Natalie—let her try! I have found out from pressing the softer, more vulnerable Svieta that the child, named Lily, is three and a half. Three and a half is six months older than we had said we would consider. We might not even *want* to bring this little girl into our family.

Alexi picks us up at nine A.M. Monday morning. With grim determination, we head for the orphanage. Alexi goes in alone, while Marc, Abe, Svieta, and I sit at the picnic table in the shade on the grounds, and watch people come in and out of the religious order across the street. Little voices float out the windows of the orphanage. No one emerges onto the grounds.

After a quarter hour or so, Alexi comes back out. "The assistant director, she says she cannot do anything without the permission of the attorney. She cannot show us the child, she cannot show us the documents proving that this Ukrainian couple exists. Only the attorney can approve these things."

"So, let's see the attorney."

"The attorney is not in until eleven o'clock."

We go back to the hotel for a cup of coffee in the orange dining room. Alexi tells us there may be another child for us in Ukraine. They are working on it.

We go back to the orphanage at eleven A.M. sharp. We all go in. Alexi goes to see the assistant director while we wait in the hallway outside the broiler-atrium. Shortly, we are ushered into the small office of a woman who manages the impossible—she is colder than the director. This is the orphanage's attorney. She is in her mid-thirties, with severely beautiful, angular features. She wears skintight white pants and a small, hot pink, pucker-knitted top. Her medium-brown hair is pulled back into a bun so tight it seems to narrow her eyes, which, like a shark's, betray no emotion. She focuses them on Alexi. I pity him.

"What you want is impossible," she opens, helpfully.

"Why?"

"Because it is impossible. This woman has been visiting this child for months. The child's behavior has improved since she's been visiting. I think she will adopt her."

So the child has had behavior problems.

"You must prove that this person exists."

"No, I do not have to prove this to you. Only to the prosecutor."

"When can you prove it to the prosecutor?"

"Tomorrow, maybe. Next week."

"This is impractical. This is impossible."

They are practically shouting at each other, and they are speaking so quickly that Svieta cannot translate everything. We are confused. We thought there was a Ukrainian *couple*. She's talking now about just a woman, apparently a single woman. Svieta shrugs. She doesn't know.

"They want to meet her," Alexi says, gesturing toward us. He knows of another case in which a Ukrainian couple relinquished a child after they met the Americans who wanted to adopt him. "Can't they just meet her, to talk it over?"

"No, we have already asked if she would like to meet them, and she says no. She is afraid. They cannot force her to meet them."

"Of course, of course, they do not want to force her, they just want to meet her."

"She will not meet them. I cannot make her. She has a lot of influence in this town."

So, the Ukrainian couple is actually a single woman who has a lot of influence in the town but is also afraid of us? No matter how hard we try, we cannot keep our eyes on the ball in this game.

"Just let them see the child, then."

"No, I cannot. What good would that do? To see her is to love her."

While Alexi and the attorney are shouting at each other, Marc confers with Abe. What if Marc addresses the attorney directly? Pleads with her? Surely it couldn't hurt. Abe asks Alexi. Alexi shrugs, and steps aside.

Marc delivers, through Svieta, the speech I hurled at Alexi a couple of nights before. "Theresa and I are both doctors. I am a pediatrician. I help sick children. This is my life's work. Theresa's work has been in child abuse and neglect, helping hurt children. We have everything to give a child. We have money, and a beautiful house, filled with toys. We will give the child the best education. We will give her our love, a sister's love."

The attorney looks at Marc unblinking while he pleads. When he stops, she says, without the hint of a smile or warmth, "I am sympathetic to you. I wish I could give this child to you. I think you would make better parents than this woman. She is a single woman. She does not have a lot of money. But there is nothing I can do. This is the law."

She turns to Alexi. "I like this job," she says. "It does not pay very much, but I like this job. Please do not press me any further, do not ask me to break the rules. There is nothing I can do."

Alexi softens. He is defeated. Whatever the truth is, he will not find it out. He asks her merely to put in writing, in an affidavit, what she has said: that she cannot show the child to us because the child is not available for international adoption. This, he thinks, will help clear the way in Kiev for our getting another referral.

We are directed out of her office into another one, also bright and nicely appointed, with a few toys on high shelves, out of reach of children. A wind-up plastic merry-go-round, a ball, a plastic-faced clown doll. Perhaps this is one of the rooms where children are first introduced to prospective parents. Abe and Marc and I walk about, dejected, idly handling the toys, putting them back. Alexi is in and out, getting paper, perfecting the wording of the affidavit. We write it out in English, and Svieta translates into Russian. After about forty-five minutes, we leave, without the affidavit. The attorney has informed Alexi that she doesn't have to give this to him, only to the prosecutor in town. Barring some miracle, we're finished here.

Abe heads home tomorrow at five-thirty A.M.

Tuesday, the day Abe leaves, there is no sign of movement anywhere. There is no point in going back to the orphanage here in Odessa. They have won, with their extra-legal means. Ukraine lacks the money and sometimes the will to enforce its laws, so the shady orphanage director has won. And in Kiev, they have yet to scare up another referral for us. Alexi promises us that today is the day; today Nina will get us a referral, and tomorrow, Wednesday, we will go to see the child, wherever she is found.

Late in the afternoon, the phone rings in our hotel room. Alexi. A little girl has been found nearby, in Bilgorod-Dnistrovsky, the town of the circus. The circus town! How surprising! In my mind's eye flash the images of the little blonde beauties across the ring from us. The child is not available for three-and-a-half weeks. However, the orphanage director would let us see her now if we want to. As a special favor. Nina will fax the referral first thing in the morning. Alexi will pick us up at nine A.M., and we will go there to see this child.

The next morning at nine we are all dressed up and waiting by the phone. Fidgeting, trying to read, playing with Natalie, talking with Sarah, pulling aside the curtains to peer down into the street. Around ten Svieta calls. They are still waiting for Nina to fax the referral. There are transmission problems. It will come soon, and they will be here.

Around eleven we call Alexi's cell phone. Still waiting. It should be soon now.

We should have known! We should have *known!* We kick ourselves for having believed. What idiots we are!

Shortly before noon, Alexi and Svieta pull up in front of the hotel. We fly down to meet them. We are off again in Alexi's van to Bilgorod-Dnistrovsky, where there is a little girl who needs parents.

"This orphanage," Alexi informs us on the way down, "it is not the best, you see. It is not the best, but it is also not the worst, not the worst. It could be better, but . . ." He trails off and ends in a shrug.

We attempt to gird our loins.

Two hours later we drive up in front of a clean-looking, sprawling white-stuccoed building placed a short distance outside of Bilgorod-Dnistrovsky. The arid island of dirt in the center of the circular driveway has been planted rather nicely with desert plants, succulents.

Sheer white eyelet curtains flutter at the open windows of the two-story building, and from the main entranceway billows a sheer white curtain.

We wait with Svieta, leaning against the van, while Alexi goes in to announce our arrival to the director. It is 100 degrees Fahrenheit, and we are trying to hold still, to avoid sweating. The bouquet of red roses Alexi has bought for us to give to the director lies wilting in its cellophane cone on the front seat of the van. While we wait, a small decrepit tanker truck drives up, dripping wet. Several women, most of them old and squat, wearing head scarves, emerge from the front door of the orphanage carrying buckets and jugs. It is a water truck. The women jostle and joke among themselves, and with the driver of the truck, as they fill their containers and lug them back inside.

Several minutes later, Alexi emerges. The director cannot meet with us now; she is very busy; many couples are coming now to see children. We will give her the flowers later. We will talk instead with the head doctor now. He can tell us everything about this girl.

Alexi leads us up a couple of steps into the building. The bright interior looks gloomy at first after the blazing sun. Soon, though, we realize that the inside is clean and fairly bright. We walk up a flight of open stairs, past a two-story Chagall-inspired blue and green stained glass window. Pretty. Upstairs we are led down a darker administrative hallway, past the director's office, and ushered into the doctor's office. Small, narrow as a hallway, with an open window at one end. Desk against one wall facing a row of chairs, where we sit, waiting. The eyelet curtains at the window blow over my hair and shoulders several times. I try to tame them, then move. Shortly, in bustles a young man who ought to be on-screen. A long lock of his curling reddish hair graces his forehead over wire-rimmed glasses. His face is boyishly handsome and extremely kind-looking. He could be playing dress-up in his white lab coat; but his evident earnestness is deeply appealing. He smiles and nods as he hurries past us with a thick brown file and sits down at his desk.

"Hmm. Let's see, let's see. It is Sniezhana you are visiting, yes?"

"Yes," says Alexi.

"I am not particularly familiar with this child. She is not one I know well." The doctor who knows her well is gone today. "Let's see what the chart says. Born December 28, 1999." He looks up. "'Sniezhana' means 'little snowflake.'" He looks from one of us to the other, and smiles.

I think about a young woman naming her baby "little snowflake" before leaving her at the hospital.

She was born on my father's eighty-first birthday. How old is she, then? Thirty-one months.

Birth weight, length, head circumference. "APGAR 7, then 8. Let's see. It says here her mother was registered with the alcohol and drug treatment authorities. We do not know why—many people are. Mother was young. First pregnancy. Mother left the hospital alone. We know nothing about this woman, the mother. She consulted a psychiatrist before leaving the hospital. Everybody does this." I can well imagine.

"What about her developmental milestones?" Marc asks through Svieta. "When did she sit up? When did she walk? Does she talk?"

"Hmm. Let's see. It says here she sat up at twelve months. She walked at nineteen months."

"That's late."

"Yes, yes. Probably she was a little neglected at first, and then the nurses started paying more attention to her, you know. Playing with her, and helping her. Then she started to develop more."

Her physical development has been poor. What about her cognitive development?

"Her language—it appears to be normal, more or less. All of these children are delayed, of course. She is not more delayed than others."

"Do you know how much she weighs now? We would also like to know her height and head circumference." This is doctor to doctor. Marc jots down the numbers, eyebrows high. "She's tiny," he says to me, quietly. He had brought growth charts from home, and would plot her growth when we had a minute.

"How is she in her social group?" I ask. "Does she play well with others?" Will she assault my little girl? I want to know.

"Hmm. Let's see. It says that she is a nice girl, that she comforts other children when they are sad. It says she gets along well with other children." He pauses, smiles. "She likes music, and she likes to dance." He looks up at us.

Alexi looks over. "Do you want to meet this little girl?"

We nod. Yes, of course. Let's meet her. The doctor goes down the hall to fetch her.

Marc plots the growth points. If the measurements are right, her head circumference just nicks the bottom of the chart. Well, that's a relief. A normal head circumference is more or less essential. But her height and weight are way, way below normal. At thirty-one months she weighs eighteen pounds, which is about average for a seven-month-old baby in America. She is not just petite. She is teensy. Could be she is stunted from malnutrition. Could be there is some other medical problem contributing to her minuteness.

We brace ourselves. We do not expect to think she is adorable, we do not expect to like her at first sight, we certainly do not expect to fall in love. We brace ourselves to recoil, to say, "No, we are not comfortable parenting this child."

We are wary when the doctor returns followed by a pretty but expressionless young woman carrying a little girl. The child's eyes, which are slightly crossed, are wide open as we look at each other. She does not blink, or smile, or cry. The caregiver sits down next to Alexi, with Sniezhana on her lap, and we walk over and crouch down in front of her. Her stringy brown hair is gathered into two topknots that make her look like a Dr. Seuss character. She is wearing a little cotton sundress that floats around her skinny little legs and arms. She allows us to touch her arms and legs lightly, but does not reach for us. She regards us solemnly, warily, through her huge dark eyes. Her lashes are improbably long.

Through Svieta we ask the caregiver about Sniezhana in her group. "She is kind," she says. "She is nice to the other children."

"Does she like music?" asks the doctor.

The impassive girl smiles. "Yes, actually, she does." She puts Sniezhana on the floor, where she stands unsteadily. "Dance, Sniezhana," she says. "Show them how you dance." The little bug sways back and forth from leg to leg, waving her hands, princess-style, near her shoulders. We all laugh. Poor little mite. She allows me to pick her up, but does not wrap her arms around me. She holds on for steadiness. She is as light as a feather. We ask to see her in her social group.

Walking through these hallways, where the children live, we are enveloped in the overpowering smells of boiled cabbage and urine. The place appears to be clean, but the odors are distinct and perhaps ineradicable. The impassive young woman puts Sniezhana on her feet, and more drags than leads her down the hallway and up a few steps toward a closed door.

We are not prepared for what we see when the caregiver opens the door to the suite of rooms where Sniezhana lives. She has been dressed and dolled up—with the topknots—to be brought to us. We walk into a room full of children in gray cotton underpants, more often than not way too big for them. They are lined up on three low benches that form a U in front of a sofa, where two caregivers sit facing them. All their little grubby faces turn toward us when the door opens. Sniezhana scampers unsteadily to her place on the bench, her left foot dragging, and settles herself facing the sofa. We look from one child to another. Sniezhana is by far the tiniest child there, but she is also one of the more alert. It is impossible to tell what the children's gender is. They're all in the same underpants, their hair about the same short length. One chubby child sits on the bench and rocks back and forth, eyes unfocused on the floor in front of her. Another child—skinny, with wide gray eyes in a long, bony face—looks up at us from where he sits rocking on the rug. A few other children look at us and grin, but stay seated as instructed.

Minutes after we arrive, the children are dismissed from the bench and told to get toys. The chubby rocker is oblivious. She stays put, in her own little world. Most, including Sniezhana, scatter to the toy boxes along one wall and select their playthings. One child, still on the bench, starts crying. We've been told that Sniezhana is empathic, and comforts the other children when they're crying. When the caregiver draws her attention to the weeping child, she goes over and kisses him a few times, then goes back and forth to the toy boxes once, twice, three times, handing him toys, bending over to peer into his face, placing her hand on his naked back. Finally she picks out a Fisher-Price shape-sorter for herself and sits down with it at a little table. She works on it all alone for several minutes, in the midst of bedlam. All around her, children are shrieking—some in glee, some in despair as toys are snatched from them by their little chums. The caregivers are largely disengaged, standing about together in the middle of the room, looking dourly around them. Besides the impassive, pretty-ish young woman who brought Sniezhana to us, there is a strikingly beautiful young woman, with very short dark hair and ruby lips. She glowers constantly. Her smile, which she occasionally slaps on, remembering we are there, is scary in its formality. Besides these two there is a more comforting presence, an older woman, dumpy, kind-faced. The warmth she would introduce into the scene is, however, nullified by the two younger furies. When the shrieks become unendurable, they intervene to return a toy. Otherwise, they talk among themselves. We watch as other children approach Sniezhana, apparently intent on snatching her toy. She surrounds it with her skinny little arms. "Nyet! Nyet!" She drives them away, one by one, and continues with her work.

We are pleased, watching Sniezhana. She does appear to be kind, at least when prompted. She is able to focus on a task. She is no pushover—she effectively defends her interests when need be.

While she's working, the doctor walks up and lifts her dress off over her head. She glances back at him, but stays at her work. He points to the large birthmark on her back, the size of Marc's palm. It's a hemangioma; it looks like a cluster of scores of small blood blisters. The doctor speaks to Alexi.

"You see," Alexi says, leaning in to us, "the doctor, he does not want to sell you a 'pig in a poke,' as we say. He wants you to know everything about this little girl."

Marc walks over and leans down to examine the mark, running his finger over it gently. He says to Alexi, "These are usually not a problem. Usually they go away by themselves." In children with normal diets and normal growth, such a hemangioma would have largely disappeared already; malnutrition has perhaps delayed its course in Sniezhana's case. "Sometimes, though, large hemangiomas like this indicate that there is an internal problem, too. Sometimes where there are large hemangiomas on the outside, there are also hemangiomas in internal organs, like the liver and brain. This can interfere with the organ's functioning. Does the doctor know anything about this? Has this possibility been explored?"

Alexi asks the doctor. We watch while the doctor nods earnestly, and explains. "Yes, yes, he knows about that," Alexi reports back. "There is no evidence of internal problems. She has had a full body scan, and appears to be fine. All the children get these ultrasound exams. She's fine."

Oh, well—that's great! I am relieved. Marc listens, smiles, nods. "Good," he says to Alexi. "That's good." Alexi ambles back over to the doctor. Marc says to me, "That means nothing. They can't do a reliable ultrasound here, let alone a CT scan. If there's a problem here, they've almost certainly missed it."

"Well," I say, worried, "is there any way to get a more reliable answer?"

"I could try palpating. Sometimes you can feel it."

"Go ahead."

He walks over and gently palpates Sniezhana's abdomen. She turns around to look up at him, and smiles. As Marc presses a little more, smiling back at her, she writhes and giggles. Then she is off— out of her chair and across the room to fetch an inflated ball. She staggers with it back toward Marc, then stops and throws it at him with a giggle. He's always wanted Natalie to play ball with him. He rolls the ball back to Sniezhana, who scampers after it and throws it back. They engage in a few gleeful rounds of ball. Sweet. Then the caregivers start gathering up the children. It is nap time. We have been watching her for about fifteen minutes. We may return in three hours if we wish.

\* \* \*

We are sitting under an arbor in an outdoor cafe not far from the orphanage, with bowls of cold potato soup in front of us. Fresh dill floats on the surface. What are the odds that we will get giardia from eating this dill? If we were going to get giardia on this trip, wouldn't we have gotten it already? We pick up our spoons. "This girl," Alexi begins, "this girl, she is good. She is not *excellent*, I think, but she is good."

We are leaning toward accepting her. In part of my heart, I already have. Already, I expect and want her to be excellent. I want everyone to agree with me that she is excellent. "What do you mean, she's not 'excellent'?" I demand. "Developmentally?"

"Yes, yes. Developmentally, she is not *excellent*. She is delayed. Not terribly delayed, but she is delayed."

"I'm more concerned about her size," Marc says. "She is really tiny."

"Yes, Marc, it is true that she is small. But you say, her head, it is on the chart, no? Yes. Marc, this is not a small-head child; she is not— what do you call it? Yes, microcephalic. She has no signs of that. This is a miniature, that's all. A miniature. But this is a *good* girl, a good girl."

Alexi is sitting on the edge of his chair, leaning forward, his elbows on the table. His clothes look like he has slept in them, and he probably has. We are painfully aware that Alexi has also been frustrated all week. He has been away from his family—his sixteen-year-old and his six-week-old and his poor beleaguered wife. He and Svieta have been sleeping on the sofa and the floor of Anastasia's tiny apartment. He expected to be here two or three days, until we had met the other little girl and made our decision. He has never had a situation like this. He is embarrassed, flummoxed. We don't understand why he didn't have all his ducks in a row before we made this trip; how could they *not* have made contact with the orphanage director before we came? How could the celebrated Anastasia have let this little detail go? We are furious about this for part of the time. Still, we feel some pressure to get this ordeal over with quickly now for all of our sakes. If we do not embrace this child, who was so hard for them to find—well, there just might not be another child to be found. This is *it*, after all: This is the child who is available to us. Can we really expect them to keep working so hard for us indefinitely? And, it's not like she's a little deaf and blind girl who can barely stand up. This girl appears to be *good*. However, however . . .

We are haunted by memories of the process with Natalie, when a lovely, robust child was chosen especially for us. Natalie came to us with all the guarantees you could possibly hope for—more guarantees than expectant parents get. We knew before we met her that she was physically healthy and developmentally fine. The referral of such a child was gratifying in every way, and accepting her referral was safe. Sniezhana, in contrast, bristles with red flags. She does seem, in the fifteen minutes we have spent with her, to have a sweet personality. Still, her physical status is deeply worrisome. What if she is desperately ill? How is it possible that we have reached this point: After all our time and money and effort, our range of choices narrowed to the vanishing point?

As we sit across from Alexi and Svieta, we look at them through a miasma of dismay and hope, a strange hopefulness born of the torments of this experience. Faced with the very real possibility of going home without a child, of breaking Natalie's heart and admitting defeat in a goal toward which we have poured immeasurable emotional energy, a goal that *should* have been realizable, a goal that *other* people have been able to fulfill—faced with such a completely depressing, perplexing, demoralizing outcome, the tiny, unsteady child we have met looks different than she would from the comfort and security of home. She looks "not bad," as opposed to not excellent. But we are hounded by our idea of what should have been.

"Yes, yes, of course," we say. "We want to go back to see her again."

When we walk into the playroom the second time, Sniezhana runs up to Marc with a big grin on her face. Her dress has disappeared, as have the topknots in her hair. Like all the other children, she is dressed only in outsized, dingy underpants. It is startling to see her this way, a little urchin. A caregiver swoops her up and throws a sundress over her head, and hands her to me. We will take her outside to spend a little time alone with her. But when we reach the outer door of their suite, she whimpers. She is afraid to go out with us. Good sign: She's attached somewhere, to something. So we stay in the empty anteroom and sit down on the old linoleum to play. The older woman caregiver smilingly delivers a baby doll and a ball, and disappears.

Sniezhana is personable. She engages all of us with her sparkling eyes. She throws a ball to Marc again, and they toss and roll it a few times. She stumbles all over the place, staggers across the room, trips every time she attempts to cross the threshold. She is handed the dolly, which she promptly begins to spank. Then she plays a loud kissing game with the dolly, which is very cute—she appears to have been kissed as well as spanked. She initiates a game of peek-a-boo with us, going outside the door and then swinging herself back into view around the edge, grinning, eyes flashing. She is curious about Svieta's purse; Svieta gives her the little bottle of antibacterial hand wash. Sniezhana stashes the dolly under one arm and hands me the bottle of hand wash. I put a drop on her palm, and gently rub it in. She is transfixed, looks from her palm up into my eyes. When that drop is gone, she shifts the dolly to the other side, and holds out her other hand. I repeat the procedure. And so does she, so that she ends up getting several drops on each palm, alternately. I rub some very gently up her wrist, up onto her inner forearm. She holds her breath, doesn't move. She loves this. She has never been touched this way. Marc gives her pictures of Natalie from his wallet. She looks at them, takes them out of their sleeves, stacks them, rearranges them, hands them out, and re-collects them. She is very engaging, playful, happy-seeming. We take turns taking videos.

There is something about this child. She seems to have an inner knowledge, against all odds, that life is fine. She seems even to have inner joy. Look at her huge eyes sparkle! Look at her confidence in approaching us. She looks right into our eyes. She scrutinizes us knowingly. She laughs. She teases! I have been afraid of a thousand things, among them that our second little girl's personality would clash with Natalie's. The worst possibility for everyone concerned is that they will be *alike*. One child like Natalie—passionate, imperious, headstrong—is a great blessing. Two would do us (and each other) in. Natalie is just like I was as a child—so much so that my siblings (who love her to pieces) snicker with glee: "Ha! You finally got yours!" This child is nothing like Natalie and me. She is a little elfin being, funny, sweet, smart, mischievous. Yet not a child who will stand by and see her interests trampled, as we witnessed with the shape-sorter she guarded so well. She will stand up to Natalie, but she will not clash head-on with her. She is perfect for us.

As I watch her, my heart quiets down with certainty, and awe dawns there. Sniezhana's spirit is awe-inspiring. Look at what this child has made of what she has been given. Abandoned in this place by a despairing young mother, neglected for her first eighteen months at least, chronically underfed, freezing cold in winter, steaming hot in summer, without running water, or a mommy or daddy or toys of her own, here she is, so funny and sweet and confident and bright. This child is, in fact, excellent. She is more excellent than I am, and more excellent than Marc. Her excellence is not visible to the naked eye. She has an amazing spirit.

"Can we go home now?" Marc has come to the same conclusion I have in the forty minutes we have spent with Sniezhana. We want her to be part of our family. Now let's get out of here until we can come back to bring her home.

Svieta fetches Alexi and he comes in smiling, relieved. The next step is to meet with the orphanage director, to make sure everything is okay. We make our twisty way through the dark passages that reek of boiled cabbage and urine, down some steps and into another, lighter wing of the building, where the smells of the orphanage are less pressing. Alexi stops at a door and steps aside to let us pass into the office of the director. It is large, lit by a long row of open windows, and dominated by an ornate old wooden desk, behind which sits the director. She half rises to lightly touch our extended hands, then sinks back into her high-backed swivel chair, imitation leather, while we settle ourselves on the edge of an upholstered bench to her left. Everything is tattered, but bright. The orphanage director has brassy blonde hair with dark roots growing out, bright orange lipstick, medium-heavy eye makeup, bright tawdry clothes. She is in her late forties, perhaps, her once prettyish face now deeply grooved, showing the hard life she has lived along with everyone else in this country. She has a perpetual smile on her face, but not a particularly friendly one—a wary, appraising, cynical smile. As she eyes us, I imagine her thinking, "You fools, you all think you're so special."

Initial pleasantries are passed back and forth. She says things about us in Russian to Alexi and Svieta that are not translated. We have to pass muster with her, apparently, before she will say that, yes, we can have this child. But Marc also wants to know about the biological mother. (There is no chance of knowing anything about the father.)

"Did the mother take care of herself during her pregnancy?" he asks through Svieta.

The orphanage director shakes her head. "We don't know."

"What about this registration with the drug and alcohol ministry?" Marc persists. "What about this visit with the psychiatrist? Do you know anything about this?"

"No. I know nothing about her."

"Marc," interrupts Alexi, scowling. "Why are you asking all these questions? She does not have to answer these questions. She is doing us a favor, seeing us now, considering us for this child, before the child is officially available."

I am embarrassed for Marc, and angry. How dare *Alexi* be impatient with *us*? I think back to what Abe said when we first met with him to talk about the Ukraine program, about the orphanage directors having all the information there is on the child, and being so happy and proud to share it with prospective parents. But that was then. Now, we're on *this* side of the looking glass.

Marc, incredibly, maintains his game face. "We are inclined to adopt this little girl," he explains to the director through Svieta. "We just don't want any unpleasant surprises."

At this, the director shrugs and waves her hand, waving us away. "Life is full of surprises," she says. "I cannot tell you anything more until the child is officially available." We are stunned, and dismissed. If we want the child, we can reserve her now, and learn everything there is to know about her when we come back in three weeks to get her.

\* \* \*

"What if this falls through?" Marc asks Sergei as we are heading back to Odessa. "What if something goes wrong, and we don't get her?"

"Nothing will go wrong."

"But how can you be sure? Isn't it officially against the law for us to claim her now? What if some Ukrainian couple pops up and wants her?"

"This will not happen. We will write your names next to her name in the book in Kiev. No one else will get her."

"Well, but—is it one hundred percent certain we'll get her?"

"Nothing in life is one hundred percent certain. But you'll get her."

"What do you want to name her?" Svieta asks me in the backseat. "We have to give them a name in Kiev."

I've been wanting to name a little girl Lana for years. "Sniezhana" is way too difficult a name for an American child. "Lana" sounds to our ears close to the last two syllables of "Sniezhana." "How about Lana?"

"This is pretty. Lana what?"

"Elizabeth?" I've always loved the name Elizabeth. "Lana Elizabeth?" This does not roll off the tongue.

"Hey." Marc twists around to face me. "Do I get a vote here?"

I smile at him. No. Svieta and I laugh. I think back to the last few names we crossed off our list of possible names for Natalie. *Sophia.* Marc's Russian grandmother's given name. A beautiful name. Wisdom. "Lana Sophia."

Even Marc has to admit that he can't do better than that.

Marc and I talk. What do we tell Natalie? "We've found a baby sister for you . . . maybe?" Like Vera? "We *think* we'll come back and get her in a few weeks?" If no one else springs from the ground and snatches her away first? If the authorities haven't lied to us?

We get home at nine-thirty P.M. to find Natalie bouncing off the walls. Thinking, perhaps, to relieve us of some pressure, Sarah has told Natalie that we may have found a baby sister, but she is not to ask us any questions. This is more self-restraint than any six-year-old can muster. Natalie is exploding with the effort.

I get her quieted down in a big chair with me. "You must have a lot of questions," I begin.

"Do I have a baby sister?" she blurts.

"We don't know, but we think so. We're pretty sure."

Natalie is stilled for a moment by this momentous news.

*"Well?"* she erupts. "What's she *like?*"

I get the video camera and play the few minutes of action we recorded before the tape ran out. Natalie watches in silence.

"Hmph," she says when the tape stops. "That's not what I expected. But I guess she's okay."

Part of the story we have always told Natalie about her own life is that the orphanage she lived in was very nice, one of the nicest in Russia, and that she was very well cared for there. Now, in the hope of inspiring a little protective feeling toward Sniezhana, I tell her that this orphanage is not nearly as nice as hers; that it's smelly, and doesn't have running water, and the caregivers are not as kind as hers were.

She takes this in, and asks to look at the video again.

"Hmph," she repeats when it's over. "She's ugly, and I bet she's stinky. My orphanage was a lot better than hers."

I am shocked and angry. *I* am the one who becomes protective of Lana. After less than an hour with Sniezhana, I have new eyes for my own child. For hours, I have been filled with deep, quiet respect for Sniezhana's strength and resilience, her capacious spirit. Now I back away from Natalie a bit, and look at her. She is beautiful and precocious and beloved. We have given her everything, everything, everything, her whole life. Now, in the eyes that have been taking in Sniezhana, Natalie looks different than I have ever seen her before. She looks quite like a spoiled little princess. I am momentarily repulsed by my beloved only child, and shocked at my own feelings.

Natalie is right to be jealous. How did she know so soon?


Back home at last in Chicago, unpacking in the bathroom, I am seized with panic. Had we lost our minds? I am suddenly certain that we have. We had acted blindly under the influence of sheer misery and confusion. We had pledged to adopt a child we never should have considered. I try to quell my panic. We don't *have* to go back to get her. Just because we said we would, we don't have to go. No one can compel us to ruin our lives. But, oh, my god, how could we put Natalie through another loss like that, after Vera? How would we explain to her that we are abandoning this child we have called her sister, that we have changed our minds? Panic is full upon me, in sweating palms and pounding heart. What on earth have we done?

I scramble around looking for the videocamera. Maybe if I look at her again, it will all come clear.

Thirty seconds into the video, I know we have done the right thing. That child sparkles with life.

# 11

## Claiming Lana

It is just the three of us this time. Mommy, Daddy, and Nattie, like always. No Abe to hold our hands. No Aunt Sarah to keep Natalie company. Just us three, who have traveled well together since we first brought Nat home from Russia five years before. We *think* we are going off to get a baby sister, but we will not celebrate until we are home again as four. No limo to the airport this time.

One of the large carry-ons I have packed is unusually heavy. It is the bag full of gifts for our Ukrainian helpers—the officials and CRA staffpeople who will facilitate our adoption. The word from Alexi was that we really didn't need to bring any gifts to Ukraine. Still, I wanted to take *something* for people, and exchanged e-mails with the sweet Svieta about what she would like to receive. She had become an intimate in one of the most difficult processes of our lives. I wanted to know what she wanted from the U.S. "Hand wash," she e-mailed back. The waterless hand wash that Sniezhana had found so fascinating when she discovered it in Svieta's purse. "We can't get that here," she explained.

Okay, that's easy enough. But what *else*?

Svieta demurred. "Well, peanut butter is extremely expensive here—a couple of dollars a tablespoon. I do love peanut butter."

Okay, I would bring Svieta peanut butter and hand wash. But what *else*?

"*Roses Are Red,* by James Patterson. In English, so I can practice. I cannot find this book here." I gave up. I couldn't get her to tell me anything of any substance she would like to have. So I bought her her book, and several bottles of hand wash and jars of peanut butter. Next to the peanut butter on Target's shelf was Nutella, an irresistible paste made of chocolate and ground hazelnuts. If she liked peanut butter, she'd *love* Nutella. So I bought her a couple of jars of Nutella as a special treat. There in the store, it was clear to me that if Svieta wanted these items so much, others would probably appreciate them as well. So I loaded my cart with a dozen containers each of peanut butter, Nutella, and water-free hand wash, and plopped on top of the lot a dozen gift bags and tissue paper to match.

Marc splutters when he sees me loading a carry-on bag with these purchases, but I am adamant. His ethnocentrism is showing. Just because *he,* with his rich Western perspective, assigns no value to these things, doesn't mean long-deprived Eastern Europeans will despise them. I keep packing.

The cabbie grunts as he lifts the carry-on full of peanut butter into the trunk. "Whaddya *have* in here? *Rocks?*" Marc snorts in exasperation. I lift my chin and sniff: We will *not* discuss it again. We climb into the backseat on either side of Natalie.

As the cab pulls away, we try not to think about the FOR SALE sign that still stands in front of our house. In the three weeks since we were last in Ukraine, we have revisited the school that wants to hire Marc, and finally succumbed to its blandishments. Marc will take the job. In the spirit of making a commitment to the place, we made a noncontingent offer on a house we had seen several times and rather love. It's one of those steps it's hard to explain later, making a noncontingent offer on one house while ours was still on the market. We just felt . . . confident. But the stock market is tanking. The real estate market in our price range in Chicago is dead. Despite two dramatic price cuts, we have had not a nibble on our house. There is beginning to be talk about a real estate bubble. Our Realtor says the next two weeks, while we're gone, will be her time to really make a push and sell our house. We wonder what she's been doing for the last several months. As we leave for Ukraine, the bids are still going back and forth on the house we have offered to purchase. We have given Marc's cousin power of attorney to act in our stead. Our confidence is withering fast. We fear that we are about to die financially. We're going to buy high and sell low—our usual strategy, but catastrophically this time.

When I tell my sister about my intense anxiety about selling the house, she wonders if I might be displacing some of my anxiety about the adoption. "Oh no," I assure her. "We're confident about this child. That's going to be *fine*. It's the house we're sick about."

We have talked with Natalie about the big, big change we are all going to experience, going from three to four. We have discussed how it won't be wonderful all the time; how sometimes she will want—we all will want—to be just us three again. How there will be a period of adjustment, months of adjustment, before it seems normal and desirable to have somebody new in our family.

I foolishly think that these talks have prepared us for what's to come.

After twenty restless hours of traveling we are finally in Kiev, starting to look about for Alexi, and Marc has been stopped by an official. We haven't declared in writing all the dollars we are bringing in, which is more than is officially allowed. We don't want the hassle of explaining or justifying or documenting, so we have stashed the excess cash in various locations on our persons and in hand luggage. We are nervous when the authorities ask us how much cash we have.

"Dollars?" the official barks.

"Two thousand," we lie.

"Grivna?" she barks again.

Oh, *grivna*! We have grivna we can declare. Who cares about grivna?

We eagerly show her all the grivna we are carrying, proud to be so forthcoming.

She frowns. "Where did you get these grivna?"

"Here, of course—on our last trip. See?" We point to the visa stamps in our passports. "We were here three weeks ago." Surely she will love us for coming back to her country so soon.

She frowns again. "Where is your declaration for these grivna?"

"What?"

"Your declaration. You were supposed to declare these grivna when you took them out of the country. You should have your signed declaration with you."

This is news to us. A vague memory stirs of Alexi's sidekick at the airport telling us just to go, not to declare our grivna. But we could not have sworn to this. We were in a daze then, as now. What are they going to do to us? Will they let us into their country? Will they take us aside for questioning? Will they decide we can't have one of their children? The woman walks away with our 500 plus grivna. It is worth about one hundred dollars.

We stand about uncomfortably. Alexi spots us, and gestures to us from behind the barricade. I walk over and explain what is happening. He shrugs. "Oh, this. They will keep your grivna, I think."

When I get back to Marc, the official has returned. "They're keeping our grivna," Marc says. Who cares about grivna? *They* do. Chalk it up as an adoption expense, another one-hundred-dollar drop in the ocean of costs.

We have told Alexi that, this time, we want to stay in a nice, air-conditioned hotel in Kiev. Irina was very sweet, we greatly appreciated her kindness, we hate to turn it down, but the heat is too much to add at a time like this. For this one night in Kiev, we want to stay in a cool, Western-style hotel, so we're neat and tidy when we go to the Adoption Center the next morning to collect the authorization to adopt Lana. We expect to spend the rest of the trip in Odessa, with Svieta, in the comfortable hotel we know from our last trip.

But Alexi's plans for us have changed. The good news is that they have already taken care of the business at the Adoption Center: There is no need for us to stop there in the morning. The bad news is that Alexi wants to drive us to Bilgorod-Dnistrovsky now. It is four in the afternoon, and the drive is nearly eight hours long. Anastasia needs us there in the morning, to proceed with official business. We will be staying not in Odessa, but in Bilgorod-Dnistrovsky, where Anastasia has found us a place to stay—an apartment, very nice, near the orphanage. Svieta will not be going with us: She is busy in Kiev. Alexi will give her the gifts that we brought when he returns to Kiev in the morning, after dropping us off in Bilgorod-Dnistrovsky. We will be in good hands with Anastasia and a driver there.

We take this in as we straggle along behind Alexi to the car. We have no choice but to trust his judgment about the best way to secure our end.

For this quick trip with just the four of us, Alexi has left his van with his wife. We cram all our luggage into the large trunk of the small car, and collapse into the springless seats, Marc next to Alexi in front, and Nat and I in back. We have never encountered seat belts in Ukraine, and Alexi's sedan is no exception. As we hit the road between Odessa and Bilgorod this late afternoon, the confidence I had on our first trip to Bilgorod in Alexi's van is shot. A few weeks ago, Sarah and I were protected by the certainty that we would not die this way. To-day, I have no such faith. We share the ragged, bumpy road with hay wagons and military vehicles going twenty and thirty miles per hour, and ancient Ladas doing their best to do fifty. Alexi goes as fast as hu-manly possible in his car, eighty or so at top speed, apparently not noticing or caring the frequency with which we are airborne. I cannot stop thinking for one minute about Marc dying as we smash head-on into oncoming traffic, or Nat and I dying as we are rammed from be-hind, or all of us dying as we fly off the bumpy road or flip into the fields on either side. The thought that Alexi has a family to go home to does not comfort me in the least, the way it comforts me to know that airplane pilots want to get home safe and sound, too. Whatever he may think, it is obvious to me that he is not reliably in control of this car. This is incomparably more dangerous than any airplane trip I have ever taken. In the backseat, I entertain and distract Natalie by making up stories with the dolls she has brought, and playing hangman with her, and drawing, in the gathering dusk, jittery-jaggedy sketches of everyday things for her to try to identify. Such is her exhaustion that, for part of the time, she puts her head in my lap and sleeps.

Finally, thank God, thank God, we are slowly cruising through the streets of Bilgorod. It is pitch black almost everywhere. It is midnight. There are no streetlights, and most of the houses are dark. A few bars are open, and cast dim light from their windows and open doors. Mostly, it is black. Alexi has been on the phone, speaking in Russian.

He slowly cruises up the street, hugging the sidewalk, then makes a U-turn and retraces a short distance to make the sweep again. Suddenly a tall white figure emerges from the inky night into Alexi's headlights and approaches the car. It is Anastasia. She opens the back door and slides onto the seat next to Natalie. Nat looks at me, her eyes wide. All I can do is return her look. I am as surprised as she is.

"Hello." Anastasia nods curtly. She does this sort of thing every day.

"Hello!" we say. She does not smile.

Then she is speaking in Russian to Alexi, giving him directions to the apartment.

There are no lights anywhere. We have no idea where we are. We creep through badly rutted streets. We turn between two walls— fences, it turns out—made of eight-foot-high concrete slabs. We turn again, into sand. I can barely see dark masses off to the right and ahead of us. There are lights in windows here and there. Dogs are barking. Are these the apartments? I am alarmed. Will we ever see home again? It seems entirely possible that we won't—that even if we are *not* murdered here by rapacious neighbors, which seems quite likely, Alexi and Anastasia could abandon us here, and we would never be able to find our way back.

Alexi pulls up in front of the building to our right and turns off the car. He turns partway around in his seat. "This is the apartment. Do you want to go up and look at it first?"

Anastasia just about jumps out of her skin. She says nothing for a moment, but she radiates tension.

Sweet Alexi. Always the gentleman. He wants to give us the option of rejecting the rooms. As if we'll go hotel-shopping in Bilgorod-Dnistrovsky, Ukraine, at midnight, after twenty-nine hours on the road.

"Oh, no, Alexi. We're sure it's fine." We are terrified.

Anastasia knows that there *is* no place else to stay. It has taken her considerable effort to find this place. She would go for Alexi's throat if we had taken him up on his offer.

As we unfold ourselves from the car, I assure Natalie that—like the place we stayed in when we went to get her, like the place we stayed in in Kiev last month, like all the apartments in the former Soviet Union—this place looks much, much worse on the outside than it is on the inside.

We trudge up the stairs with our suitcases, Alexi carrying more than his share, as always. We walk five flights up. Five stinking, badly made, dirty flights of stairs up to a door thickly upholstered in burgundy Naugahyde, replete with covered buttons, that swings open before Anastasia's meticulously manicured nail touches the buzzer. Smiling and nodding in the warm light of the open doorway are two lovely women: one young, about sixteen, and her mother, about forty. My fear about being robbed and murdered evaporates. These people will not hurt us, and probably do not live in a dangerous place. The daughter is proud of her good English.

"Welcome. We are glad you are here. Please, let us show you your rooms."

When we step inside, we are shocked. The place is clean, as we expected. But it is as decrepit inside as outside. The doors, where they exist, are made of particle board, and do not latch. The particle-board French doors to the living room, which will serve as Marc's and my bedroom, have empty frames with only protruding nails where glass and curtains are supposed to go. This room is two steps from the kitchen, where Luba and her mother will cook for us three times a day, beginning very early, way too early, tomorrow morning. Wallpaper is peeling off everywhere from the bottom up in large swatches. In the bathroom, tiles are missing from the walls. Floor tiles shift and grate under our feet. There is no mirror over the sink, and no shower. The single faucet swings from tub to sink. When we lean on the edge of the bathroom sink to examine the faucet arrangement, the top tips off. There are several pots and pans on the floor of the bathroom, and we notice—because we have removed our shoes to walk through the house, as is the custom—that the floor is warm. It takes us a while to realize that it is warm because the pots and pans are full of hot water, which Luba and her mother have heated for us to wash in after our long trip. They have needed to do this because, as Luba informs us as we survey the apartment, there is no hot running water in the summer, anywhere in the town. Cool running water is available—generally—ten hours a day, from six to eleven in the morning and from six to eleven at night. There is, of course, no air-conditioning. There are no fans. There are coarse screens on two small windows in the kitchen. The other windows are screenless. The two beds are stiff couches that fold down, creating two narrow, rounded surfaces joined by a deep, wide crevice. When we sit on the edge of the bed in the room we will use, it tips over, nearly spilling us onto the floor. When we attempt to move the bed slightly away from the wall, the arm falls away. When we try to move a table next to the bed, the top lifts off. It is as if the place is booby-trapped. Outside, stray dogs roam the weed-filled lots, and bark unpredictably. Occasionally, cat fights increase the din. If we open the windows, we will be eaten alive by mosquitoes and deafened by the stray animals. If we close the windows, we will still hear the animals and will risk suffocation. It has been 100 degrees again today, and we are on the fifth floor.

We take all this in in our stuporous state. Anastasia and Alexi look at us soberly, matter-of-factly, assuming everything will be fine. Luba and her mother beam at us and hover, eager to determine if they can do anything to make us more comfortable. More hot water, perhaps?

Something to drink? Are we hungry? "We have food here, lots of food for you," says Luba eagerly.

We will be staying here for at least a week. We need to be alone now, to acclimate ourselves. We agree to pay fifty dollars a night for the lodging and three meals a day. We locate the bottled water and glasses, then send everyone away as soon as it is decent to do so. Luba and her mother will be back at seven A.M. to begin our breakfast. Anastasia will pick us up at nine A.M. to go to the orphanage to see Lana.

The everyday heroism of our kind hosts is not what we first absorb. What we first understand is that, for us, this could be a rough trip.

A couple of hours later, I lie awake, wondering why in god's name they don't use the stray dogs that howl and bark outside all night for target practice. *I* would. I would begin target practice that very minute if I had a gun. Later, guiltily, I conclude that it's a sign that the people have retained some hope, some sense of themselves as decent, as human, that they let the dogs live.

During the week, Marc and I argue frequently about the windows. He wants them open, for the air, despite the mosquitoes. I would rather hold very, very still and brave the heat than contend with swarms of possibly plague-carrying mosquitoes. Nobody wins reliably. The windows open and close all night long, every night we are there.

Marc begins quickly declaring that this is a nightmare. I disagree. This is definitely *not* a nightmare. A nightmare would involve our physical illness, or danger. One of us would have to become sick, perhaps dangerously sick, for the experience to qualify as a nightmare. Or we would have to be afraid for our well-being. We are not sick or afraid, just uncomfortable.

A few sweaty, sleepless days into our travail, however, I *am* tempted to say that a more tormenting situation could not have been devised. But we decide that I can't get away even with that. Because it would definitely be more tormenting if vermin were involved. With one of us sleeping on the floor every night, the presence of cockroaches or rats or other vermin would definitely substantially worsen our situation.

"Why *aren't* there any vermin, do you suppose?" I ask Marc in the middle of one night, the dogs barking and howling behind me. It doesn't take him long to answer.

"Because there is nothing for them to eat."

Of course. The people throw out almost no food, and what little food they *do* throw out is immediately consumed by the dogs. We see the dogs cleaning out the trash cans all over town all the time. Maybe that's another reason they don't shoot them.

We are inspired and shamed by how well-turned-out the Ukrainians around us are. Anastasia is always impeccable, but Anastasia is in a class by herself. More telling is virtually everyone else we see on the street, beginning with Luba and her mother, who always look well-scrubbed, carefully made up, and nicely dressed. How do they do it, in these conditions? We feel like we are camping.

A few hours after the dogs and I finally go to sleep the first night, Luba and her mother arrive, as promised, to prepare breakfast for us. They are bright-eyed and cheerful. While we struggle to wake up and groom ourselves, they lay out a delicious meal of hot sausages, egg pie, buttered toast, tomato salad, and cold sliced cheese and meat. We let Natalie sleep as long as possible, then roust her easily enough with the whispered reminder that this is the day she will meet Lana. She is instantly alert and up, eager to get going.

What images did she have in her head? A darling little girl, throwing her arms around her, listening to her every word, asking her advice, following all her instructions, and disappearing when she was no longer wanted. An inflatable-doll sister, who is completely submissive and can be made to vanish on command. Something like that, probably. Who could blame her?

We are full of anxiety for Natalie. Her well-being is the primary reason we are here. We would never have persisted in this insane quest for ourselves alone, or out of some highly determined altruistic impulse. It is essential to us that these girls love each other. We have prepared Natalie to be a big sister by telling her how much Lana will love her; that she will be one of the most important people in Lana's life forever; that Lana will want to do everything she does; that she can't expect to love Lana every minute of every day, but that Lana will become her best friend for the rest of her life. Now Lana has to prove us right. She has to *be* lovable, to not hurt our baby, to accept and return Natalie's love. We feel a fierce protectiveness toward Natalie as we help her get ready to meet her sister for the first time.

We are ready for Anastasia when she comes, on the dot at nine A.M. We had loaded up our small backpack of goodies for Lana: the dolly and blanket Aunt Sarah had brought last month, a little wooden music box that plays "Round and Round the Mulberry Bush" when you crank the handle, the flap book *Dear Zoo,* a rubber ball. In the car with Natalie on the way to Bilgorod last night, I had written down all the children's songs we could think of that had interesting hand movements to entertain Lana. Our list is in the backpack. So are a sippy cup and a can of PediaSure, a nutritional supplement for sick or malnourished children. A developmental pediatrician colleague of Marc's, looking at Lana's growth curve back home, had suggested that we start feeding her PediaSure as soon as we could. Our luggage bulges with the heavy cans.

As we head for the door, Anastasia stops and turns back. "Do you have a gift for the director of the orphanage?"

"Oh! Yes!" I say. "I brought some peanut butter, and some hand wash."

Anastasia looks confused. "No," she clarifies. "I mean a gift, a gift for the director."

I am not sure whether Anastasia and I haven't understood each other, or Marc was right about my choice of gifts.

*Marc* is sure. "Ther*ee*sa!" He glowers.

I ignore him. "Well," I say to Anastasia, suddenly abashed. What if Marc is right? I'll feel like such a fool. And we'll be here empty-handed! "I have little gift bags, which I was going to fill with peanut butter, and hand wash, and this chocolate spread."

She looks at me a moment, uncomprehending. She turns away, sure it's her English that's at fault, and heads toward the door. "Do not worry. We will pick something up."

My face is burning from more than the heat as I follow her down the stairs. I am not completely persuaded. I need more evidence. But I have to admit that, at first glance, Anastasia's reaction definitely weighs in favor of Marc's argument. I'll ask Luba about it later.

Outside, handsome young Slava leans against the door of a beat-up old Lada, waiting for us. Slava can't be more than nineteen—younger, probably, than his car. He is tall and lanky, with dark hair falling over his huge, dark, long-lashed eyes. His beard isn't all the way in yet, and he blushes easily. He will be our driver in Bilgorod where, like Luba, he has grown up. He smiles shyly and ducks his head as we all shake hands, then folds himself into the tiny car.

In the bright morning sunshine, we can see where we are. The markers of Soviet domination are unmistakable. All of the countries of the former Soviet Union have a unique ugliness about them. The buildings, new and old, are very badly made—concrete blocks stacked atop each other, held together with mortar crudely placed, splashed all over, frozen in place oozing out from between the blocks. The buildings seem to be plopped down randomly, and are joined by dirt paths worn smooth by the residents. There is no landscaping, no sense of landscaping—no grass, just weeds and dusty ground. Some flowers, planted by the more hopeful and cheerful residents, add surprising dashes of color here and there. Walls and roofs are often of corrugated steel, unpainted or once-painted, now half-painted and peeling. Slava drives, for the most part, very slowly, because the roads are more pothole than road. All of the cars weave along trying to connect the dots of intact road. The car ride becomes a game of chicken, since all the vehicles are trying to use the same tiny fragments of the road. Sometimes Slava just gives up and stops, creeps down into a pothole, then creeps back up the other side. We pass eight-foot-high fences made of poured concrete slabs, crude holes punched in the sides of the slabs where they are held together with thick wire wound round and round, rust stains streaming off the wire down the concrete. The place is crushingly ugly.

The orphanage, though, is not. It is not so bad, from the outside.

Inside, as we turn a corner into the children's wing, trailing behind Anastasia, the stench of urine and boiled cabbage rushes to greet us. We hear the din before the door to Lana's suite of rooms open to us. Children shrieking, tearing about. Free play time. When we step into the room past the caregiver, Lana streaks across the room toward us in her ungainly gait. Like all the other children in the room, she is unadorned, clad only in those large gray underpants. She is happy to see us! We beam at her, relieved, as she approaches. We urge Natalie forward a bit, so Lana gets to Natalie first. Natalie crouches down a little, smiles at her, and holds out her arms, waiting. Lana lurches past her, past all of us, and throws her arms around Anastasia's legs.

Anastasia's face melts into a huge grin. Ah! Here is her warmth. She scoops up Lana and nuzzles her neck. She has been visiting Lana occasionally since our last visit. She brought Lana the family pictures we had sent, and had explained to Lana that we would be coming for her—her mommy, and daddy, and sister. She and Lana have grown fond of each other, waiting for us. We stand by awkwardly and watch their lovefest, wondering when Lana will be delivered to us.

A caregiver intervenes to take Lana to the sofa for grooming. We didn't see this woman on our first trip. Like the other two who are in the room, she is new to us, and seems kinder than the ones we met on our first trip. She is older, softer. She situates Lana between her knees, pulls a sundress over her head, and begins brushing her hair into the Seuss-like topknots they love. Lana stands still and smiles, shooting the occasional glance at us, relishing the special attention involved in being groomed.

As we wait, a little moon-faced girl we remember from before runs up to us, grinning, and throws her arms around Natalie. Natalie looks up at me, startled, uncertain what to do. This is what Lana was supposed to do. Natalie is delighted, but this isn't her sister. Is it okay to react? I smile permission, and Natalie leans down, takes the little girl by the hand, and tries to talk with her. I glance about the room. There's the skinny, bony-faced boy, the floor-rocker, ambling about distractedly. There's the chubby bench-rocker, still rocking, a few feet away from where we saw her last month. And then, there she is—in the doorway all the way across the room, eyeing her suite mates, the little girl who *should* have been ours! What a cutie! Plump, blonde, with big blue eyes in a pretty, round face. Fear and dismay and jealousy leap into my heart and jostle madly. What if we got the wrong child? What if we were supposed to have that one? She looks so much more like Nat's sister. She looks so much healthier than Lana. Who got her? Why didn't we?

What I *know*—that I don't know that child, that I don't know Lana, that I don't know, in fact, which girl would be better for our family. My knowledge is no match for my jagged feelings. I use it, though, as best I can as my only shield against the doubt that wants to seize my heart.

Now it is our turn. Lana is handed to me, and Anastasia points out some lesions we haven't seen before. Beneath both ears and along the bottom of her hairline are bright splotches of scarlet red. We will have to have a doctor examine these when we get home, Anastasia tells us. Maybe go to the hospital. She shrugs them off. They are nothing. Then we are shooed outside. Lana has apparently been prepared for this moment by Anastasia, because she goes with us without a murmur, a game look in her eyes.

The day is blistering. Part of the yard is devoted to Soviet-era playground equipment mired in dust. This is treacherous stuff you would never let your child near, and indeed the caregivers at the orphanage do not venture onto the playground with their charges. The only children we ever see there are accompanied by prospective adoptive parents desperate for different modes of distraction and interaction. There is a homicidal slide made of thin, rusting metal emerging at a 60-degree angle from the faded mouth of a once-garish clown, reached by climbing a narrow flight of rickety, rusty stairs. There is a formerly four-seated merry-go-round with one of the seats missing, rusted to immobility in the dusty weeds. There are two one-person swings on frames, one of thin wobbly metal with peeling paint, but at least movable, the other made of stiff heavy wood and almost impossible to budge. Surveying these options, we retire to a damp concrete step in the shade alongside the building. There, we turn to our bag of tricks, hoping that something inside will interest Lana.

We all try to amuse her at once. Look at this! Look at this! We have no plan. Look at this! I try to settle her on my lap to look at *Dear Zoo*.

She struggles for control of the book as I try to turn the pages, and finally I let it go. She turns it upside down, leans over, and bangs it hard against the concrete step, looks at it closely again to see what's happened, then throws it with all her might into the leaves across the narrow walk. She wriggles off my lap and darts after the book. Natalie tosses down the little music box she's been furiously cranking, and goes after Lana. Lana picks up the book, throws it again. Rushes over to it, kicks it. Has this child never seen a book before? She's treating it like a ball. Not wanting my first words to her to be "Stop that this instant!" I rush over to rescue the book while Marc and Natalie distract Lana with a game of Kick the Leaves. I stow *Dear Zoo* in the backpack for a quieter moment, and dig out the small ball we've brought, which I toss to Marc. Then I settle myself on the step to watch.

They dart back and forth in the leaves, looping around trees, following the ball. Lana is responsive. She chases Natalie, then Daddy. She and Daddy chase Natalie, then she and Natalie chase Daddy. She copies Natalie: when Natalie stops, she stops; when Natalie waggles her arms, she waggles her arms. There is squealing and giggling, and Marc's shouts of encitement. It looks like success from here.

After a bit of this, we decide to try our luck with Lana in the one mobile swing. Natalie jumps on first. "Look, Lana! Swing!" We push her a bit, showing Lana how it's done. Then Lana takes over the pushing. Then Nat jumps off, and I put Lana on the seat. Nat begins swinging gently. A grin spreads over Lana's face. Wow! What a revelation this movement is! We try putting Lana on Nat's lap on the swing. Nat so wants Lana on her lap. But Lana tolerates this constraint for less than a minute before she wriggles free. She wants to swing alone or not at all. Natalie is hurt. While we watch Daddy swinging Lana, I try to explain the world from Lana's perspective, to allay the pain Nat's own perspective is causing her. But Natalie is six, and her clock has been turned upside down, and she has had almost no sleep for a couple of days now, and she's in a very strange and uncomfortable place, and this isn't at all what she expected. The hurt dims a bit, but a suspicion has been born—I can feel it there in her heart: This baby sister deal might not be as great as she had imagined it would be.

My anxiety ratchets up to meet Natalie's pain. I have to make this work. Lana is going to have to conform a little more closely to my baby's dreams.

Nat and I walk a little distance away, kicking up the playground dust. We'd love to be somewhere familiar and cool, alone. We'd be reading, or playing American Girl doll or Barbie. Then Lana is clutching my leg. She has wriggled off the swing and come to reconnect—not with Natalie, but with me. I get Natalie to help me try to interest Lana in some of the songs with motions we wrote down on the bumpy road to Odessa. How about "Where Is Thumbkin?" No? How about "Five Little Ducks"? No? How about "This Old Man"? No? I try to humor Natalie, to keep her engaged. But she flounces off to Daddy in disgust, and I am left with Lana, who is working her fingers into the dirt at my feet. I look at Lana, and try to be mature. She is just a mite, a helpless little mite. She has never had anything. She doesn't know anything. But my maternal heart is relentless: If this child hurts my baby, she will have me to deal with.

Not a moment too soon, playtime is over. It is time for Lana's lunch and nap. While Natalie goes with Anastasia to return Lana to her suite, Marc and I compare notes.

"I thought that went pretty well!" I chirp.

"Oh, man." Marc is used to my attempts at sunny optimism, and is not moved. "She didn't want to play with Natalie! She kept going to you and me."

"Well, of course, she kept going to us. She's *used* to other kids. She wants attention from *adults*. She'll come around." I desperately hope I am right.

"No! The *other* kids are more attracted to Natalie than *she* is!"

"Well, some are. But this will come, honey, this will come."

"I don't know." Marc is feeling Natalie's pain. He is more protective of her than I am. "Why's she so *little*?" he continues.

"Because she's fed nothing but cabbage?"

"They're all fed nothing but cabbage. She's by *far* the littlest one. It's not normal."

There is no getting around the fact that Lana is a peanut. Some of the kids in her group are double her weight. She is the youngest one in the group, true, but she is way, way smaller than normal. Natalie weighed considerably more at thirteen months, when we brought her home, than Lana does at thirty-two months.

Obviously, Marc has some ideas he wants to share. "What are you thinking?" I ask obligingly.

"I'm not sure. I just wonder if there's another hemangioma somewhere. I bet it's in her liver."

I scrutinize him. Is this Marc the brilliant doctor talking, or Marc the neurotic worrier? I can't tell. Could equally be either. For once, I want to see the worrier.

"Also, I couldn't get her to make good eye contact with me."

"Really? She did fine with me." This I was sure about—the child did hold my gaze, and sought it out.

"Not with me. I kept trying, but she kept looking away."

Anastasia and Nat come out the door. I look for signs of Natalie's heartbreak, but see none. She looks tired, but not overtly distressed. She feels big, having gone alone with Anastasia to take Lana back. Like Marc and me, she's ready for a break. We will go back to the apartment for our nice, hot, fat-soaked lunch and a rest. Anastasia will come for us again around two o'clock.

Back at the apartment, Marc helps Nat wash up, pouring water from a bucket over her hands to wet and rinse them. I can hear them goofing around in the bathroom behind me while I stand at a bedroom window, looking out. Trashcanistan. That's the irreverent name bestowed on the former Soviet states by a recent cover story in *The New Republic*. It fits. I am startled to notice for the first time that we have a view of the fortress from here. A pretty good view, actually, with the huge bay sparkling in the sun and wrapping around the pristine profile of the ancient site. And stretching from our apartment building to the edge of the bay, shacks with corrugated steel roofs, randomly placed; their residents, big-bellied guys in white undershirts standing swaybacked in front of their shacks, holding beer cans, scratching their paunches; stray dogs crisscrossing lots covered with weeds; cats fighting; chickens scratching in the dirt; dirty kids playing on piles of building debris—rusty wire, corrugated steel, broken concrete. No unexpected beauty jumps out to surprise me in this tangle of ugliness from the window to the sea.

Look at this place. It's just awful.

What if Marc is right? What if she is sick? What if we are about to ruin our lives?

"Um, Theresa." Luba's quiet, kind voice interrupts my reverie. "Your lunch is ready."

On the way to the orphanage in the afternoon, we stop in town. "We will buy some treats for the children now," Anastasia says. While Slava waits in the car, we four walk across a dusty intersection and step into a completely unexpected place: a pretty little soda fountain, cool and dark. When our eyes adjust to the light, we see fine dark wood paneling, a high ornate ceiling, and a couple of pretty tables with red-checkered cloths. Can we *stay* here? It is the only air-conditioning we encounter in Bilgorod. But Anastasia completes her purchase quickly—twenty lollipops for the children, five grivna—about a dollar for the lot.

At the orphanage, we walk into the suite as the children are finishing their afternoon snack of watery cocoa and a half slice of bread. They sit at their little tables, four to a table, in their gray underpants. All eyes turn toward us as we walk in the door. Lana starts out of her chair, but is restrained by a word from a caregiver. Anastasia gets permission to distribute the suckers, and Natalie walks from table to table, putting them into eager little hands, while Marc films. Caregivers follow in Natalie's path to help little hands unwrap the treats. Soon, sticky drool runs down sixteen chins.

Marc and I have decided that I'll hang back this afternoon, so that Lana will orient more toward Natalie. I'll try to get out of the way of their bonding. So, while they play with the dolly on the shaded step and chase each other again in the leaves, I wander away to the playground. There is another couple there, with a young boy. The woman hangs back a bit, but the father and son seem to be having fun. The mother and I gravitate toward each other. She and her husband are tall, attractive, dark-haired, vibrant. Ten years younger than us, like all other parents of young children in the world. They are from Austin, Texas. They are adopting a five-year-old boy. He looks cute, active, bright—like a normal kid, though we don't put much energy into examining him. They have another one at home. This seems odd—adopting a child the same age as one you already have, without involving your first. Sibling issues become more complicated: Who gets the privileges associated with age? The special dispensations accorded to the youngest? The couple made their connections in Ukraine through their church group. They are bright, personable, articulate. Like us, they have been confused and jerked around by the system in Ukraine. They are impressed with its inefficiency. They are game, though, and determined. They have brought smart toys for their new son: a ball, sand toys, a truck. The mother and I smile our farewell as we rejoin our families.

When the time comes, Nat wants to go up alone with Anastasia, but Marc goes, too. He wants to talk to the caregivers about Lana's eating habits. Maybe she's so small because she doesn't eat as much as the other kids. Maybe she has poor appetite. As I wait, leaning against the old Lada, Slava dozing inside, a couple emerges from the orphanage, moving slowly through the white curtains that billow from the front door. They are dressed in jeans and T-shirts. They look to be early middle-age, not very wealthy. The woman is crying, her face in her hands. The man looks pained; he puts his hand on her shoulder, drags on his cigarette, pulls her head onto his chest. They appear to me as a vision of the loss involved in adoption. They must have left a child there. All the books are right about the heartbreak at the core of adoption. I am struck by the juxtaposition of their grief and others' imminent happiness, maybe even ours.

Later, sadly, I tell Marc about what I have seen. He thinks I'm nuts.

After talking with the caregivers, he has a new theory about the cause of Lana's size. It's dire. He'll fill me in when we're alone.

It is rather important right now that we stay in contact with home. We have the bid on the new house to track, hoped-for bids on our own house to field, family and friends to reassure about our well-being. Marc needs to respond to issues that arise at work, pursue negotiations on his new position. We were able to keep in touch with people on our last trip via public Internet connections in Odessa and Kiev. Here in Bilgorod, it's another story.

Anastasia understands our need to make Internet connections every day. She is a college teacher of computer science herself, during the regular school year. Being an adoption facilitator is a sideline, something she does both out of love and out of the need to keep the post-Communist wolf from the door. She is happy to get us to one of the public Internet places in town every day. This first full day in Bilgorod, after Lana has been redelivered to her suite for supper, Anastasia says, "So, now we go to use the Internet." We are delighted. A connection to civilization.

Slava parks on the street across from a row of shops in a pink stuccoed strip. A glittery sign over one of the doorways reads INTERNET CLUB. Promising. We follow Anastasia into the gloom and down a steep flight of stairs into a stinking, stuffy room. It is noisy, and smoky. Noisy not with the sound of voices, but with the sounds of violent video games. As we look around, we see about a dozen computers lining the walls, and at each station one to five young men are gathered about, to play or watch. One of these computers, it turns out, has a dial-up connection to the Internet. That is the one we will use to try to communicate with home.

The manager of the club easily shoos away the clump of young men who surround one station. They look at us with more curiosity than resentment. They don't often see Americans. While the club manager, proud of his rough English, bends over Marc instructing him how to log on, elegant Anastasia and I sit on the only surface available—a filthy couch against one wall. Natalie sits on my lap swinging her legs and looks about, dazed. I take the opportunity to clarify with Anastasia about the peanut butter.

"Anastasia," I begin. "When we were getting ready to come back here to get Lana, I asked Svieta what she wanted me to bring her from America." Anastasia nods, serious. "She told me she would like to have peanut butter and hand wash." Anastasia shrugs, nods. "So, I thought maybe a lot of people would like to have peanut butter and hand wash, and I brought some more as gifts."

Anastasia frowns slightly. Perhaps she hasn't understood. "I think this is only for Svieta."

In my heart, I know I'm doomed. But I need another answer. I shift my weight so I can see more clearly into her face, which floats white before me in the gloom. "I mean, Anastasia, I brought a *lot* of this stuff to give to people here. Svieta said peanut butter was very expensive, and you couldn't even get hand wash."

Anastasia relents. "Okay, yes, this is okay." But I know she is humoring me. Now we will have to go shopping in Bilgorod.

Marc labors for a good forty-five minutes at the computer. I find out later that he takes so long because the connection is extremely slow and unreliable. It takes minutes to log on, minutes to move from message to message, minutes to send. Sometimes it just shuts down, and you have to start all over again. He is in a foul mood when he joins us outside, where we have retreated from the stench of smoking, sweating, poorly washed boys.

On the way back to the car, Natalie walks a few paces ahead with Anastasia, and Marc says to me, "I think she's ruminant."

"What?"

"I think Lana's so small because she's ruminant. She's not eating her food. She spits it out. The caregiver said she puts her fingers in her mouth sometimes, and spits out her food."

I had read about rumination in psychology courses. As I recalled, it was an emotionally disturbed response to psychosocial deprivation. It could be bad. It could cause malnutrition, and even death.

"Mo-omm!" Natalie's plaintive wail puts an end to our conversation for the night. We go home to sleep as best we can through a stifling night of barking dogs and yowling cats, our first night with the image of Lana hovering among us all.

The next morning, I am standing on the other side of a small patch of pine trees, quietly watching Lana and Daddy and Natalie interact. My stomach is leaden. Every so often, a wave of nausea rises and subsides. What are we doing? What are we doing to our family? As I watch Lana, it is obvious to me that her constant good cheer is pathological. How could she actually be *happy* in this place? She is already deranged. Maybe her mother *was* insane, and Lana is following early in her footsteps. Life in the orphanage is bringing it on quickly.

Feeding her this morning, we watched like hawks for the slightest sign of rumination, and saw it. We brought a banana, and her second can of PediaSure. Some of the PediaSure went straight down; some of the banana, too. But some of both came burbling back out of her mouth shortly after it went in. Chew, chew, chew, blurt. Mashed banana inching down her chin. Then she smiles at us. "*No, Lana, no!*" we hiss, sickness rising in our stomachs. This child is starving herself. It's a game.

Perhaps she *also* has an internal hemangioma. Those red patches behind her ears and at the nape of her neck—perhaps these are hemangiomas as well, obscured by the pink medicine they slather on. The more external hemangiomas she has, the more likely she has internal ones as well—maybe in her brain as well as in her liver.

We are about to condemn ourselves to inescapable torment.

With Natalie, the fact that adoption is forever didn't faze us. *Of course* it's forever. That's the idea. She needed parents, we were childless: This was a perfect forever fix. Now, the fact is that, if we make a disastrous mistake by bringing this child into our lives, we cannot fix it, we cannot undo it, we cannot go back. Now this fact makes me sick to my stomach. Hoping to augment our happiness, we could in fact destroy it. What if this child is terribly sick, and all of our time and money and anxiety are taken up caring for her? What if she is deranged and does something awful? What if we all fall in love with her and she breaks our hearts by dying or being sick or crazy?

As I watch Natalie engaging with Lana, responding to Lana's unhinged smile and laugh, my vision tunnels and my head spins. How can we turn back? If we turn back now, *we* will break Natalie's heart. And what would we be telling her about adoption? A child can fail an audition? "Sorry, kiddo—that just wasn't the right baby sister for us." We had done that with a dog when Natalie was three—a miniature poodle that couldn't be housebroken and wouldn't stop nipping at her. We had taken her puppy away and "given it back to its mommy" because it "wasn't the right dog for us." We could never risk conveying to her that it works the same way with children. And besides, there will always be another dog—one that *can* be housebroken. There won't *be* any more baby sister candidates. This is our only chance.

I take some deep breaths to try to get ahold on myself.

I look up. There is my Natalie, all flushed and tired, trying so hard to have fun with Lana. Lana seems to be cooperating. She imitates Natalie appropriately. She *does* smile a lot, but surely this is better than being glum. She seems to want to do what Nat and Marc want her to do. Maybe it'll be all right? I amble over to join them.

I smile a wan smile at Marc, who grimaces back at me. We have not been able to talk at any length since we left home; Natalie is ever-present, including at nighttime. She's always been a night owl, and so far on this trip we have fallen asleep getting her to sleep. But I'm not sure Marc and I actually *want* to talk privately anyway. I dread speaking my thoughts out loud; maybe he does, too.

Just then, the little girl who was supposed to have been ours—the one I saw across the room in the doorway yesterday morning—arrives at the playground with her new parents and eight-year-old brother. My attention is riveted.

I can't just stare at the other little girl, so I strike up a conversation with the parents. They are strapping, wind-burned, Irish. I love their brogue and their openness, their good humor and common sense. They have been here already for two weeks. They hope to go home in another couple of weeks. Their agency is having some problems. I can't imagine languishing here for that long. They are tolerant, patient. It *is* difficult, but it will be over. As we talk, their little Christine is tearing about. She picks up a handful of sand and runs over to her daddy, hurls it at his knees. The couple chuckle.

"She's a wee wild," they say, fondly.

She tears away for more sand and runs back, hurls it this time at her mom. As she tears around, I notice that she's actually a little chubby. How'd she get that way here? And her face, which looked so cute from across the room . . . up close, it looks more scrunched up, more plain. A little mean-looking.

"No, no, Christine," they say, a joke still in their tone. "No sand-throwing! Nyet!"

She tears off for two handfuls of sand, which she does not so much hurl as slam into the father's legs. He tries to pick her up to distract her, but she writhes like an octopus out of water. He puts her down, and she streaks off for more ammunition.

"We're in for it," the mother says, ruefully. "She's just like her brother, that one is."

I stare at her, incredulous. I have long known that having another child as spirited as Natalie would do me in. One is life's greatest gift; two is too much of a good thing. This mother seems to be taking in stride the prospect of having two ungovernable children. The brother, meanwhile, has taken refuge behind some weeds a few yards away, where he is ambling about. He's had enough of his little sister, it seems, until he can safely pound her to smithereens.

I look over to where Natalie and Lana are playing quietly. They are shoveling sand into empty water bottles, pouring it out again, adding fresh water. Lana does not throw sand or hit. Lana is following Natalie's direction. Lana appears to be tractable.

I am embarrassed by my fickleness. Lana is obviously much more the right child for our family than little Christine would be. I do not know yet whether Lana is safe for us. But I am at least relieved of the illusion that the right baby for my family is just an arm's-length away, tragically switched at referral, missed by a witless twist of fate. Seeing Christine in action stops my wandering eye, at least for the moment.

As we are gathering up our children to return them to their suite for lunch and a nap, I notice across the playground the couple I had seen on the steps the day before, a tableau of the tragedy at the root of adoption. They are with a little boy, about five years old. Everyone is smiling broadly. Christine's mother informs me that the couple is here from Italy to adopt the little boy. Ah! So I *had* been wrong, as Marc suspected. Good.


Lida squeezes in beside me in the back of the Lada, then turns to face me with an impish grin. I love her face: pretty, round, flushed, freckled, carefully but lightly made up. Her intelligent eyes twinkle. Her short hair is nicely cut, with one long skinny tail trailing halfway down her back. A touch of punky color is splashed here and there in her hair. Lida was Anastasia's English teacher at University, and will provide extra translation services for our afternoons of official visits and paperwork. We learn later, during the interminable waits that are part of all official business in Ukraine, that Lida lives with her mother, to save both of them money. She has a friend from New York, who is a Peace Corps worker in Bilgorod.

"So!" she says perkily, after we have made our introductions. "How you like our town?"

I glance at her, aghast. Slava is inching the car down into a pothole. How we like your *town*? Your town is a *pit*! You need to get out of here *as soon as possible*. But the look in her bright eyes is proud, expectant. I am supposed to name the good things about her town now.

"Actually," I splutter, "we haven't seen very much of your town. We've only been to the orphanage." Through my speechlessness, I have made a miraculous save.

She nods, satisfied. "You will see. You will like our town, I think."

I think not. "We're eager to see the rest," I agree cheerily, as Slava inches out of the hole.

We have finished our nice, hot lunch. Natalie is asleep on Daddy's lap next to me in the backseat of the car. We are headed for an afternoon of waiting in anterooms in official buildings. No official is ever on time for one of our appointments. We carry a bag of coloring books, markers, dolls, and fairy tales to help Natalie get through the excruciating afternoon.

\* \* \*

We are sitting beside the desk of a city official who is signing some necessary papers and talking with Anastasia in Russian. Natalie is awake now, her eyes wide, sitting bolt upright in Daddy's lap.

"Mommy," she whispers. "I can see her bra!"

"I know, dear," I whisper back. "Shhhh." We raise our eyebrows at each other. She smiles knowingly and sinks back into Daddy's chest.

The woman, neither young nor thin, is wearing a see-through black mesh top over a black bra. As she signs our papers, she converses with Anastasia.

She looks at us for a moment, and looks at the papers in front of her again. Speaks to Anastasia.

"What does she say?" Marc asks.

Anastasia smiles gently. "She says you are not young."

I am shocked. *So?* "Tell her I might not be young, but at least I'm not wearing a see-through top," I think.

"She says this is good," Anastasia continues. "You have experience, and patience. You will need this."

I am abashed and afraid. I had thought we were being insulted; we were being praised. And why are we going to need so much patience?

The papers are signed, and we are on to our next stop.


It is Thursday, our third morning in Bilgorod. Natalie fell asleep with us again last night: We still have not had a chance to talk alone.

I try valiantly to battle my terror. I breathe deeply. I remind myself of our robust first impressions of Lana. I talk to myself about probabilities. Sometimes I am okay. More often I live in dread. My stomach churns. We could wreck our family here. We are on an ocean liner that has begun its inexorable progress into the open sea.

Natalie is exhausted. The novelty has worn off. "I want to go hooooooome," she wails when we wake her up.

"So do weeeeeeee," I want to respond.

When Anastasia picks us up to take us to the orphanage she is thrumming with anxiety. "This is a big day for me," she says with a tense smile, "a very, very big day. There is much to do today, much to get done." She throws her hands in the air and shakes her head, as if it will be a miracle if she accomplishes all she has on her plate.

We nod our empathy, wide-eyed, and hurry out the door with her. In the gloomy stairway, her white pants glow in front of me. When we get outside, I capture the full impact of her choice of wardrobe for this critical day. She is wearing bright white pants that cling to her trim body like a bodystocking, and are sheer enough to reveal the white lace front panel of the thong she is clearly wearing underneath. Does she *know* that this shows? She might as well be wearing her underwear on the outside of her pants. Her bright white and lemon-yellow flow-ered knit top is just as close-fitting, hugging her pert little breasts. Around her neck, on a fine gold chain, a small gold cross dangles in-congruously. Her makeup is perfect.

At the car, she turns on us with a tense, official smile. We scurry into our seats.

At the orphanage, Marc and I are hanging back, trying to give Natalie a little time alone with Lana, time to be a big sister, to get into, as she has said, her "big sister skin."

We lurk on one side of the concrete-block lean-to at the edge of the playground, while Natalie and Lana play with the doll from Aunt Sarah. They lay the blanket in the dirt, plop the baby doll atop it. Lana drags the doll off, into the dirt, seats herself on the blanket, scoots along in the dirt. A tiny part of me is impelled to rescue Sarah's loving handiwork from such hard treatment. But Sarah's own spirit supports me in calm restraint. This kind of play is why god made washing machines.

We watch in silence. We shoot some footage. We do not yet love Lana. But perhaps she and Natalie will be good together as sisters? *Perhaps?*

I sigh, and turn to Marc. "If we bring this child home it will be the mitzvah to end all mitzvahs."

When Marc had expressed some anxiety to a Jewish friend between our trips, anxiety about the impact on our lives of bringing this child home, of taking responsibility for her forever and ever and ever, the friend—a dear man, an idealist—had asked, "But what about the mitzvah? What a mitzvah this would be!" Easy for him to say. Easy in theory to bring into your family a stranger who could shred all of your hearts.

Marc looks at me, surprised. A shiksa, I never talk in these terms. "Yes," he says at last. "It would be."


That afternoon, we are sitting again in an official place. This time, the room is large, the light is bright, the table is long. We sit on one side, acres of table stretching beyond us. Anastasia sits across from us, and the official—a woman, neither young nor thin, fully dressed—sits at the head. Polite remarks are exchanged between Anastasia and the official.

"Do they know about the diagnoses?" the official asks Anastasia.

Anastasia nods, waving her hand, as she translates for us. Yes, yes, we nod automatically, our heads moving up and down with hers. We know about the diagnoses. But then a warning bell goes off in my head. *Do* we know all the diagnoses? With a child like Natalie, the goofy diagnoses cooked up to make the child available for international adoption are one thing. With a child like Lana, the diagnoses take on a completely different meaning. I wonder if there's something there we've somehow missed. I whisper to Marc. He shakes his head, shrugs in disgust. The medicine is so bad here, the diagnoses are probably worthless anyway.

Anastasia is in my lap, swinging her legs, dutiful. All of a sudden, it is done. The official puts down her pen and closes the book. Anastasia leaps up, beaming. "It is official!" she crows. "Lana is yours!"

We are paralyzed. Lana is *ours*?

Anastasia strides around the table behind the official and embraces us warmly. We smile as best we can.

"Oh! That's great!" Our voices echo desperately in the empty hall.

My heart is in my throat. *They cannot make us take this child home.* We are free to leave any time we want, with or without this child. We are *free*.


Finally, Natalie has fallen asleep while we are still conscious. We face each other, Marc sitting on the edge of the folded-down couch, me on the floor, atop my bedding.

"Oh, my god."

"Yeah."

"What do we do?"

"I don't know."

"I feel like throwing up."

"Me, too. I've felt like throwing up for days."

We cast our eyes about the room, looking for answers. There are no good answers here.

I take a deep breath. "The question is, really . . . the question is, would it be more harmful to our family to leave her here, or to bring her home? That's the question."

Marc nods. That *is* the question. Now we have to sort it out.

It comes out, at last, on the side of bringing her home. The odds of her being desperately ill are pretty good. Quite good, actually. Perhaps an internal hemangioma, even more than one, lies at the root of her failure to grow. Perhaps she has a genetic malabsorption syndrome that prevents her from processing fats and some proteins. Malabsorption could account for her increasingly strange odor, too. Perhaps rumination was causing or contributing to her low weight. Perhaps the emotional disturbance underlying the rumination is a precursor to severe mental illness. All of these things are distinctly possible. But the odds of damaging Natalie emotionally by leaving Lana here now—after they have played together, after they have been called sisters—are even better. And there is the question of our own emotional damage. Could we live with ourselves if we left her behind? Could we live with the thought of her here? With the memory of her sparkling eyes and dazzling smile and little wriggling form? Could we live with the memory of her sense of humor and oddly knowing spirit? With the fear of what we had done to Natalie by abandoning Lana? With the knowledge of what we had done to *Lana* by abandoning Lana? With the suspicion that we had been governed by irrational fears instead of sober reason?

We talk long into the night, while the dogs and cats howl. At about ten P.M., the people in the next apartment begin a rehab project, hammering at the other side of the wall in the bedroom where Natalie sleeps, and employing for minutes on end a machine that sounds for all the world like a jackhammer. We stare at each other in open-mouthed amazement; we leap up and stalk about in impotent fury, waving our arms. Natalie sleeps on. The racket lasts for over an hour. By the time it has subsided, our decision is firm: It is likely to be better for our family to bring Lana home. We are to take custody on Monday.

On Friday, Lana's odor is distinctly unpleasant, a mixture of urine and boiled cabbage and something else. I sniff. Please, God, let this be the smell of orphanage clinging to her; let these smells wash away once we get her home and clean and cabbage-free. Let her emerge smelling sweet and normal, like a normal kid. I think there is a good likelihood of this. That orphanage smell of urine and boiled cabbage has begun to cling to *us* after less than a week: It gets in your nose, in your clothes, in your skin. It's hard to get out. I sniff at her again. Is there any element her own little body is contributing? Is her smell especially peculiar, above and beyond the stench of orphanage? Is there a smell here that could signal a metabolic disorder that would help explain her puniness? I can't tell. I am dismayed that I am reluctant to nuzzle her, hesitate to hold her close.

A long bright hallway between orphanage buildings is broken up with colorful kid-sized statues of gnomes. "Guh-nomes," Anastasia says to Lana every time we pass them. "Guh-nomes." "No, Mommy," Nattie hisses to me, tugging urgently at my arm, "it's *nnn*nomes, *nnn*nomes, not 'guh-nomes'!" I too am distressed by this funny little thing. We don't want Anastasia to teach Lana English *wrong*! But soon none of this will matter in the least. "I know, honey. It's okay." But it's not okay with Natalie, and it's not okay with Marc: It bugs them. And in truth, it bugs me, too. This is about possession.

\* \* \*

On Saturday, we are to take Lana to the market for undies, shoes, and visa photos. The poor child reeks to high heaven. Then it strikes me: They must bathe the children just once a week. Maybe today is bath day, or tomorrow. A week's worth of orphanage crud has accumulated on her skin and under her nails and on her scalp. She is presented to us with four topknots in her hair, which I attempt to brush out to make her more presentable for her passport photo. But her hair ends up all pouffy, in a weirdly shaped little bouffant, because I can't smooth the bumps out.

Lana has never been in an automobile. She has seen them, though, and is curious. When we approach the car with her, she clambers right in. It's like a play structure—she wants to climb all over it.

"Sometimes they are very afraid when the car starts," warns Anastasia.

We settle in, Marc in front with Slava, and Natalie between Anastasia and me in back, Lana on my lap by the window. When the car starts to move, she starts to scream. She screams and screams, very high-pitched, and flails like a monkey on speed. I am talking softly to her, trying to gently restrain her, but I am having no effect. She tries to climb out the window, screaming. Anastasia reaches across Natalie to pull Lana off my lap and into hers. I resent her for it. What makes her think she can calm Lana better than *I* can, her mother? But she can, of course, since she knows her better and can speak her language. The elegant Anastasia enfolds the stinky, flailing child on her lap and puts her mouth to her ear as she rocks her back and forth, talking to her softly in Russian. Lana's screams quiet to whimpers, she struggles less hard to flee. By the time we arrive at the market she is quietly miserable.

As I have done all week as we made our official rounds, I find myself at the market scrutinizing the faces of passersby, wondering,

"Could *that* be her mother? What if her father were like *that*?" This guessing game thrusts itself upon me involuntarily. I stop it as quickly as I can, because there are a lot of people around whom I do not want to imagine as the parents of my child. I do not need this complication. I cannot know what her parents look like; I can never know who they are. She will have to stand on her own with me, acceptable or not on her own terms. She emerges from nowhere, of no parents, like Venus rising from the ocean.

The market is crowded with people this Saturday morning. Lana's big brown eyes are wide as she quietly takes it in. There are some small permanent shops lined up on one side of the road, but by far the most commerce is taking place in the open-air market, which is indeed very large for a town this size. Along the periphery are farmers perched on overturned crates selling fruits and vegetables and eggs. Inside is every other material good one needs in life. When we find a stall with underpants tiny enough to fit her, we buy more than a dozen pairs. We will not be able to find these in the U.S.—undies this size do not exist in America. We buy her two pairs of adorable shoes, a sporty pink pair with kitties on them, and a dress-up red pair with embroidery and lace. When we put the red ones on her feet to check the size, she says "Wooooooh!" and does not want us to take them off. She keeps looking at them and touching them as we make our way slowly through the market. She wriggles with pleasure in my arms. She has a beautiful smile, lively eyes.

On the way back to the car, Anastasia is dabbing at her eyes. "Are you okay?" I ask.

"I am okay, yes. My eyes, they are irritated from the makeup, that's all. I buy Lancôme makeup, you know this makeup?"

"Yes, sure. I know Lancôme." I *wear* Cover Girl, but I do know Lancôme.

"I buy it because I think you might like this. But I am allergic to it."

It takes me a few moments to process this. Anastasia thinks I can identify makeup *on*? And she is so concerned to impress me that she wears makeup that she knows will make her eyes itch and run? With this revelation, Anastasia comes into clearer focus for me. The ice queen demeanor that has often put us off stems not from a lack of feeling, but from an abundance of it: She is highly anxious about making a good impression on us. I feel foolish and cold myself.

"Oh, Anastasia—I'm sorry the makeup is bothering you."

"Oh, it's okay," Anastasia says. "The lady who sold it to me, she said I could bring it back if it hurt me. I think I will do this."

I think about the used makeup this woman is selling from her bazaar booth. If I had considered buying any makeup here, I wouldn't do it now. "Oh, well, that's good," I say, and let the matter drop.

In the car on the way back to the orphanage, Lana is less hysterical, and lets me hold her. Natalie and I begin singing to her to distract her, and soon she is huddled against my chest, her smelly scalp tucked under my chin, just whimpering.

As I sit cradling this child who is mine but whom I do not yet love, my thoughts drift back to a realization I had the night before. It had dawned on me with the force of an unpleasant but inescapable fact that one reason Marc and I are not more drawn to this little girl is because she does not make us feel proud—of her or of ourselves. We were proud to have been chosen as the appropriate parents for Natalie, the princess of the orphanage. Natalie's glory reflected well on us. Lana, in contrast, puny and sickly as she apparently is, fails to elicit the pride that could jump-start the bonding process.

Disgusted with this view of myself, I try to fight it. But I have to admit that it feels like the truth. In the middle of the night, my narcissism has been revealed to me. And it makes me wonder: How *does* love get started if you don't, looking at your child, feel pride? Marc and I cannot fall back on the knowledge that we created her—one basic claim on parental narcissism of every biological child. Marc looks for and finds Lana's beauty on film. She appears to be very smart. She has a wonderful spirit, remarkable resilience. That laugh, if it's not deranged . . . Still, our pride wounded, our biological role nil, we are groping for our footing for loving this child. I sigh and peer into Lana's flaky scalp as she huddles, trembling, searching for safety in my lap.

While Marc labors to activate Bilgorod's other Internet connection, Luba, Natalie, and I amble outside. It is a beautiful, bright, sunny Sunday. Anastasia has told us that the orphanage is closed, but we have heard different from the Irish couple, who will be visiting their wild Christine today. This morning, when we pressed Luba to check with Anastasia—we wanted one more visit with Lana before we took custody—Anastasia assured her that the orphanage was closed.

"But we *know* it's open!" we said in exasperation to Luba, after she had hung up the phone.

"I think we will do what Anastasia says," our sixteen-year-old keeper had replied firmly. And that was that.

Thwarted in our attempt to see Lana, we determined at least to put the day to good use. Once Marc had accomplished his near-impossible mission to communicate with the outside world, we would buy a fan for the apartment. We wanted one in part for ourselves, and in part to help Lana be comfortable when she came home with us tomorrow. We would use it for the couple more days we would be here, and leave it as a hostess gift for our landlady.

Natalie, Luba, and I have fled from the stifling Internet club and into the large park behind the building. In the distance there seems to be a playground of some sort, so we make our way toward it. As we approach a bench where two middle-aged ladies sit looking at us, Luba leans into me and whispers, "Do not talk to these ladies. These are dangerous ladies." Dangerous? I look at them, trying to see the danger, but it escapes me. I can clearly see the danger, though, in the young man who seems to be shadowing us. He is unshaven, his hair tousled, his clothes rumpled and dirty. I noticed him when we walked into the club. Now he is behind us as we walk toward the park. When we stop to look at a tree-trunk sculpture, he passes us and sits on a bench a few yards ahead. This danger I can clearly see, and keep an eye on. But the ladies?

They mumble a bit as we walk past them, but do not accost us. As we get closer to what we thought was a playground we discover instead an abandoned amusement park. An old man and an old woman sit on folding chairs alongside a shed. Otherwise, though, the park is deserted, the rides still as death in the yellow Sunday sun. It is eerie. About half of the equipment is rusted and out of use, surrounded by weeds. Here are bullet-shaped cars on once-swinging arms, rusted and still. Here is a platform with teacup-shaped cars tilting this way and that in a frozen circle. Here is a small Ferris wheel, its once-bright paint faded and peeled. This is the Ferris wheel of my nightmares, the one that begins an inexorable slow-motion topple to the ground when my basket is at the very top. We wander through. About half of the equipment appears to be in working order. Natalie wants to climb on everything, but I think of slips and cuts, rust and infection. The answer is no.

"Where are the children?" I ask Luba. "It seems odd that there are no children here on such a beautiful day." Luba has no explanation. It *does* seem strange, she admits.

The old lady calls across to Luba, and they converse briefly.

"She wants to know if Natalie would like to ride something."

"NO."

"Mamma, *please?*"

"Absolutely not. Honey, this stuff could fall apart at any moment. It's not safe."

Natalie's agonized shrieks split the silence. They go on for a long, long time. She jerks at my arms and my clothes, trying to drag me toward a ride. She stands feet planted, arms folded across her chest, refusing to budge. She sobs as if her heart were breaking. She throws herself on the ground and screams how she hates me. She has needed this outlet. I try to take it in stride. The dangerous old ladies and the dangerous young man watch from their respective perches, wondering, perhaps, when I will fling my purse to the ground and start battering my child.

"It is good, how you let her cry," Luba says.

"You think so?"

"Most Ukrainian parents, they would not allow this."

I am interested in knowing how they would suppress it. "She's been under a lot of stress—she needs to blow off some steam."

"Yes, this is what I think, but most people here would not agree."

I finally get Natalie calmed down enough to move back toward the Internet club. Her sobs are subsiding, her feet are moving one before the other, when behind us a creaking sound draws our attention backward. One of the rides has started up—a tall pole that rotates, sending the seats attached to it by long cables floating out in a wide circle all around it. One little girl sits in one of the cars.

Natalie's wails resume, full pitch.

"This park," Luba says to me as we creep back to the Internet place trailing Natalie like a broken pull toy, "it used to be so nice. Eleven, twelve years ago, you know—everything was so nice in this town."

This is a theme we have heard before. Sitting at lunch one day with Anastasia, at a nearly empty outdoor cafe, Natalie off chasing a scruffy little striped kitten from table to table, we heard the same refrain: It was so much better in the old days, when old age was secure, when babushkas knew where their next dinner was coming from. Now, no one is secure, ever. Everyone has to work very, very hard, even into old age, or be trampled. Look at Anastasia—she works three jobs! Our mothers, both of them, they need our money in order to pay their rent. No, no, we do not want to go back. There is no going back. But it was better then, almost everything was better. It was good not to have to work so hard. And now, we don't feel it's entirely safe to say anything bad about the president, and we can't get rid of him either. What was the point?

As we approach the front door of the Internet place, Luba is adding, it was good to have order enforced, to have juveniles under control instead of out vandalizing our parks. Marc steps out, fuming. "The electricity has gone out!" He had just come to the end of a long response to a colleague when the screen went dark.

"I can't believe it!" He had managed, after several minutes, to make a phone connection but had been defeated at a more basic level.

"It is the government," Luba explains helpfully. "They do not always manage to keep the electricity on."

Natalie, seeing her father's dismay, recovers somewhat her own equanimity.

"Mommy," she says, tugging at my dress. "Why does the *government* turn off the *electricity*?"

To compensate Nat for the loss of a death-defying carnival ride, we buy her some ice cream as we amble toward the flea market. Luba's mother will meet us there to buy an item we missed on Saturday—a little plastic toddler potty for Lana. When Luba tells her mother that we also want to buy a fan, she frowns. "A fan? I do not think these stores are open today. The stores that sell fans."

"Well, let's just see."

"Okay, okay, we see." In the strip of little permanent shops across the street from the flea market we readily find an electronics store that sells fans. There's a fine fan right inside the door: a floor model, three speeds, rotating, stainless steel.

"What about *this* fan?" we ask.

Luba and her mother frown and shake their heads. "We think this fan, it is too expensive."

We check again. It is 114 grivna, about twenty dollars. "No, it's not too expensive for us. We're happy to buy this fan. Would you like to have it for your apartment?"

They confer again. "This fan, it is cheaply made, we think," Luba reports. "It is way too expensive for what it is."

It doesn't look any more cheaply made than fans in America. They must be trying to save us money. "It's okay," we say. "It will last awhile. We think it will be good for Lana to have this fan, to cool her a little bit. And then you can use it for other guests."

As Luba translates, her mother shakes her head vigorously, and expostulates in Ukrainian. Luba turns to us. "Ukrainian children, they no like fans. They get sick. Ukrainian children do not like fans."

We can't endanger the Ukrainian child. We give up on the possibility of moving the air in the apartment.

As we walk out of the store, a car halts abruptly in front of us and Anastasia leaps out. "I've been looking for you for an hour! We can go, we can go!" She has discovered that the orphanage is open, and on her way to find us has purchased another round of lollipops for the kids. The glum day opens up. We clamber into the car.

When we arrive in her suite, we can just glimpse Lana in the back

226

room, seated on a plastic potty in a circle with other children similarly engaged. The plump, smiling caregiver waves us in. Lana and her confreres do their business in a patch of sunshine that is flowing through the tall open window. In addition to the plastic potties there is one toilet in the room, two little child-height sinks with bar soap, a couple of little towels hanging up. Behind a white wooden screen on a platform off to the right is a bathtub. Damp towels hang over the sides.

When Lana sees us, she starts jumping up and down, knocking over her potty. This is the sort of move that would account for the urine-saturated stench of their bathroom. The caregiver supervising the children's toileting, though, is kind. She firmly but lovingly returns Lana to her potty. I am impressed by her gentleness, and by her indulgence. She talks to the children in a steady stream of Russian, and allows them to putz around a bit in the water as they wash their hands. Watching, I hope that it will be this woman, and some of the other kind women we have seen in the last few days, who will be there tomorrow to receive our gifts, not the young ice queens we met on our first visit.

Do we want to see where Lana sleeps? she asks. Of course. As she leads us to the sleeping quarters—a large, airy room lined with identical cribs, completely free of toys—she detours to a shelf near an easy chair and from the top picks up the family photos we had sent ahead for Lana's enlightenment. She gestures to the pictures, to us, to Lana, beaming.

We have an easy visit with Lana. Her weekly bath has transformed her. She smells good, her scalp is fine, the redness behind her ears is gone: It was a rash, not hemangiomas. The caregiver reports that Lana hadn't vomited or had diarrhea during the night—so she had been able and willing to keep down the PediaSure and banana we'd fed her the day before. Maybe she is only *mildly* ruminative, maybe she digests her food normally.

Carrying her toward the playground, I stop at a juniper tree and pluck one of its fragrant berries. I dent it with my thumbnail, and hold it up for her to smell. My mother, a biology teacher, had introduced me to the juniper this way. Lana sniffs, looks at me, smiles.

On the playground, she and Natalie sit side by side, playing quietly in the sand, for a long time. My heart starts to settle.

Walking by myself back toward the orphanage to go to the bathroom, I come upon an old nursemaid sitting in the shade in the courtyard of the building, surrounded by hanging laundry, her drooping body draped in a faded sundress. In the carriage that she joggles are two adorable babies, no more than six months old. They look healthy and alert. She gazes at them, coos to them, smiles at them, fusses over their bonnets and blankets. She picks one up and nuzzles its neck. It pierces my heart, this sight of what Lana has missed, what Natalie missed. What I have missed. I wish suddenly again with all my heart that I had had Natalie from birth, indeed that I had had her inside me. I wish I could have stroked her from the moment she was conceived, stroked her through my own skin, the way I see pregnant women doing all the time, let her know through my hands circling and patting and stroking my belly that she was loved and safe, that my love for her was infinite. I wonder if I will soon feel the same way about Lana, and think that perhaps I will. I take in the scene, tears prickling behind my eyes for just a moment, and keep moving. There is nothing for it.

When it is time to leave, no one wants our visit to come to an end—a novel experience. Lana cries and reaches back for us when we hand her to her caregiver at the door to her suite. She is ready to come with us. And we are as ready as we will ever be to take her. We needed these last few hours together more than we had known.

Natalie heaves a big sigh as we walk down the reeking hallway. "Well," she concludes with satisfaction as we emerge into the late afternoon sunlight. "She loves me, that's for sure."

# ~❀ 12 ❀~

# Escape from Ukraine

"We spent a year in Bilgorod last week." Today is our day to take custody of Lana at last, but, like the strictest Puritans, the Ukrainians have determined that our gratification will be delayed until the last possible moment. We will not take custody until suppertime, after we have completed more official work, shopped for gifts for the orphanage and the caregivers, and picked up our last round of snacks for the children.

Our first stop is to see the judge, who is late to work. We wait, and wait, and wait, all dressed up, outside the judicial building, across from the army barracks, in the sun, sometimes in the car. It is hot and windy. The dust is blowing up everywhere and we are soon filthy. A woman from the orphanage is here, a social worker we have never seen; a woman from the Education Administration; Lida, the perky translator ("How you like our town?"); Anastasia, of course. We pace and mill about for twenty minutes, forty minutes, sixty minutes. The little re-freshment cart outside the judicial building has no cold beverages. We cannot go anywhere, lest we miss the judge. While I sit in the car col-oring with Natalie, Marc watches soldiers slowly sweep the dust from one side of the sidewalk to the other with brooms made of branches. Then the wind comes and moves the dirt back, and they begin again, in slow motion. No need to hurry.

Suddenly, we must go in! The judge has arrived! We hurry up the large, airy staircase, smooth our hair, brush dust from our clothes, compose ourselves. Wait a moment outside the judge's office, are ush-ered in. He is intelligent-looking, good-humored, balding, trim. He sits in shirtsleeves behind a neat desk, with one of the floor fans we saw at the market swinging from side to side behind him, ruffling the edges of the documents he holds. He is at ease, and soon we are, too, sitting across the room from him on plastic chairs. He looks at Marc, speaks to Anastasia with a smile. "He says American men aren't as good-looking as Ukrainian men," she says to Marc with a laugh. Everyone chuckles. Marc jokes that, earlier, a woman had said he was old, and now this judge is saying he's ugly! The judge laughs.

He asks, still good-humored, "Is America going to invade Iraq?"

We groan. "We hope not! Most Americans do not like the idea."

The judge smiles, nods, signs the documents. "Okay, then, you can adopt her." It is cordial, quick, done.

Our next stop is the notary. There is a long line outside the notary's office, which is in an ancient-looking, olive-colored stuccoed building on a tree-lined street. Anastasia elbows her way in and is told to come back at two o'clock. We will go shopping for the orphanage instead.

Anastasia wants it to be clear that we do not have to buy anything for the orphanage. We are not to think that bribes are necessary. If we do not want to buy anything, that is just fine.

We tell her that we have expected to buy a gift for the orphanage, we want to buy a gift for the orphanage. What do they need?

They need a few things; we can choose. They need music in Lana's suite. Their tape machine is broken and so they have no music. Okay. What else? They need a heater. There is no space heater for the suite. Last winter, the children were very cold. They had to wear many layers of clothes inside. We try not to think about this. Okay, a space heater. What else? That is all. What else? Cookies. They would like cookies for the children. How about some healthy cereal for the children? Yes, this is good, too. Cereal would be fine. So we go shopping. Except for whole-grain cereal, we find and buy everything, plus chocolates for the children who are staying behind, and chocolates and champagne for their nurses.

At two o'clock, back at the notary's door, the street is deserted, and no one responds to our knocks. Wait, wait. Finally, someone opens the door. Inside are two women in an office. One of them operates the only computer we have seen in operation in an official function. As she clicks away at the computer, the other woman is sewing our documents together with a large needle and heavy thread. There is a fly strip hanging from the ceiling light in the middle of the room. Natalie finds a fly swatter and starts chasing flies as we sit across the desk and wait. The women joke kindly with Anastasia about giving Natalie a job controlling the flies.

On our way out, we run into the attractive couple from Austin, who are adopting the five-year-old boy. We smile, greet each other. Almost done! Whew! Congratulations!

Then, finally, we get to go to the orphanage. Natalie is jumping out of her skin. But before we see Lana we must present our gifts to the director. Now, finally, a few minutes before we are to take custody, we can ask her about Lana's birth mother.

We are excited to be giving so many nice gifts. We watch proudly as Slava brings the gifts from the car and piles them on the director's desk and floor: the twenty-five-pound box of cookies, the space heater, the tape player, the tapes of children's songs, and, for her, a glittery gift bag with a silk scarf, a beautiful wallet from the local department store, and peanut butter and hand wash. When we enter, she does not stand up. She sits sideways in her armchair, her legs crossed at the thighs, the standard chilly smile on her face, surveying the gifts. We are nonplussed. She's not even going to thank us? She looks at us. "Yes? So you take home—who is it?—you take home Sniezhana today, eh?"

"Yes, we do," Marc replies through Anastasia. He is trying to be upbeat. "We wonder if we can ask you a couple of questions."

She raises her eyebrows. We can ask all we want. That doesn't mean she'll answer them.

All the books and common sense tell us to be sure we know Lana's habits and preferences: What is her schedule? When does she eat? What does she eat? When does she potty? How does she get to sleep? What are her special comfort objects? Marc starts down this line of questioning, the orphanage director glancing occasionally at Anastasia as she begins the translation. She waves them off. "You can ask the nurses these things."

No touchy-feely here. No "Climb Every Mountain." This is pure business.

"Well," Marc recovers, "and we also wanted to know what you know about the birth mother."

The director listens, shakes her head. "We don't know anything, really. She was very young, it was her first pregnancy. That's all we know. She left the hospital quickly. We don't know her height, her weight, her eye color—we know nothing, just her age."

And that is it. She waves us off and turns back to her desk.

Up in the suite, Lana is delivered to us naked, just as Natalie was. They even want the rubber bands holding the topknots in her hair. When we pull out the pink, sparkly dress we have brought for her to wear home, she says, "Ooooooh!" and does a little happy dance, wiggling and waving her hands above her head. We hand out the gifts to the caregivers; it is the set we first met, with the young ice queens, whom I did not want to reward. But they seem rather kind today, and they accept the gifts graciously. Natalie hands out the chocolates to the children. They sit in their underpants on their bench and eat chocolate. My last picture of the group shows them wide-eyed, intent, their faces smeared with chocolate. Then everyone says good-bye to Lana, and we leave.

When we arrive at the apartment, Luba and her mother are leaning out the balcony windows, looking for us. They rush downstairs and fawn over Lana as if she were a princess. They have dinner ready for us. For Lana they have prepared a special soup, a thin, watery, cabbage soup, like she's been used to in the orphanage. This is precisely what we *don't* want her to have.

"Let's feed her some of these potatoes," Marc says. "Do you have any extra butter?"

"Oh, but Ukrainian children, they love soup," Luba and her mother protest.

But this child is ours now. We pour a can of PediaSure into a cup, mash potatoes with butter, cut meat into minuscule bites, and sit down to feed Lana. She eats like she's been starving. We slow her down. We watch like hawks for signs of rumination. "No, Lana! No! Keep your food *in* your mouth!" She grins at us as she blurts a little back out, but she keeps most of it down. We'll probably *give* her an eating disorder if she doesn't have one already.

After dinner, Natalie and Lana take their first bath together, in the washtub inside the bathtub, splashing around, squealing in universal child language. We watch from the edge of the tub, ready to catch a falling body.

"Look at her tushie," Marc says to me quietly.

I look. "What about it?"

"Look how the bones protrude there."

Toddler tushies are funny-looking. Lana's looks like a skinny toddler tushie to me: funnier-looking than most, but fundamentally normal.

"I wonder if she has some weird dwarf syndrome. Maybe *that's* why she's so small!"

I snort. "*Marc!* Don't be ridiculous!"

He falls quiet, but he's sure he's right.

The girls are to go to bed in the same room, Natalie in the fold-out bed, Lana in a chair that folds flat, that Luba and her mom have made into a bed. She climbs onto it, and crash! Like everything else in the apartment, it falls apart, collapsing under the weight of a malnourished toddler. Lana sits on the bed angled like a slide, looking startled, but not yet crying. Luba rushes in, apologizes, fixes it. Lana tentatively crawls back onto the bed, smiles when it stays upright, and curls up to go to sleep. Natalie falls asleep quickly, too, in a room with her sister.

Marc and I sit in the living room, in shock. We have another child.

About an hour later, the rehab work begins again in the next apartment. They are hammering on the wall of the room where the girls are sleeping. We rush in, expecting the girls to wake up afraid. I look at Lana's little body, splayed out on the bed. It is objectively adorable. I can see that it is adorable, but I am not moved. I stand looking at her a moment, and wonder: When will I find this body adorable? When will I kneel down beside her bed and drink in the vision of her sweet face? When will I feel compelled to stroke her and kiss her while she sleeps? I want to know, right now, exactly when this amazing transformation will occur in my heart.

They sleep on. Eventually, we do, too.

Our first day of full custody of Lana, Anastasia picks Marc up at five-thirty A.M. to run all over the countryside finalizing paperwork and getting Lana's passport. They have to go to the tiny village where Lana was born to get her original birth certificate. They pass through Moldova. ("Do not say anything," Anastasia instructs Marc. "It is best if they do not know you are American.") They have numerous other stops. I try not to think of Marc being hauled all day over Ukrainian roads in an old Lada. It is without a doubt his most dangerous day on the ground.

If their day goes well, we will leave Bilgorod tomorrow. We have tried to prepare Natalie for the long trip home by making it sound like a great adventure. We will leave very early in the morning to drive from Bilgorod to Odessa so that we are in time to catch the morning commuter flight from Odessa to Kiev. We will stay a day or two in Kiev, where we must go to the American embassy and to a doctor who must clear Lana for adoption into the U.S. Then, we will fly to Warsaw, where we will again visit the American embassy, this time to get Lana's visa. We will stay in Warsaw a day or two while the visa is processed. From Warsaw, we will fly to Amsterdam for one more trip through Schiphol Airport, and from Amsterdam, finally, we will fly home to Chicago. Four airplanes! Imagine! we say to Natalie. What an adventure!

We will take this one leg at a time.

While Marc and Anastasia bounce around Ukraine all day, Natalie and Lana and Luba and I play on the apartment-building playground. Its decent equipment's grounded in a combination of dirt and sand. The good-looking children who are playing on it scrutinize us speaking our English, and alternately approach and exclude Natalie). We amble over to the seawall and watch frogs leap from the slippery steps that are crumbling into the Black Sea bay; Lana scrambles to follow them, and I almost lose my grip on her. Back on dry land, Lana pulls a few berries off a nearby bush, and holds them up to my face. I look at her, uncertain what I'm supposed to do. She holds them up to her nose, sniffs. She is remembering the juniper berry I had offered her to smell on Sunday. I sniff the red berries she holds up again to my nose. "Mm-mmm," I say, nodding and smiling at her. She grins back. I got it. We play in the apartment. Take baths. Natalie is solicitous of Lana. I am hopeful, anxious, worried, tired, not yet in love.

Marc returns at the end of the day, thank god, with Lana's pale blue, improvised-looking passport. It has been sewn together by hand. She peers sideways out of the picture uncertainly, lips apart, eyes wide, hair in the lumpy bouffant left by the topknots.

Lida comes up with Anastasia to say good-bye. They are pleased and proud for us. "I think that now you are a happy mommy," Lida says. I look at her sharply. Is she joking?

"Why?" I ask, forcing a smile.

"Because! Now you have two girls. My mother, she had two girls, and she says, this is what makes a mommy happy, a happy mommy!"

I smile as best I can and bob my head. Sure enough! I'm a lucky mommy. My family is complete. I have my two girls. I pray for the day my heart affirms this decision.

The next morning we waken the girls at four-fifteen A.M. in order to reach the seven-forty-five A.M. flight from Odessa to Kiev. I am relieved and impressed by Lana's game attitude. She smiles, scrambles out of bed. Our kind and valiant hostesses have been there since three-forty-five, getting breakfast for us. We leave the rest of the peanut butter and hand wash for them, the suitcase we brought it in, and cash.

All of us in the car are groggy and quiet, watching the sun come up as we crash over nearly empty roads toward Odessa. Eerie sights of lone individuals walking out in fields, dark shapes before dawn. What are they doing? The country is just beginning to stir. In the blue morning dusk around five-thirty A.M. people start tending their fruit stands by the side of the road.

The airport in Odessa is an old one-story brick building, with a couple of gates. The waiting area looks like that of an old bus station—high ceilings, cracked tile floors, wooden benches like church pews. Waiting people, poorly dressed, slouch sleepily on the pews or mill about, smoking unfiltered cigarettes. At boarding time, Anastasia and Slava help marshall us toward the gate, and in a flurry of arms and legs and boarding passes and bags, we kiss quick good-byes and burst out of the terminal onto the runway. We follow the line snaking under the back end of the small jet. People disappear up the jet's tail, and we follow. The airplane, about forty years old, looks like something out of a *noir* movie. Small doorless bins hang over the two rows of tattered green seats. The tray tables are thin sheets of metal, like guillotines. As the pilot revs the engines, smiling plump stewardesses walk up the aisles offering hard candies to suck during takeoff. They are back during the flight with paper cups of sparkling water and orange soda. As we near Kiev, a fat, slovenly man in a dirty pilot's uniform, shirt untucked, staggers to the back to take a leak. Nevertheless, we land.

It is a Wednesday morning in August in Kiev. Alexi and Ivan meet us at the airport and separate us, Marc going off with Alexi and our passports to accomplish more paperwork, the girls and I going off with Ivan. Ivan takes us to the Oil and Gas Ministry for Lana's appointment with the embassy-approved doctor. (He is unimpressed with Lana's development delays: She will catch up, he says.) Ivan ushers us to the photo store next for the visa photos we will need in Warsaw, then to our apartment. We have asked for an upgrade, but didn't expect this. Ivan leads us into an old beaux arts–style limestone building just off cathedral way in the heart of Kiev. Up one flight, he opens the door to a huge, recently rehabbed and beautifully furnished apartment. Everything is new. Nothing falls apart. There is a large bathtub with a big, shiny showerhead. The water runs hot and clear. The sink is clean and whole; the tiles stay in place; there are mirrors where we need them. Doors close and lock. It has high ceilings, and huge windows looking out into a small central courtyard, with very deep window wells. It is beautiful, European.

"Man!" I have been groaning to Natalie. "I cannot *wait* to get back to civilization."

"What's cilivization, Mommy?"

"Oh, honey—it's hard to explain."

I say to Natalie as we are walking through the apartment, "This is really very close to civilization, honey." I hate to be grudging, but still—there is no air-conditioning, no potable water. But it's *close*. We could live here easily. They had wanted to spare us the expense of this apartment on our first trip; it is twenty dollars a night more than Irina's apartment.

The large color television, the first we have seen in a home since we left Chicago, looks alien and vaguely menacing. Marc is watching CNN report that the U.S. stock market is tanking. One of our favorite financial gurus is saying that the real estate market may be the last bubble, just waiting to burst. Dread sinks into my stomach. We have had no offers on our house. Will we be ruined just getting *out* of the contract on the new house? We cannot cope with this much stress right now. We click off the set and turn to our girls, who are bouncing on the bed in the other room.

The woman who will be cooking for us arrives carrying shopping bags full of food she has prepared elsewhere, which she begins laying out for us. Special, for Lana: gruel!

Marc is firm. "No, *no!* We do not want her to have this!"

"Oh! Well, what do I know?" she says, in her rough English. I cannot tell if she is offended—which seems to me appropriate—or if she is genuinely humble. We put her specially prepared gruel away, and instead feed Lana the high-fat meats and cheeses the kind woman has prepared for us.

After this late-afternoon dinner, we set out to find an Internet cafe. We must reconnect with family, work, Realtor, lawyer. I strap little Lana to my body and collect appropriate accoutrements for the impending weather, for the summer evening has grown quite cool, and dark: We grab a blanket to throw over Lana, a jacket for Natalie, an umbrella. As we walk about in the deepening gloom looking for the Internet cafe that should be just around the corner, it starts to rain. Then it starts to pour, and soon it is pouring in sheets. We cannot find the place. Drenched, we run back to the apartment, everyone ready to cry.

Ivan is to pick us up at eight-thirty A.M. for our nine A.M. appointment at the American embassy. We are hurrying to be ready on the dot. The cook hasn't been here to give us breakfast, and we are hungry, but we don't care. We are leaving Ukraine. We are exuberant. We are on our way home!

"Where are the passports?"

"I don't know. *You* had them last."

"I put them on the coffee table. They're not there now."

Right. Marc *had* put the passports on the coffee table when he'd arrived the night before. He'd put the passports and the money belt with about twelve hundred dollars left in it on the coffee table where

Lana could scatter them to the winds. I had moved them to . . . the drawer in the bedside table, I was pretty sure. But they weren't there.

I had had custody of the passports and money belt for the entire trip, and had kept entirely appropriate fanatical watch on them at all times. Yesterday afternoon, for the first time, Marc took the passports to transact his official business with Alexi. Now neither one of us knows where they are.

Marc is getting panicky. I try to stay calm. "They're here somewhere," I say with a tinge of condescension. Does he think they dematerialized? "But *where*?"

"I think I saw them on the windowsill," he accuses.

I have the vaguest memory, yes, of maybe putting them on the windowsill. I *might* remember deciding that the girls could still get them from the bedside table. So I had put them in one of the deep window wells and closed the blind over them, shutting them from the girls' view. I might have done that.

But they are not in any of the window wells. I am rifling through my purse again when Marc issues a stark cry from the other room. It sounds as if he has found his mother's battered body. "They're *gone*! The passports are *gone!*"

The girls are starting to sense our dismay.

"Good god, calm down!" I hiss. "Of course they're not *gone*. They're here somewhere. Where do you think they *went*?"

"Out the window, that's where!" He is glaring at me, but he is seeing his mother's bloodied body. He hates me with all his heart. *I* have done this terrible thing.

"Out the window?! How could they go out the window?"

"Somebody *stole* them, Theresa!" He spits it at me. "You put them on the window ledge, where everyone in the courtyard could see them, and somebody stole them while we were out! Don't you remember that the windows were open when we came home last night? Don't you remember that we had to close the windows?"

"Mommy? Daddy?" Natalie's voice hums with anxiety. Theft is Natalie's greatest fear. Since she has been able to formulate the thought, despite all of our efforts at reassurance, she has been afraid that someday *she* will be stolen.

"It's okay, honey," I say hurriedly. "Everything's really fine." I am trying to reconstruct last night. True, we did have to close the windows against the pouring rain and cold when we got home from our walk, but they are tall, narrow windows that open like a "V" from the top. How could somebody get in that way? Plus—I looked out the window into the courtyard—how could anyone get up to our second-story window? There aren't any ladders out there. There are no toe-holds in the sides of the building.

"How could they get *up*?" Marc howls back at me. "A million ways!"

"No they couldn't! Not without everyone seeing!"

"So?! Everyone *saw*! Nobody *cared*! *They* don't care if our money gets stolen. *Everybody* wants American dollars and American passports. Oh! They're *gone*! We're *never* going to get out of here!"

In the blink of an eye, it seems to me possible that my sense of safety here has been stupidly naive. My blind trust in the benignity of the neighbors in our courtyard, of the benignity of the people in Ukraine, suddenly looks fatuous. I have deceived myself. I have comfortably assumed that the people around us are sort of like us, not different people with different experiences and different world views and possibly malign intent toward us.

"For chrissakes, honey," I explode in my dismay. "You have the passports for *one day* and you lose them! I've kept perfect track of them the whole trip, and you have them *once,* and lose them!"

Natalie starts to wail. "Why would somebody steal our passports?"

"Well, honey, people *do* want American passports. They can help you go places. And then, of course, everybody wants money."

"It's the cook!" she shrieks.

"What?"

"It's the cook! *She* took them! I never liked her!"

"Honey, no—the cook wouldn't do that!"

"I'm telling you, Mommy, it's the cook," she seethes. "She came in while we were gone and took them!"

There is a certain plausibility here. It's more plausible that the cook let herself in and took them than that someone scaled the outside wall and squeezed through the tiny "V" at the bottom of the window to take them while all the neighbors cheered him on.

I fight my rising panic. "They *must* be here somewhere. Keep looking! They're here, I'm telling you." I paw through suitcases and toy satchels and drawers.

"Oh my god," Marc wails, "we're *never* going to get out of here. I'm sorry, Theresa, I'm sorry. I'm so sorry." He's standing in the middle of the room, weeping.

I'm horrified, and rush in with fortifications. "Honey, honey, it's *okay!* We *both* let our guards down. We both felt so good that we're finally going home, we just *relaxed*. We stopped paying attention!"

He agrees that it's all my fault. "You *should* have been paying better *attention!* Why did you *move* them?"

"*Jesus!* Because *you* put them where the girls could get them! This is *not* my fault!"

Then he has a revelation. "Theresa! *Do you have copies of the passports?*"

That had been my job, too—managing the paperwork. Copies! Yes! I *do* have copies. I can find them! With copies, we're okay.

But my heart is clutching in terror as I pull out the file of paper-work because *I know* that I have not made copies of Natalie's passport. I have copies of Marc's and mine, copies galore, but out of some stupid oversight, some stupid sense of security, I have not made copies of Natalie's. What if it's hard to get a replacement passport for Natalie? She is a Russian citizen. What if they make it hard? The old nightmares of their wanting her back seize me. Now *I* am afraid of her being stolen.

And, of course, there has been no time at all to make a copy of Lana's strange passport, that unique little pale blue booklet that Anastasia ran all over southern Ukraine for days to acquire. Oh my god. What if we have to go back? *We can't go back to Bilgorod.* I *will not* go back to Bilgorod!

I know that when I alert Marc to the fact that we have no copies of the children's passports, a tsunami of rage and grief is going to break over my head. I try to steady my voice. "Um, honey . . ."

He experiences complete despair. *We can't go home! It'll be weeks!* He is striding around the apartment, waving his arms, wailing. Natalie is crying, "Mommy, Daddy! It's the cook, I'm telling you! It's the *cook!*" Lana is gazing from one to the other of us, completely baffled, but not crying. She has been kidnapped by Martians.

I am trying to calm Natalie and myself; I am trying to calm every-thing. As my heart thuds with terror and dismay, I tell myself desper-ately, "This is not the end of the world. This is another week or two, that's all. It's just money. I'll get a job! This is a very nice place to spend extra time. We can get to know Kiev! We will make the best of it. Watch, this will turn out to be a *good* thing!" I say, "Honey, I don't think it was the cook," as the cook enters and Natalie runs up to accuse her.

"*You* took them, didn't you?" she snarls. She is crying, furious. "*You* took our passports!"

The cook, thankfully, is uncomprehending. She looks at me as I hiss at Natalie. "*Stop* it, honey! She didn't *do* it!" I look at the cook, wondering if she did. Natalie is dead certain, and turns on her again.

Then Ivan knocks at the door. Marc flings it open. "Ivan, Ivan, our passports! They're missing! They've been stolen!" Ivan, though he speaks very little English, does know the word "passport." Marc makes his point clear, and Ivan flushes deeply, looks urgent. "Wait!" he says. "Wait!" He calls Alexi on his cell phone, thrusts it at Marc.

"Are you *sure*?" Alexi bellows.

"Yes, I'm sure! We've looked everywhere!"

"Are you *sure*? Look again!"

Marc thrusts the phone back to Ivan, and tears back to the bed-room. One last time, Marc rifles through his suitcase. "Aieeee! They're here! Here they are!" His mother has risen from the grave. He tears into the living room waving the passports, which have been buried at the bottom of his suitcase, where one of us—we will never agree who—had hastily stowed them.

I am absolutely furious with him. Spitting recriminations at each other, we hurl everything into open suitcases with no regard for any-thing except getting out of town. Natalie throws herself on the bed and weeps in relief. Lana waits for instructions.

At the U.S. Embassy, Ivan politely escorts us past throngs of waiting Ukrainians to the head of the line and inside the building to a large, clean, empty waiting room abundantly furnished with toys. CRA has put all of our documents in perfect order in a single bound notebook. Embassy personnel easily find everything they need. We feel, belatedly, as if we have been in very good hands as we watch the only other cou-ple in the waiting room comb through two different FedEx folders and a bulging file looking for the documents they need.

They have a pretty, small baby from somewhere in Ukraine.

I don't even feel envy. I don't want a small baby. That is their life. This is ours.

Kiev is a big city. It takes us an hour in a Lada over bumpy, stinky, careening roads to get to the airport. I am holding Lana on my lap, and when we get to the airport, I unload her first, onto the pavement right beside the car while I step out behind her. As I step out of the car she begins: She leans over and vomits, thoughtfully, without a whimper; she just leans over, again and again, and deposits on the ground a vast quantity of food. It seems to be everything she has taken in for days. Marc looks at me, eyebrows raised. Malabsorption. She hasn't digested anything she's eaten in days. No wonder she's so small.

Ivan and Alexi put us on the plane for Warsaw—happy, no doubt, to be rid of us at last. What a job they have.


When we reach the Sheraton on Embassy Row in Warsaw—which has a very forgiving "adoption rate" for people at this extremely trying point in their lives—we heave a deep sigh of relief.

"Woooow," says Natalie, as she takes in the crystal chandeliers, marble pillars, ankle-deep carpeting, towering clusters of fresh flowers.

"*This,* sweetheart, is civilization," I say. She gets it completely.

Lana does not say, "Wow." She stops, looks all about her wide-eyed, and pushes her foot into the carpet a few times, experimentally. She's never seen anything like this before. Then she drops full-length to the floor, cheek against the carpet, and waves her arms and legs, making a carpet angel. That's her wow.

We have not been able to change our flight out of Warsaw to an earlier flight. We are going to be here for a few days. So we go to a mall, where we buy the only umbrella stroller we can find, the most expensive one we have ever seen, and buy some healthy food to stock our mini-fridge in the room. We do not want to make Lana sick by packing her diet with too much high-calorie food, but we do want to start her on healthy eating. This is more easily said than done. When I offer her a whole wheat roll with peanut butter on it, she grabs it eagerly, takes a bite, chews with a growing look of outrage on her face, then spews out what's in her mouth and hurls the rest to the floor. This is the fate of much healthy food. Finally, we give up and feed her french fries and sweet rolls—whatever it takes to get a little meat on her bones.

In Warsaw, around the corner from our hotel, is the largest park playground in Europe. It is beautiful, brilliantly designed. We spend time there, Lana on her first first-world playground. A revelation, swings that swing, a bouncy play surface, clean sand, and climbing frames. A shallow man-made stream full of rocks and sand, amazing to explore. Warsaw is a beautiful city.

In the hotel at night, Natalie and Marc and Lana play tag in the room and up and down the halls, and squeal in delight. We order lavishly from room service, and fight Lana to keep the food in her mouth. Lana refuses to take off her shoes, sleeps in shoes and socks, adorable. I am not yet in love with her, but I can feel love stirring. I can see that she is adorable there in her crib, sleeping in her shoes. She has been fun today, really game. And she can't digest the little bit of food she allows into her tummy. I look at her and think, "Well, you have to get into our hearts in order to crush them," and know that this is beginning.

In Warsaw, by phone with our attorney, we kill the real estate deal because of an unacceptable inspection report. Thank god for deferred maintenance. We hate to lose the house we love, but it's better than losing our shirts.

We note that Lana does not vomit when she rides in a Mercedes.

The flight to Amsterdam and the layover in Schiphol Airport are uneventful. Marc and I are working our tails off to keep up spirits. I have taken, for the time being, Natalie, and Lana has glommed onto him. It is on the last leg, the long leg, from Amsterdam to Chicago, that things fall apart. It begins before takeoff, because Marc has to go to the bathroom. When he puts Lana on my lap so he can execute this small escape, she pauses for one stunned moment before letting loose a shriek that has everyone on the 747 alert within seconds. This shriek is so penetrating, so demanding, it uses her entire body as a sounding board. She is rigid in my arms and shuddering all over from the effort involved in producing this shriek. Nothing I do has any effect on the noise she is emitting. It is so overpowering that Natalie soon begins to cry. I am not far behind. I am horrified. What is this creature I am holding? Who is this? Why is she in my lap? Take her away from me! I try to calm her, and try with mounting effort to keep myself from throwing her into the aisle, until, finally, Marc reappears. "What's going *on*?!" and she looks at him and stops. I hate him, I hate her, I hate my life. I just want to go away with Natalie, and we'll start over, the peaceful two of us.

The entire flight, Lana will not sleep and will not sit still and will not take comfort from me. Marc is exhaustingly busy. Despite my efforts to shield her, Natalie watches *Spider-Man*.

"Doesn't that scare you?"

"No."

"Honey, don't watch this part."

"I *want* to!"

"Honey, stop."

We wrestle with the headset.

"Honey, you're going to have nightmares."

"No, I'm not. *Stop,* Mother!"

I stop. We both watch. Marc chases Lana up and down the aisles until he can't stand it anymore, and it's my turn. The real nightmare, it seems, is in our midst. Toward the end of the flight, a man three-quarters of the way back, a man traveling with his wife and two older children, reaches out his arm and collects Lana. He pulls her up onto his lap and starts to play with her. She loves it. She lets him hold her, and play with her. We are disturbed. She shouldn't be so easy. She'll walk away with anyone. We look back there with mixed resentment and relief. Again and again, she runs up the aisle, and he mercifully gathers her into his lap. He smiles at us. We can rest. We smile back, tentatively, resentful and grateful. Guiltily, I think, "Let him have her."

We are finally in O'Hare. One last jot of paperwork. It is Sunday morning and we've been traveling without sleep for more hours than we can count. We have in tow our own beloved Natalie and a scrawny little child who spits out her food, doesn't absorb what she takes in, will go to anyone, and is immensely charming and cute. We are de-toured from the main arena into a vast barren hall. The glass-and-steel ceiling is thirty feet off the ground. Acres of terrazzo surround us. A row of plastic seats lines one wall. We are the only ones here. They're going to process some essential INS paperwork for us while we wait.

Natalie, Marc, and I sit, exhausted, while Lana squirms out of Daddy's arms and onto the floor. She makes a break for the grand open spaces before us. Marc and I each start to drag ourselves off our seats to pursue her *again*. And from Natalie begins a low wail that builds into a howl and soon is ricocheting off the walls of the vast empty space: "*This* . . . is the *worst* . . . *day* . . . of my . . . *entire* . . . *life!*"

# 13

## Falling in Love Again

My mood has become an issue at my house. It's the rage. The other day Natalie said to me, "Here's our family now: Daddy—stern. Mommy—angry. Lana—yuk. Natalie—wonderful!" She said to me, "Mommy, you used to be such a *nice* mommy. You used to be a *happy* mommy. Why are you so mean now?" My protestations bore no weight with her, as they contradicted her direct experience and were, anyway, full of self-doubt. This morning, Marc said, "Do you think you could be premenopausal?" We were in our bathroom, trying to get ready to go, with a two-and-a-half-year-old, who had already been up for two hours, darting between our legs opening drawers and cupboards, scattering their contents (ignoring the dozen or so toys of her own that we had imported for her amusement), stepping in and out of the shower, falling down, climbing in and out of the tub, falling off the ledge, demanding to be picked up, asking for more food she wouldn't eat, whining, laughing, flirting, and chattering unintelligibly in Russ-glish. It was one of my days to be at home with her—after we drove back and forth through the Loop to drop off Natalie at school. I was running late, as usual.

I answered Marc's question with a piercing look. I didn't want to risk opening my mouth right then. About two minutes later, though, I asked Marc if he would drop off a vitamin to Natalie when he kissed her on his way out the door. I had woken her up ten minutes earlier, but she was lingering in bed until the very last possible moment, as usual, when I would go in and threaten her with a squirt from the misting bottle and she would emerge screaming with rage into the bathroom. Marc paused. "Does she *like* it?" he needed to know. If she likes the vitamin, he's happy to give it to her. If she doesn't like it—if there could be a battle involved—well, then, that's *my* job.

I *could* be premenopausal, it's true. One of the alarming facts that has become as obvious as sidewalk since we got home with Lana is that the biological clock stops ticking when it does for a *very good reason*. What was I *thinking*? Do I want to spend hours every day tearing around after a very active two-year-old? *No,* I do *not*. Here I am, at an age when premenopause is a distinct possibility, parenting a toddler. The Gap is running an ad for cashmere in which an impossibly young couple and their beautiful eighteen-month-old baby twine around each other in sleep. I study this ad, probing my recent wound: That's what a mother of a toddler is *supposed* to look like. I have never felt so old. I have never *been* so inappropriately aged for the task I'm engaged in. I know a couple of mothers of six-year-olds who are as old as I am; I know *no* mothers of two-year-olds who are my age. I don't want to be a decrepit old mom for my children. Cranky, arthritic. I want to be young and fun, like everybody else's mom.

It is not premenopause per se that is turning me into Mommie

Dearest: It's trying to parent a toddler during premenopause, and about a thousand other things. After years of active misery in his job, Marc is a complete tangled mess of indecision and reservations and fears and rage and sorrow about leaving for a plum position elsewhere. I am supposed to manage my own complex feelings about work— mine and his—and the impact of work on our marriage, in order to be his primary source of decision-making support and wisdom. I am stalked by grief about the prospect of leaving Chicago, my longtime home, the beautiful city I love passionately, home to my best friends and my work life and a very large chunk of my identity, which is no longer the best place for my family to live. And, of course, our house is on the market and no one wants to buy it, and no one knows what houses are going to be worth in the next few months, and at every moment I am ready to vomit with anxiety about money. And, because we are trying to sell it, even though I have a new two-year-old, the house is constantly supposed to be immaculate on (effectively) a moment's notice. Even without a new two-year-old, the current state of our lives creates blinding anxiety, a lack of sleep, a certain irritableness.

And then there's the galling fact that Marc gets to walk out the door and go to work every morning because *he's* the one who makes all the money. And that he's so clearly relieved to go—and wouldn't I be, too—because about seventy percent of the time, maybe more, when he goes, *and* when he calls home to check in, there is screaming going on. Most often Natalie screaming at Lana to get away from her things and her mommy, and often me screaming at Natalie while she's screaming at and simultaneously trying to dismember Lana. Sometimes Lana's screams can be heard in there, too—either her screams of fear and pain, or her angry screams in Russglish, for it turns out she has quite a little spirit, this kid, and she'll stomp her foot and put her hands on her hips and deliver herself of long tirades whose syntax is perfectly clear and discernible but whose words are unintelligible. Since we've been home, Nat has cried and cried, "I want a sister who's fun to *play* with! I want her to speak *English!* I want her to *imagine* with me!"

"Welcome to my *life,*" I say bitterly to Marc, when one of these scenes breaks out in his presence and he looks at me in astonishment.

Surely I should be able to manage better. I should be able to prevent these scenes in the first place, or bring them to a quicker close once they begin. Surely it is *me*; *I* am mishandling the whole thing.

But I feel like I am losing my mind. Or not so much my mind, as my self. My mind is intact, but I no longer recognize myself. I am no longer funny, or pretty, or young, or happy, or sexy, or competent. Despite my weak denials when Natalie brings it up, I can feel it, too: I am turning into a witch. I have no patience with this new child, who gets up two or three times during the night, and never sleeps past five-thirty A.M., who is hungry and desperately needs to eat, who asks for food, and then, when I hopefully, lovingly put food before her—even specially prepared food she has eaten happily before—cries and whines and angrily pushes it away. "Nyet!" she shrieks. "Nyyyyyyeeettt!" as she shoves it off her tray, kicking and flailing, then slumps in her seat with her head down and cries.

Natalie's crying right now is very different. Natalie is in the battle of her life, *for* her life. "I have lost half my parents," she has wailed. "I have lost half my parents, and half my toys, and all of my time alone with you!" And the grief associated with this astute analysis is expressed in wracking sobs. She lies on the floor of her room, or in her former play space in the great room off the kitchen (now dubbed by a babysitter "The Battle Zone"), and sobs, eyes closed tight, mouth open as wide as it can go, her head thrown back, her body rigid, sobs originating in the tips of her toes and coursing through her body in waves. One time, I tried to snap her out of this state: I said to her, sternness itself, "Knock it off! We have given you the greatest gift we can ever give you by bringing Lana home. We have given you a *sister,* and it cost a fortune, and even though it might not seem so right now, she will be your best friend for your whole life. So *snap out of it!*" This did actually get her attention for a minute, and inserted into her brain a new and more comforting idea. However, it did not address the need of that moment, and of many subsequent moments in the months that followed, which was to accommodate herself to her excruciating short-term losses. Sometimes, when she is in one of her states, I lie on the floor with her and hold her and stroke her and kiss her wild wet face. Sometimes, I just leave her to sob, because I don't feel that I am helping, or I am at my own wits' end, or Lana needs me.

I do not understand why it is not the same as watching your lover make love to someone else—watching your beloved mommy and daddy, who have only ever hugged and kissed *you* that way, hugging and kissing someone else. I feel that I need to show affection to Lana freely, but I feel guilty every time I love her up in front of Natalie. This seems like wanton emotional torture of my beloved first child. "If I died," Natalie has hurled at me, her anger dissolving into sobs, "you wouldn't even *care*—you'd be happy with Lanaaaaaa!"

Lana is about a thousand times easier than Natalie. It's true that she is disturbing our sleep regularly, and is very trying to feed; but her temperament is so much more easygoing. She is so much less intense. She is funny, and smart, and affectionate. Her eyes sparkle with fun and life. She has a little "happy dance" she breaks into spontaneously when she's delighted. She is extremely sweet, the sweetest child I have ever seen. She is gentle. She starts fights only, ever, by existing in the world as a torment to Natalie. She walks by one of Natalie's toys, and Natalie lands on her like a Fury. She settles into the crook of my arm, and Natalie is at us both, pulling down my arm, trying to yank Lana out of it.

Natalie's reaction to Lana is making our lives hell. I have invidiously compared the two girls: Lana—easy. Natalie—impossible. I hate myself for this betrayal, but the comparison is inescapable. I don't know what to do with Natalie.

One night I dream about Natalie in one of her fits of grief, and instead of getting frustrated and angry with her, the defense I can resort to easily during the day, I feel her pain in my dream. I wake up suddenly, engulfed in grief, as if my mother has died, or my lover has been flagrantly unfaithful. Both of these things have happened to me, and I have not wanted to experience that pain ever again in my life. Lying in bed in the middle of the night, I realize that I have been more distant with Natalie than I should have been now, at this most difficult time in her sweet life, because I do not *want* to feel her pain. I cry in the dark, cursing myself for my betrayal of her, my refusal to enter into her feelings and support her there, when she has needed me the most.

And then, like Natalie, I resent Lana for coming between us.

One day I realize, "I don't have to deal with this all alone! I'm sure OSLA must have some resources for people like me, a support group for parents of newly adopted toddlers," and I call Ruth, my favorite social worker at our local agency, and ask her.

"Hey, how's it going?" she asks, all bright and chipper, her children grown, herself safely ensconced in a full-time office job.

"Tough," I say. Already I have started to cry.

"Ooohhh," says Ruth, crestfallen. "What's *wrong*?"

"It's just . . . it's *hard* bringing home a toddler!" I squeak. "Natalie's fighting with her all the time—it's just hard."

"Oh. I'm sorry."

I feel like I should still be impressing this woman with my coping skills. But I can't. "Do you guys have any support group or anything for people who've adopted toddlers?"

"Us? No, no, we don't have anything like that."

I'm so surprised I stop crying. "Well." I sniffle. "Do you know of any in the city?"

"Hmmm." She pretends to think. "No, I don't. But try CHEER." CHEER is the all-volunteer group of parents who have adopted kids from Eastern Europe. We're members. They don't have anything.

"That's it? CHEER?"

"That's all I can think of."

I may be at my wits' end, but I think I can objectively say that this is *not* okay, to put together extremely challenging family constellations and then walk away. I hang up, abandoned, angry for the first time at the wonderful Ruth.

It's Saturday morning. Marc is at work, and I am home alone with Lana. Natalie shares my own biological clock: late to bed, late to rise. She is sleeping in while I play with the new little girl who doesn't sleep, the one who's early to bed, and early to rise, several times during the night. This in itself is an obstacle to bonding for me. I am not trained, like my doctor husband, to wake up polite and alert in the middle of the night. I wake up like most animals whose sleep is broken into repeatedly: dangerous. This morning, we have already been up for a couple of hours when we repair to the playroom where all toys are jointly owned. This will be, I reason, a good time for us to have fun alone together, out of Natalie's eyesight. And Lana is fine, happy, busy. But Natalie is stalking my heart. Everything I pick up betrays evidence of Natalie's fertile imagination—a purse full of rocks and paper scraps, half-peeled sticks, tons of artwork, scattered crayons—and I am wracked with grief, almost as if she is dead. I miss her so much. I just want to be with Natalie. I am stricken with guilt at the impatience I have had with the messes she creates in the process of pursuing her imagination. I am wracked with grief about all the times

I have been less than perfectly loving with her. I follow Lana around the room, playing, throwing balls, exclaiming at the wooden train, pushing cars back and forth between us, catching her at the bottom of the slide, sobbing. I just want Natalie back. I just want to be cuddling with Natalie, curled up with her, one.

And I realize as I stagger around, blinded by tears, that I am missing Natalie, yes, just Natalie in her own particularity and the character of our vanishing time alone together, but also that I am crying about death, about life's being gone so fast, about our ultimate parting soon, the loss of all the opportunities of life. I am crushed, thinking about the yawning afternoons at the playground impatiently endured for what has felt like years on end, when the actual years of her childhood are flying away from me forever, so fast I can barely detect them as they pass. And then there is, of course, my own mother, who died thirty years too soon, who would have been such a source of wisdom now. Why can't she be here with me, explaining my feelings to me, interpreting Lana? She was a baby-whisperer. She would have known what to do.

Marc comes home and finds me in this state. "What's wrong?" he asks.

"I just miss my baby," I wail, bleary-eyed. "I miss Natalie!"

Marc throws his hands up. He is distraught. He wants to make me feel better, but he doesn't know how. He fears we have made a mistake, bringing Lana home. Maybe we should have just stayed the three of us.

That night, I dream about death. It is right there before me, in the knotted end of a balloon that is cut off. *Whoosh!* All gone! You're dead.

The next day we are at Grandma Martha's for brunch. Marc and his father and Lana are outside, when Grandma says something to Natalie about going to heaven. Natalie says, "I don't believe in heaven."

"You *don't?*" Grandma says. "What do *you* think happens when you die?"

"When you die, you just shrivel up, and you're nothing," Natalie replies, unfazed.

"That's what happens to your body, yes," Grandma admits. "But what happens to your *insides,* you know, to the rest of you?"

Natalie, stumped, looks at me.

"Grandma means your *soul,* honey. You know—like *who you are.* And, actually, nobody really knows what happens after you die. People believe lots of different things, but nobody really knows." I don't know what this grandma believes, but I can't worry about her right now.

"Well, but, Mommy, are *you* going to die? You and Daddy?"

"Yes, honey, we are." I need to spare her pain. I spin. "But my plan is, after we die, we're going to wait for you, and then when you die, we'll all be together again forever."

She lights up at this idea. "Really?"

"Really, really."

"Is your mommy waiting for you?"

What a great idea. "Yes, honey, she is. She's waiting for me, and we'll all wait for you, and then we'll all be together forever. She'll love you so much!"

Natalie grabs the ball and runs with it. "And then, we'll do everything *I* want to do, and we'll go where all the animals talk."

Even spinning out this fantasy scenario, my gut reaction to the idea that *she* would call the shots is "I don't *think* so!" Happily, I squelch this thought and say, "Absolutely. You can be in charge, and we'll definitely go where the animals talk."

Then, tentatively, dutifully, I suggest, "And Lana can come, too."

Natalie's light dims. "I don't think so."

I don't want to include Lana either just yet, so I let it go. Maybe I shouldn't have brought it up. We want to wrap ourselves in the comfort of the story we have spun, of being together forever, with each other and Daddy and my mother, in the land where the animals talk. But the idea of Lana nettles just a bit, a pinprick hole in the cocoon.

I wonder: When will I care? When will I want to spend eternity with Lana as much as I do with Natalie? This is an extension of the question I have asked myself every night: When will I be compelled to go into her room and gaze in wonder at her sleeping form? When will I want to kneel by the side of her bed in the dark, drinking in her sweet warm smells, moving damp hair off her face, kissing her precious flushed cheek?

Maybe when she loves me as much as Natalie did from the beginning. Loves *me,* specifically, uniquely, irreplaceably. Because right now she loves everyone the same. Natalie literally attached herself to me for weeks after we brought her home, and only very slowly—to the grandparents' dismay—allowed anyone besides Daddy and Mommy into her intense affectional orbit. She offered and drew from us a profound and focused attachment. In the orphanage, this capacity for love had worked very well for her: She had come to us at thirteen months plump and healthy, clearly well cared for, probably well loved. Lana, in contrast, was so easy in the orphanage, so undemanding, that she was pretty seriously neglected until somebody noticed that she was eighteen months old and still not walking and thought maybe they should do something about it. This easiness of Lana's is nice in many ways: It's a relief to have a child who is easy to amuse, easy to distract, easy to transition. But I never had a child who so easily took to anyone in the vicinity who might do something for her. And I was not prepared at all for the effect of her infidelity on my own feelings.

It started with the guy on the airplane who swept her up, unresisting, into his arms. Turns out it includes any other mom on the playground who can help her up onto the bouncy bridge. Any perky young babysitter. One morning when I am getting ready to leave,

Lana falls from the high chair she is climbing on and starts to wail. The beautiful young babysitter and I both rush to get her, and she turns away from me to be gathered into the babysitter's arms. This is the first time Lana has seen her. I step away, flushed with embarrassment and anger and hurt. Another morning, I bring Lana downstairs and she hurls herself from my arms into those of another young babysitter, a carefree girl in her early twenties who, unlike old hag Mommy, never stops smiling. I am too old to be attractive as a mother to such a young child. I'm not lovable to her. She wants to love somebody else, somebody younger and more fun. Soon Natalie will want that, too, and even Marc. And no one will love me.

Each time she reaches for a stranger instead of for me, my heart is pierced. It is starting to get flinty in self-defense. I am stunned by what I am seeing in myself: I am reacting as if this child is an unfaithful lover. I have reached out for her, and she has reciprocated, and we have started to have an understanding, an intimacy. We are starting to fall in love with each other. Then she spurns me, swiveling effortlessly toward someone else for comfort and aid.

One day, after Lana and I have dropped Natalie at school, we are back at home alone. I need to clean house for a showing later in the day. I put on Alison Brown, sweep Lana off her feet, and dance with her. We had danced to Alison Brown after dinner last night, Marc, Nat, Lana, and I, but it was difficult. Natalie wanted to be dancing with both Marc and me at once—wanted to prevent Lana from dancing with either of us. Wanted to be danced with as Lana is—held in the arms and twirled around. But Natalie weighs over fifty pounds now. It was physically exhausting and emotionally fraught. Here, alone, out of Natalie's eyesight, I dance with Lana, who can't get enough of it. I nuzzle her neck and kiss her all over her face; we gaze into each other's eyes, grinning. I am falling in love again, lucky me. But gazing into her eyes, my love curdles. Dancing around the messy room with her, doing fancy footwork among the scattered toys, I suddenly feel like an idiot, a sop. I could be anyone to her. This little girl makes love to everyone she meets. I look into her eyes, and like a jealous lover, think, "You look at everyone like this, don't you? I'm not special to you the way you are to me." And Natalie's passionate jealousy of our love for Lana becomes real for me. I feel like I am having an affair. I am guilt-stricken about cheating on Natalie. Natalie, with all of her difficulty, is at least faithful, discriminating. This one, the easier child, loves the one she's with. I put her down and start cleaning house, troubled.

We had dismissed attachment disorder as one of the risk factors with Lana. We had been focusing on what the experts call "inhibited" attachment, the kind everybody knows about from the mass media's standard "Eastern European adoption nightmare story": the child doesn't make eye contact, doesn't interact well, isn't affectionate, never learns to love you.

About a week after we got home, we got an e-mail from Lida and Anastasia in Bilgorod. Did we know, they asked, that that couple left their child at the airport?

What? I wrote back for clarification. What couple? What child? What airport?

That couple from Austin, Lida replied. The couple that was adopting the five-year-old boy from Lana's orphanage. They left him at the airport in Kiev. They decided not to take him home. "They said they could not find relation with him," wrote Rita.

We are stunned. How awful! How awful for that child! How could they "not find relation with him"? How hard did they try? This was the couple with their biological five-year-old son at home. We had thought that was going to be tough—integrating into your family a stranger the same age and sex as your beloved only child. Maybe they had just decided they couldn't do it—or, at the airport, couldn't see *how* they would do it, and left him. We were intimately familiar with their terror. We were a little in awe of what it took to do what they had done. Did it show extreme callousness, or had they perceived (or thought they perceived) in their week with this child a profound inability to connect?

When we related this story to some good friends, they related another about a couple they knew slightly who had brought home Russian brothers, four and seven years old, a few years ago. These boys, according to their adoptive parents, could not attach. They manipulated and deceived and damaged their home and lashed out at their adoptive parents and eventually began stealing from them. The parents, in desperation, finally shipped these boys off to some institution, with the explicit understanding that they would never see them again. The parents were paying tens of thousands of dollars a year to unload these kids—whom they had doubtless spent tens of thousands of dollars to adopt—and were moving and changing their name, so the boys could never find them.

Marc and I listened dumbfounded to this Eastern European adoption horror story *par excellence*. We didn't know private institutions existed that would take permanent custody of your children. If it weren't for the source, we would have doubted the truthfulness of the account; even given the source, we had to wonder what was wrong with the adoptive parents—were they emotionally remote rich people who drove these boys away while seeming to embrace them? Or were they really good people, people like us and the people from Austin, who just couldn't, despite all their best efforts, "find relation" with unattachable children?

We knew from the first time we met her that Lana was not of this ilk. She connected readily, with her big smile and flashing eyes. But it had seemed to us that she had connected appropriately—she hadn't climbed all over us, or thrown herself into our laps. She had been game, but appropriately tentative.

Since we've been home, though—in fact, since we've taken custody—we've seen that she completely lacks discrimination in her attachment behaviors. I have learned that this pattern, too, has a name: *indiscriminate*. The "inhibited" child makes no one happy. The indiscriminate child, like Lana, makes lots and lots of people happy, quickly and easily. She's a charmer. Grandparents and babysitters love her to pieces because she crawls into their laps immediately. The flamboyant older woman I called in desperation—the minute I could locate the phone after we got back—to come in to help me with Lana is completely agog over her. She regales me with breathless stories—"Isn't she amazing?"—of how Lana puts up her arms to everyone, won't let a new acquaintance put her down after he has held her for fifteen minutes, cries when a virtual stranger leaves. All of these behaviors, of course, I have interpreted as signs of love for me, specifically, and for Marc and Natalie. I study the sitter while she is reciting this litany of Lana's infidelities. She seems just innocently to be reporting behavior that she finds delightful. But it feels like she is willfully torturing me. It's as if she's saying to me, over and over again, "See? She loves me and my friends as much as she loves you."

Inside the orphanage, seducing all the people who might be of service to you can be a good survival strategy. But in a family, it backfires. Because—I ask myself—if she's as happy with anyone else as she is with me, why kill myself for her? She holds my love cheap. My heart draws away from her, angry.

Surely I should be bigger than this. Surely I should be mature, disciplined, principled. I should be able to call on my education to explain the child's behavior and overcome my emotional reaction to it. But guess what? This indiscriminate child has taught me something profound and humbling. She has taught me that when I put love out I demand love in return. So much for the satisfying image of myself as a big-hearted woman who could just pour out free love to needy children. So much for myself as someone who could perform the mitzvah to end all mitzvahs, dispensing love without regard for its being requited.

Why does the lamb love Mary so? Why, Mary loves the lamb, you know. Mary loves the lamb because the lamb loves Mary because Mary loves the lamb. I love Lana because Lana loves me because I love Lana. Or not. If the lamb trots away from Mary and starts following somebody else home, well, forget that lamb! Mary might feed the lamb occasionally when the lamb comes by, but she's not going to devote herself to the lamb. She's going to devote herself to the lamb that devotes itself to her.

Who knew this principle would apply to my love for a child? This is a killer self-discovery.

I know that withdrawing in response to Lana's apparent lack of love for me, or her failure to distinguish me from all the other loving faces in the crowd, is the most damaging thing I can do. But it takes a heroic effort *not* to withdraw. Because, she teaches me, I do not give away real love for free. Without reciprocation, it is not real love: It is policy, it is a position, a stance. Giving away "love" without reciprocation might enhance my self-image, but it doesn't enlarge my soul, it doesn't warm or expand my heart. I am not interested in bestowing love without reciprocation. I want something back for so much of me, and I want a lot back—I want the same amount back. You should get what you pay for. What you sow, you should reap. This is the logic of the heart, even in relation to little kids. Lana's failure to return my love in kind has taught me this.

One morning, after she has shoved me aside to get to a babysitter,

I think, hurt and cold, "Okay, I can raise her, I guess, as long as I think she's going to be Natalie's good sister for life." But I think this with a hollow, empty feeling. And how could that really work? How could I raise without love a good sister for a child I passionately love? Wouldn't the difference in my feelings for them be apparent to them and interfere with their love? But, I think, she *has* to love Natalie. *I* can get along without Lana's love: We hadn't been clamoring for another child to love for ourselves. We relentlessly pursued a second child so Natalie would have a sister to love her whole life long. But—the thought seizes me—what if she doesn't form a deep, specific attachment to Natalie, either? What if Natalie, her sister, is just another face in the crowd for her? What if she breaks Natalie's heart by not returning the huge gift of love Natalie will want to lay at her feet after she's done killing her? I see how Natalie is hurt when she tries to kiss Lana and Lana shoves her away (rarely, but occasionally). Natalie is cut to the quick, and often lashes out in anger. I quickly try to interpret and encourage: "Lana, look! Natalie's hurt because she wanted to kiss you and you pushed her away. Natalie, Lana loves you, but for some reason just doesn't want to be kissed right now. Don't let your feelings be too hurt." Natalie now *commands* Lana to kiss her: *Kiss, Lana, kiss. Hug!* And she almost always gets it, even when she's recently pounded on her sister, perhaps because she is so threatening.

If this little girl hurts my baby, she will have me to deal with.

Only for Natalie—for Natalie, I will try to fall in love with someone else, with Lana, so Lana will fall in love with me, so Lana will fall in love with Natalie. I will hurt Natalie doing something I don't particularly want to do in order to secure for Natalie future happiness with her sister.

Reluctantly I face an obvious truth: If I spent more time with Lana instead of handing her over to babysitters, she'd almost certainly attach to me faster. If I want to reduce the child's confusion about the source of love and food and other goodies in her life, I should reduce the number of people bestowing these treasures. I need to spend my days *with* the child, instead of writing about the child.

But I just can't, this time. I was so smug about the benefits of spending so much time with Natalie. But I know that, this time, I would go stark raving mad if I stayed home with a two-year-old all day long. I'm just not in the same place. And, my friends and husband and sister assure me, it wouldn't facilitate bonding if I spent all my time with Lana wanting to be somewhere else. It wouldn't be best for her, or for me.

The only way Lana seems to single me out is for abuse. I am the only person I know of whom she hits and bites and pinches. She does it mainly when I am least able to defend myself, when I am leaning over her strapping her into her car seat. Okay, so she doesn't like the car seat, but isn't this extreme? She doesn't do this to her babysitters. She tries, often successfully, to kick my head; she pinches my hands, hard; she hits me in the face. I have been afraid that she will assault Natalie, but instead she is assaulting me. It is extremely difficult to maintain my composure, and sometimes I don't.

And then one day, despite me, it happens. Lana proves she loves me best. Despite my age and anger and anxiety and absence and incompetence, Lana loves me best. It happens on the same day she thrusts herself away from me to get to one of her babysitters. I am so upset, so hurt, so worried, that I call my dear friend Maureen after I get to my writing desk and say, "I just have to come to see you." A single mom, Maureen adopted a little girl from Southeast Asia. She's the one who, before adopting, had subjected herself to the angry young woman saying, "Why don't you just give all your money to the birth mothers?" We have been sharing traumatic adoption experiences for years. Maureen understands and forgives everything. Her heart is huge. She takes in my story and we agree that I will bring the girls over after Nat's school lets out, and we will talk.

As we sit there at her kitchen table, our two-year-olds play between our knees, Lia between Maureen's, and Lana between mine. Mo and I talk about everything: what I should do, whether Lana will bond, what it is reasonable to expect of her, Marc's torment about his job, my grief about leaving Chicago, our terror about selling our house, losing our shirts. While Natalie sits in front of the television, the two little girls go back and forth to the toy pile, fetching toys to enhance their play between our knees. Then, one time, Lana walks away, and Lia comes over and takes Lana's place between my knees. In a flash, Lana is back. She is gentle, but firm, the way she had been in defending her toy the first day we saw her. "No," she says to Lia, putting both hands on Lia's upper arms and moving her away from me. "This *my* mommy." Lana steers Lia back between Maureen's knees, and resumes her rightful place at mine. Then she looks into my eyes and grins, her little hands resting on my knees. Maureen and I look at each other and burst into laughter.

It is not a smooth path, or a straight one, from here. There are still many ups and downs, misunderstandings and hurts, battles and painfully rendered apologies between Lana and me. But almost always, from this moment on, I take only pleasure in seeing Lana love up other people, and seeing them bloom and glow under her dazzling smile and sweet wet kisses. She is a charmer. She is making up for lost time. She is a child of the universe. But mostly she is mine.

We have moved. The house deals turned out okay—we didn't make a mint, like (it seems) everybody else did, but we didn't lose our shirts.

Natalie has lots of friends in her new school. Lana is in a wonderful, loving, home day-care setting most days, while I write. Her exhaustive medical work-up has revealed no special problems—none of our fears, thank God, have come true. The girls and I have a lot of time on our own, after school, while Daddy works. Lana now intentionally starts fights with Natalie by sneaking into her room and pilfering her treasured objects. She runs out of the room and tears past Natalie, waving the object above her head. Natalie streaks after her, shrieking, and Lana tears toward me, thrilled. I am able to scoop her up, usually, just before Natalie seizes and pounds her. Their battling now feels like completely normal sibling strife.

They spend hours in their rooms playing together, heaven knows what.

They soak in the tub together, floating like twins, toes to each other's ears, only their eyes, noses, mouths, and little round tummy mounds clearing the surface.

Lana imitates Natalie all the time, to Natalie's public disdain and secret delight.

One day, a few months after we had arrived home with her, Lana peered into my eyes, put her hand on my arm for emphasis and, as if she had just figured it out, said, "I Lana!" I looked closely at her, and realized: I have no idea what this child has gone through—spending her first years the focus of no one's love, crossing the world with perfect strangers, working her way into our tight-knit little family—and I never will. The other day, I came upon a picture of us that Marc's mother had taken on the day we arrived home. I am holding Lana, with her head over my shoulder, facing away from me, into the camera. She looks exhausted and baffled and deeply concerned. She looks the way I felt that day. I am nailed to the floor, peering at that picture, thinking: *We might have left her there.*

The three of us, Nat and Lana and I, drive around our new town on errands and come home from school, singing the girls' current favorite at the top of our lungs. "Babba Ann, Babba Ann," Lana hollers the minute we get into the car, and I crank up the CD. " 'I went to a dance, looking for romance, / Saw Barbara Ann so I thought I'd take a chance . . .' " Not with Vera, not with Daria, not with the mystery girl in Odessa: We found our romance with the little snowflake in the broiling circus town.

Marc and I steal into her room now in the middle of the night and kiss her all over her sweet face. In the daytime, she makes a joke of wiping off our kisses, and we warn her sternly: If you do that, we'll have to put them all back when you're sleeping! She gleefully continues to wipe them off.

Lana has increased her weight by more than half in the last six months. She does still play with spitting out her food a bit—I think there was a little something there. But she is fundamentally fine. She is not a dwarf. Her hemangioma is fading fast. She smells like a million roses.

It is amazing, how the universe steered us toward this particular little girl—through a maze of baffling obstacles and our own human obtuseness and hesitation, steered us toward the perfect little girl for our family. It's enough to make a believer out of you.

# Coda

You know what I love? I love waking them up in the morning. I love burrowing into the covers to find their faces, loosening the bedding just enough so I can see them, but not so much that cold air rushes in to wake them before I get my fill of gazing. I love the imprint of the sheets on their soft, warm skin. I love their goofy morning hair. I love their eyelashes against their flushed cheeks. All children look like angels when they sleep. I love to kiss them awake, planting my lips on their cheeks next to their ears, whispering that I love them, that we have a fun day ahead. Most of the time, they wake up happy.

Right now, one of the first things Lana does as she comes to consciousness is to look for two rubber fish my sister sent for Nattie's bathtub play years ago. They're never far from hand. Lana has pressed these generic fish into service as "Nemo's daddy" (Marlin) and Dorie. When I have finished dressing her, as she waits for me to activate the harder-to-roust Natalie, she sits on the end of the bed, moving her fish in the air just above her head, telling their story of finding Nemo.

*Finding Nemo* is a brilliant, beautiful movie (written and directed by Andrew Stanton) that, for me, is about learning how to let go of your kids and hold them close at the same time. Lana is captivated by the adventure-filled tale. We recently made the happy discovery that "Nemo" provides a nice way to help Lana understand her adoption story. Just as Nemo's daddy looked all over the ocean and beat all kinds of odds to find him, we looked all over the world for Lana, and found her in the most unlikely place. "Just like Nemo!" she trills. It's a start.

Once you become a parent through adoption, you experience all the joys and worries, exasperation and delight that biological parents experience. And then some.

At adoption conferences, parents routinely fret and sometimes fume over ways in which the word "adoption" gets used. "Adopt a highway" is a pet peeve for many. At one conference, I heard a keynote speaker splutter, "You don't *adopt* highways! What does such usage tell our kids about their lives?" Personally, I think this is a little over the top. Are our kids really going to be confused about the nature of our relationships by "adopt a highway" slogans? Mine aren't that literal. They know that we use lots of different words in wildly different ways. I think mobilizing against "adopt a highway" or "adopt an animal" programs is a waste of valuable energy. We have bigger fish to fry.

I knew that Natalie's kindergarten teacher had read E. B. White's book *Stuart Little* to her class, so when Nattie and I were browsing the kids' section of Hollywood Video one night for the requisite movie for our family's sacred "pizza Friday" I didn't object when she latched onto the movie version of the classic book. I'd heard a few mixed reviews when the movie came out, but hadn't paid them any mind; and

Nattie said she'd seen part of it at a friend's house, and wanted to see the rest. So we took it home.

Ninety minutes later, Marc and I were in the grips of the creeping and then roaring dismay that overcomes adoptive parents when we see our children being hurt by some boneheaded popular representation of adoption. *Stuart Little* (the movie, not the book) is terrifying and confusing for adoptive kids. First there's the depiction of the adoption process: "We want another child," the couple says, in effect. "Let's go pick one out at the local orphanage." As if, perhaps, the orphanage is kind of like the local pound. ("Oh, my god, honey," we say to Natalie as the scene unfolds. "That's not what it's like *at all!*") When their son goes off to school (with the words, "Pick a good one!"), the parents go and look over a scene of wild, school-aged, uniformed kids careening around a large room (has an orphanage *ever* looked like this, outside of the movies?), and choose to bring home, instead of a child, a mouse. (Child, mouse—who cares?)

*"What!"* we say to Natalie. "A mouse isn't like a *child*. That's so stupid. Honey, let's turn this movie off. This isn't right."

"No, no! I want to see what happens." She's already seen part of it at a friend's house. We can't help her sort it out if we don't know what she's seen. We leave it on.

Then the adoptive parents' biological son and extended family reject the adopted mouse because he's *different* from everybody else. Obviously, he is not *one of them*. (It has never occurred to either of our girls that their extended family might do anything but embrace them with love.)

"Oh," we say, with some uncertainty, "those people aren't very nice." On the other hand, they *are* looking at a *mouse*.

Eventually, the family comes to accept and love Stuart; but Stuart is troubled by thoughts of his "real" parents. "Something's just missing," he confides to his adoptive parents. He's empty inside, because he's not with his *real* parents.

"Oh my god," we say to ourselves. What do we say to Natalie about the movie's suggestion that all adoptees quite naturally feel a piece missing, since they are, after all, not with their "real" parents? Do we say, "*They're* his 'real' parents, because they're raising him— even though they are of different species"? What we do say is, "Honey, let's turn this off. Let's watch something else. This movie is bad." But she insists on watching—and we, like Nemo's daddy, accept the fact that we can't protect her from all potential harm, and leave it on.

Then, an impostor mouse couple comes to the family's home, and say they're Stuart's real parents. His adoptive parents, remembering his words, "Something's just missing," readily give him up to strangers.

"Oh honey," we moan. "What a horrible thing to do. How could they not hold on to Stuart?"

Eventually, Stuart and his adoptive family are happily reunited, and the moral of the story is the line that is almost always music to the ears of transracial families: "Just because we don't look alike doesn't mean we don't belong together." But the makers of this insipid, disastrously wrongheaded movie have done so much damage to the families they're ostensibly supporting that the line is a saccharine insult.

When the movie is over, Marc and I heave a sigh of relief and disgust. "Well, that was a really dumb movie," Marc says.

"It sure was," I confirm.

Natalie shrugs it off and disappears.

Marc goes downstairs to check his e-mail, and Lana, oblivious to the meanings in the movie, tags along to play. When I go into the master bedroom to begin getting ready for bed, I find Natalie almost literally bouncing off the walls. She is stalking around the room, talking nonsense at the top of her voice. I put myself in her path. "Honey," I say, looking her in the eyes. "Are you upset by something?"

"Yes," she answers, looking at me warily, weaving like a caged creature who has been hurt. I try to hold her eyes, but she dodges around behind me.

"Honey, can you tell me what's upset you?" I ask, whirling to follow her movement.

"No! I can't!" she cries, careening and chattering.

She's behaving really weirdly. My heart sinks. She has been hurt. "Honey." I keep moving in her direction, looking for her eyes, wanting to lock her in. "Was it the movie?"

She bobs in place for a moment and lapses into baby talk. "Yeth. It wath the movie. Yeth." She nods emphatically.

"Mommy and Daddy hated a *lot* about that movie. We thought it was terrible. Can you tell me what part of it bothered you?"

"No. *You* tell *me.*"

Where to start? The first idea that comes to mind is the right one. "The part we hated the worst was when that mouse couple came and took Stuart away. That was just awful. Is that a part that bothered you?"

Natalie slows down, making smaller circles and ellipses in front of me. Her baby talk persists. "But that could never happen to me, becauth if anybody came to our door, you would say, 'No, her mommy is in Russia. You can't be her mommy.'"

I will tell you, it just breaks your heart, helping your child sort through the emotional ramifications of the fact that, for whatever reason, her first mommy and daddy chose not to parent her. Her wounds become yours.

"Oh, honey," I say, looking her right in the eye, "we will never, ever let you go. We could never be happy without you. No one can ever come to our door and claim you, because you are ours forever."

She finally lets me touch her, and I gather her in, and we do the "one, two, three, jump" routine that we do now that she's grown too big for me to pick up. She jumps onto my hips, wrapping her legs around my waist, and we bury our faces in each other's hair, as close as we can be, breathing each other in.

In the adoption process, kids are inevitably objectified to some degree. You have criteria you want a child to meet: race and health, at least, for most couples; age and sex, for many. Some couples are even more specific in the traits they hope to find in a child. You go through kids-on-paper until you find one that fills your criteria, and then, when you adopt your child, she becomes a precious, unique little flesh-and-blood human being, and the very idea of criteria is deeply offensive. But it is unrealistic to expect adoptive parents to go in search of children with no criteria in mind; we all have our wants and needs. And yet we can be blinded by what we think we need. We would never have accepted Lana on paper; she was way too risky on paper. And look. The little sparkling self that made us move past our fears in the orphanage has filled our lives with joy. But who knew?

Many people regard adoptive families as different from biological families. Here's a dirty and weird little secret: Even *I* do sometimes. When I know that a relationship is adoptive, a little flag goes up in my brain, and lurking around the base of that flag is mild curiosity and suspicion. My inclination is to discreetly scrutinize the actors to see what their relationship is like, to see how they love each other, because my suspicion is that there might be gaps in that love. Now that I'm an adoptive mom I am highly aware of this reaction of mine, and I am appalled, even offended, by my own prejudice.

My prejudice doesn't, of course, apply to my own family, because I am *inside* my own family, and I *know*; I have personal experience of our love. But looking from the outside at another adoptive family, I feel this little flag go up, and I confess this unpleasant fact because it is important: It is a sign of how the culture's longstanding suspicion of adoptive relationships has seeped into me and persists in my brain even after my heart has been completely taken over by love for my own kids. Harvard Law Professor Elizabeth Bartholet, who has children through both biology and adoption, calls this pervasive prejudice the culture's "biologic bias" (in her very important book, *Family Bonds: Adoption, Infertility, and the New World of Child Production*). This bias holds that biologic family ties are stronger, more secure, more rightful than ties created through adoption.

Several riddles rely on just such usually invisible prejudices. You know the one about the boy who is riding in a car with his father, and they are in a terrible accident. The boy and his father are rushed to the hospital, unconscious. The surgeon called in to work on the boy refuses, saying, "I can't operate on him! He's my son!" Who is the surgeon? Pause for thought. Ah—the surgeon is the boy's mother. This riddle works (when it still does) because we don't expect female surgeons. The assumption that the surgeon must be a male is like the assumption that adoptive families are different (and suboptimal). It is culturally ingrained; it often operates without our awareness. And it can change.

You think you don't have this prejudice. But you might, without realizing it. Even if you are aware of having this prejudice, you will be reluctant to admit it. Now that the U.S. can fairly be described as an "adoption nation" (the title of Adam Pertman's terrific book), admitting to questions about the emotional ties in adoptive families is as politically incorrect as admitting to racial prejudice. But, like racial prejudice, these doubts about adoptive families persist and are much more widespread than anyone wants to admit. They are a motivating factor for the tens of thousands of couples who spend millions of dollars annually and endure extraordinary physical and emotional pain feeding the biotech-reproduction industry.

I was shocked to hear another adoptive mom express the "biologic bias" the other day. We were talking about adoptive family support networks in our community, and this other mom, who has two biological children and one adopted child, was critical of the quality of the interactions she saw between adoptive fathers and their children at one play group. "I don't know," she said, shaking her head. "There's something about that biologic tie. Some people aren't able to have babies for a reason." Another mom of two biologic kids, who was sitting at the table with us, nodded her assent. Both of these women are exceptionally nice and thoughtful. If *they* harbor such thoughts, the biologic bias is very widespread.

You might think, "If they were so nice and thoughtful, why would they say something so hurtful in front of you, who is a mom solely through adoption?" I think the answer is where hope lies. It didn't occur to them that their comments might be hurtful to me, because they knew my family from the inside, as I do; they don't think of my family as "adoptive" anymore, because they know us. Their knowledge of the quality of our relationships exempts us from the category. So their hurtful comments paradoxically inspire hope, because as adoptive families proliferate and become known as friends rather than as "adoptive families," we, in effect, disappear.

But *is* there "something about that biologic tie"? It depends upon what the meaning of "is" is. There is something about that biologic tie when it works as it's presumed to work, the way it's supposed to work. That is, there is something about it when there is something about it. Obviously, however, biologic ties do not prevent the physical and emotional abuse and neglect of children that is rampant in the U.S. and other countries. Biologic ties do not prevent the cold-hearted abandonment of biologic kids. Biologic ties do not prevent the kind of settled disaffection expressed by an acquaintance the other night who growled, "Bad genes," as the explanation for his biologic son's dissolute life. To a considerable extent, our reverence for the biologic tie is ingrained cultural myth that flies in the face of much conflicting evidence. We adoptive families will become more normalized as more people get to know us better, and learn that controlled studies routinely find that adoptive families are at least as close, loving, and high-functioning as biologic families. Someday, some biologic parent having trouble with her kids is going to muse, "There's something about that adoptive tie . . ."

I don't want to say that I think about adoption all the time, because I don't want to scare you away from it. But I kind of *do* think about it all the time. When you become a parent through adoption—just as when you become intimately connected with a member of any marginalized group—you see the world differently. You see the world through the eyes of your child, who has to make sense of the fact that her first parents gave her up, that the parents she knows and loves didn't make her, the way most of her friends' parents did. Movies, books, television shows, stray comments are filtered through a new awareness of this different-from-"normal" reality. A movie that most find harmless, if badly made, becomes inimical; another movie, loved by many for a range of reasons, becomes a metaphor for the adoptive parents' search, the lost child's need.

But my hovering awareness of adoption is not colored by the tone of "but" (". . . but they are not mine"); it exists in the tone of "and" (". . . and I am so lucky"). It is rather like the awareness of death, handled well. People who handle the awareness of death well (I am not yet reliably one of them) are able to use their awareness of death to enhance their appreciation of life. They live the meaning of Wallace Stevens's immortal line, "Death is the mother of beauty." The awareness of adoption is the mother, in me, of a reverence for the gifts I have been given in these children.

We have completely bollixed up bedtime. We have read all the books, we have tried—I am not kidding—*everything,* and we have never managed to get Natalie regularly to go to sleep in her own bed. Once she could climb out of her crib, the gig was up. For months, despite all our well-informed efforts to establish a peaceful and orderly "bedtime ritual," the only ritual we could count on was hours of nightly battles to get Natalie to cooperate. Her little wail from down the hall, "I just want to be with youuuuuuu!" finally did us in. We folded. She falls asleep in our bed nearly every night, and usually wakes up there as well, since if we move her during the night she inevitably wakes up and comes back, waking us again as well.

When we first brought home Lana, she was the ideal little sleeper. Having slept in a crib until we brought her home, and having been under the strict scrutiny of the orphanage caregivers, for weeks she didn't even know she *could* get out of her bed on her own steam. We would put her into bed, kiss her, turn off the lights, and—*voila!*—like magic, like the books say she should, she would *stay* there and sleep. It was heavenly. Now, of course, being a smart little girl, she's on to the whole bedtime scene at our house, and has begun to insist on sleeping in our bed, too. What an incredible treat for her, to go from an impersonal good-night from nurses, to a big bed filled with the warm bodies of people who love her! And, for our part, how could we leave her out in the cold? How could we say no to her, while we say yes to Nattie? So, very often, we are all in bed together. And, very often, I am not sleeping when they are, because I *can't* sleep, because I'm all squished. And even as I bemoan the mess we have made of bedtime, I lie there in the semi-dark with one girl's head on each of my shoulders, smiling up through the ceiling, my heart filled with gratitude. I like to think that my mother is smiling back.

# Adoption Resources

Here is a quick outline of this resource list. You can start anywhere, but if you read "Why I leave certain things out," other comments sprinkled throughout the list will make more sense. I hope you find it helpful!

**INTRODUCTION**
   Purpose of this list
   Why I leave certain things out

**GENERAL RESOURCES**

**BOOKS**
   Policy, Trends, Data, Theory
   How-to and Decision Making

Adoptive Parenting
   Addressing Adoption in the Schools
Books for Children

**ORGANIZATIONS**
   General Interest and Domestic Adoptions
   International Adoptions

# Introduction

*Purpose of this list*

A wealth of books, articles, and websites has devoted to adoption in the last twenty years—so many, in fact, that the range of choice can be mind-boggling. Everyone who is considering adoption should have an experienced "buddy" to help them through this maze of resources. I hope this highly selective list can help serve as your long-distance buddy, wherever you are in the process. I will update the list periodically as new resources emerge. You can find the latest version at www.theresareidbooks.com.

*Why I leave certain things out*

I am listing books and websites I have found most helpful and interesting. A major criterion for me is that the featured work be based in rigorous studies and careful thought, not in myths. As you search for useful information about adoption, you will find books, articles, and websites that, subtly or blatantly, denigrate adoptive relationships. These materials are grounded in the belief that biological kinship is naturally superior to adoptive kinship, and that the severing of biological ties irreparably wounds all separated parties. *There are NO reliable data to support these claims.* If you come across claims like this in your search for good information, ignore them. *Do not allow anyone to cause you to doubt the rightness, beauty, and depth of your love for your children, and theirs for you.*

I appreciate your feedback on resources you find helpful. Please register that feedback via my website: www.theresareidbooks.com.

# General Resources

As an adoptive or pre-adoptive parent, you need to know about these general resources:

*Adoptive Families* magazine offers a wealth of information online and in print, including its annual adoption guidebook. www.adoptivefamilies.com

**National Adoption Information Clearinghouse (NAIC),** a service of the U.S. Department of Health and Human Services, is a tremendous source of information about all aspects of adoption, for all members of the adoption triad. www.naic.acf.hhs.gov

**Perspectives Press,** run by Patricia Irwin Johnston and based in Indianapolis, has published some of the best work out there on adoption and infertility, including Johnston's own outstanding books (referenced under "How-to and decision making"). www.perspectivepress.com

**Tapestry Books** is the original purveyor of adoption-related books. Tapestry offers a wide range of books on all aspects of adoption from many different publishers on a searchable website. www.tapestrybooks.com

**Adoption.com** at www.adoption.com and www.adoption.org. This is a media company whose websites you are certain to find immediately if you are searching for adoption information online. These free commercial sites have a very different feel from those of dedicated nonprofits. They do not always provide the in-depth information you will need, but the beginning information is good and reliable, and the links go on and on and on. . . .

# Books

*Policy, Trends, Data, Theory*

Elizabeth Bartholet, *Family Bonds: Adoption, Infertility, and the New World of Child Production* (Boston: Beacon, 1999).

> Harvard Law Professor Bartholet names "the biologic bias" in this book and traces its effects in the culture at large and in adoptive families. This is a groundbreaking and essential work.

E. Wayne Carp, *Family Matters: Secrecy and Disclosure in the History of Adoption* (Boston: Harvard University Press, 1998).

> E. Wayne Carp, Professor of History at Pacific Lutheran University, gives the first detailed history of the shifting attitudes and practices about secrecy and openness in the history of U.S. adoptions. Exhaustive, enlightening, and sane.

Harold Grotevant and Ruth McRoy, *Openness in Adoption: Exploring Family Connections* (Thousand Oaks, CA: Sage Publications, 1998).

> Harold Grotevant and Ruth McRoy, Professors at the Universities of Minnesota and Texas (Austin), respectively, cut through the dense

myths and ideology in this volume, reporting recent research on the effects of various levels of openness in adoption.

H. David Kirk, *Looking Back, Looking Forward: An Adoptive Father's Sociological Testament* (Indianapolis: Perspectives Press, 1995). Order directly from Perspectives Press at www.perspectivespress.com.

> Sociologist H. David Kirk is the father of contemporary adoption research and theory. His contributions to the field are incalculable. In this farewell address delivered at a major adoption conference, he assesses progress in the field and thinks about its trajectory.

H. David Kirk, *Shared Fate: A Theory and Method of Adoptive Relationships* (Port Angeles, WA: Ben-Simon Publications, 1964).

> This is Kirk's first book about adoption. One of its critical contributions is its recognition that the challenges faced by adoptive families are not inherent in the institution but created by the culture's suspicion and devaluation of adoptive relationships. This is a cornerstone of contemporary adoption literature.

National Council for Adoption, *Adoption Factbook III* (1999). Available through NCFA's website, www.adoptioncouncil.org.

> In the wars over open records, the National Council for Adoption has consistently fought for privacy; hence, it is vilified in many areas of the adoption community. However, NCFA publishes perhaps the most comprehensive compilation of facts about adoption to be had. You might disagree with some of the opinion articles in the *Factbook,* but as a data source it is excellent.

Adam Pertman, *Adoption Nation: How the Adoption Revolution Is Transforming America* (New York: Basic Books, 2000).

> An adoptive father and journalist (and now executive director of the Evan B. Donaldson Adoption Institute; see later, under "Organizations"), Adam Pertman authored one of the very best books ever written about contemporary adoption and how it is changing America. Pertman is a major open adoption advocate and strongly criticizes the National Council for Adoption for its fight to keep records closed, making Pertman's book both a fascinating record of and document in the current adoption debates.

Katarina Wegar, *Adoption, Identity, and Kinship: The Debate over Sealed Records* (New Haven: Yale University Press, 1997).

> Associate Professor of Sociology at Old Dominion University, Katarina Wegar analyzed historical records and policies, popular representations, activist newsletters, and academic articles for evidence of unconscious bias, and found plenty—most of it destructive to adoptive family relationships. This is an important book that concludes with a discussion of ways to avoid perpetuating the harmful images of all triad members.

## How-to and Decision Making

Books in this section help you deal with infertility, decide whether or not to adopt, decide what adoption route to take, and then learn how to cope with the process.

Christine A. Adamec, *The Adoption Option: A Complete Handbook* (New York: Crown Publishing Group, 1999).

*Adoptive Families* magazine's annual *Adoption Guide* is indispensable. Available from their website, www.adoptivefamilies.com.

Tracy Barr and Katrina Carlisle, *Adoption for Dummies* (New York: John Wiley and Sons, 2003).

The Dave Thomas Foundation for Adoption, *A Child Is Waiting: A Beginner's Guide to Adoption*. Available to download or order from the Dave Thomas Foundation website, www.davethomasfoundationforadoption.org.

Lois Gilman, *The Adoption Resource Book: All the Things You Need to Know and Ought to Know About Creating an Adoptive Family* (New York: Harper Reference, Fourth Edition, 1998).

Mary Hopkins-Best, *Toddler Adoption: The Weaver's Craft* (Indianapolis: Perspectives Press, 1997).

Claudia L. Jewett, *Adopting the Older Child* (Boston: Harvard Common Press, 1979).

Patricia Irwin Johnston, *Adopting After Infertility* (Indianapolis: Perspectives Press, 1992).

———, *Adoption Is a Family Affair! What Relatives and Friends Must Know* (Indianapolis: Perspectives Press, 2001).

———, *Taking Charge of Infertility* (Indianapolis: Perspectives Press, 1994).

Cynthia Martin and Dru Martin Groves, *Beating the Adoption Odds: Using Your Head and Your Heart to Adopt* (New York: Harcourt Brace, 1998).

Trish Maskew, *Our Own: Adopting and Parenting the Older Child* (Morton Grove, IL: Snowcap Press, 1999).

John H. McLean, *The Chinese Adoption Handbook: How to Adopt from China and Korea* (iUniverse, Inc., 2004).

————, *Russian Adoption Handbook: How to Adopt from Russia, Ukraine, Kaza-khstan, Bulgaria, Belarus, Georgia, Azjerbaijan and Moldova* (iUniverse Star, 2004).

Lois Melina and Sharon Roszia, *The Open Adoption Experience: A Complete Guide for Adoptive and Birth Families—From Making the Decision to the Child's Growing Years* (New York: HarperCollins, 1993).

Bruce M. Rappaport, *The Open Adoption Book: A Guide to Adoption Without Tears* (New York: MacMillan, 1992).

Cheri Register, *"Are Those Kids Yours?" American Families with Children Adopted from Other Countries* (New York: Free Press, 1991).

Gail Steinberg and Beth Hall, *Inside Transracial Adoption* (Indianapolis: Perspectives Press, 2000).

Michael R. Sullivan and Susan Shultz, *Adopt the Baby You Want* (New York: Simon & Schuster, 1990).

## Adoptive Parenting

As I say in *Two Little Girls*, "Once you become a parent through adoption, you experience all the joys and worries, exasperation and delight that biological parents experience. And then some." Even the happiest, most secure adoptive families have to come to terms with a host of issues: birth parents' decision not to parent their child, and your child's feelings about that; your own feelings about birth families; the culture's feelings about adoption; attitudes about adoption your child encounters at school; and, in closed and international adoptions, lack of sometimes critical information about genetic background. Some adoptive families have additional challenges, most prominent among them attachment difficulties.

The books that follow address all of these issues. My one caveat with some of these books is the authors' failure to consistently qualify their statements about adopted children and families. Although every author notes, typically in the book's first chapter, that every family is different, authors all too easily drop qualifiers and start talking about "adoptees" and "adoptive families" as if they were all alike. All adoptive families do have to cope with issues specific to adoption; but how those issues affect the children and families varies tremendously. Typically, when qualifiers are dropped, subtle pathologizing of adoption is going on. You know how I hate that!

If you find unqualified statements about adoptive families in any of these books, add your own qualifiers and read on. A great deal of help is to be found here.

Vera Fahlberg, *A Child's Journey Through Placement* (Indianapolis: Perspectives Press, 1994).

Karen J. Foli and John R. Thompson, *Post-Adoption Blues: Overcoming the Unforeseen Challenges of Adoption* (New York: Rodale Press, 2004).

Gregory C. Keck and Regina M. Kupecky, *Adopting the Hurt Child: Hope for Families with Special-Needs Kids* (Colorado Springs, CO: NavPress Publishing Group, 1998).

Joyce Maguire Pavao, *The Family of Adoption* (Boston: Beacon Press, 1998).

Elinor Rosenberg, *The Adoption Life Cycle: The Children and Their Families Through the Years* (New York: Free Press, 1992).

Holly Van Gulden and Lisa Bartels-Rabb, *Real Parents, Real Children: Parenting the Adopted Child* (New York: Crossroad Classic, 1995).

Mary Watkins and Susan Fisher, *Talking with Young Children About Adoption* (New Haven: Yale University Press, 1993).

## Addressing Adoption in the Schools

Marilyn Schoettle, *S.A.F.E. at School: (S)upport for (A)doptive (F)amilies by (E)ducators, A Manual for Teachers* (available from the Center for Adoption Support and Education [CASE], at www.adoptionsupport.org).

Lansing Wood and Nancy Ng, *Adoption and the Schools: Resources for Parents and Teachers* (Available from Families Adopting in Response [FAIR] at www.fairfamilies.org or P.O. Box 51436, Palo Alto, CA 94303).

(For a wealth of resources for use in schools, see www.adoptivefamilies.com /school/index.php.)

## For Children

Believe it or not, I make only three recommendations for children's books. Hundreds of books have been published to help children understand and feel good about adoption. Many of these books are excellent. However, the books that are best for you will depend upon how you talk with your children, how old they are, the circumstances of their adoption, their temperament, etc. So I urge you to explore this very rich bookshelf yourself—if possible, in person. I have bought many a children's book online that was disappointing for any number of reasons. So browse in a real bookstore, if possible, and find what fits for you and your child. I think these three, though, are excellent for all adopted kids, school-age and up.

Jill Krementz, *How It Feels to Be Adopted* (New York: Knopf, 1982).

This book is a series of interviews with adopted adolescents by adoptive mother and photographer Jill Krementz. Although I first recoiled from the title, *How It Feels to Be Adopted*—as if there is *a* way adoption feels—I was won over by the frank, varied, and wonderfully sane interviews. Although the photos look a bit dated now, more than twenty years after they were taken, the voices are evergreen. This is a wonderful resource for adoptees 10 and up, who will be relieved to find some of their private thoughts openly discussed.

Marc Nemiroff and Jane Annunziata, *All About Adoption: How Families Are Made and How Kids Feel about It* (Washington, D.C.: Magination Press, 2004).

Delightfully illustrated by Carol Koeller, *All About Adoption* is straightforward, thorough, and upbeat. Ages 4–8.

Marilyn Schoettle, *W.I.S.E. UP Power Book* (Silver Spring, MD: Center for Adoption Support and Education, Inc., 2000). Available from www.adoptionsupport.org.

The *W.I.S.E. UP Power Book* is one of the best resources I have ever seen for adopted school-aged kids. It gives kids explicit, age-appropriate, empowering guidance in how to respond to remarks about adoption from people of all ages. In the process, it raises their consciousness about prevalent adoption myths and attitudes, and reminds them that they're among millions of adopted people living in the United States Indispensable.

# Organizations

*General Interest and Domestic Adoptions*

**AdoptUSKids.** Online at www.adoptuskids.org. On land at Adoption Exchange Association, 8015 Corporate Drive, Suite C, Baltimore, MD 21236. By phone (toll free) at 888-200-4005.

> AdoptUSKids is a program of the Children's Bureau of the Administration on Children, Youth, and Families of the U.S. Department of Health and Human Services. In partnership with several leading child welfare organizations, the Children's Bureau launched AdoptUSKids to help recruit permanent families for the 120,000+ adoptable children in the U.S. foster care system. The website has lots of information for prospective parents and for and about waiting children.

**The Center for Adoption Support and Education, or C.A.S.E.** Online at www.adoptionsupport.org. On land at King's Park Professional Building, 8996 Burke Lake Road, Suite 201, Burke, VA 22015. By phone at 703-425-3703. Also on land at 11120 New Hampshire Avenue, Suite 205, Silver Spring, MD 20904. By phone in MD at 301-593-9200.

> As stated on their website, "C.A.S.E. was created in May 1998 to provide post-adoption counseling and educational services to families, educators, child welfare staff, and mental health providers in Maryland, Northern Virginia, and Washington, D.C." But C.A.S.E. has generated invaluable publications available nationally, including the *W.I.S.E. UP Power Book for Kids* and *S.A.F.E. at School* (both cited in the previous section). C.A.S.E. also offers nationally accessible training and consultation and, through its website, valuable information about other resources in the adoption community.

**Dave Thomas Foundation for Adoption.** Online at www.davethomas foundationforadoption.org. On land at 4150 Tuller Road, Suite 204, Dublin, Ohio 43017. By phone at 1-800-ASK-DTFA.

> I love the Dave Thomas Foundation for Adoption. Established by Wendy's founder Dave Thomas, himself an adopted person, the DTFA encourages adoption of children from the U.S. foster care system. The Foundation publishes the *Beginner's Guide to Adoption* (referenced under "How-to and Decision Making," and download-able from the Foundation's website), provides extensive information on how to secure financial assistance for adoption, sponsors research, and supports adoption in many other ways.

**Evan B. Donaldson Adoption Institute.** Online at www.adoptioninstitute .org. On land at 525 Broadway, 6th floor, New York, NY 10012. By phone at 212-925-4089.

> Founded in 1996, the Evan B. Donaldson Adoption Institute's mis-sion is "to improve the quality of information about adoption, to en-hance the understanding and perception of adoption, and to advance adoption policy and practice." Now headed by Adam Pertman, author of *Adoption Nation* (cited here under "Policy, Trends, Data, Theory"), the Institute is a vital source of new research on issues in adoption and of reliable information about current events in adoption.

**National Adoption Center.** Online at www.adopt.org. On land at 1500 Wal-nut Street, Suite 701, Philadelphia, PA 19102. By phone at 1-800-TO-ADOPT.

> The National Adoption Center (NAC) works to find adoption op-portunities for children throughout the United States, particularly

for children with special needs and those from minority cultures. NAC was begun in the early 1970s by two adoptive mothers in Philadelphia, who worked from their kitchen tables to find families for "hard-to-place" children. Their website has lots of valuable information for families considering adopting these kids, including information about waiting children.

**National Adoption Foundation.** Online at www.nafadopt.org. On land at 100 Mill Plain Road, Danbury, CT 06811. No phone listed on website.

Bless the National Adoption Foundation (NAF). As they say on their website, no loving family should be unable to adopt because of financial barriers. The NAF is the only national resource dedicated exclusively to providing financial support, information, and services directly to adoptive families. Their website is the place to apply for their own small direct grants ($500–$2,500) and to learn about other ways to finance adoption.

**National Council for Adoption.** Online at www.adoptioncouncil.org. On land at 225 N. Washington Street, Alexandria, VA 22314-2561. By phone at 703-299-6633.

Founded in 1980, the National Council for Adoption (NCFA) "is a research, education, and advocacy organization whose mission is to promote the well-being of children, birthparents, and adoptive families by advocating for the positive option of adoption." As I mentioned before in the listing of NCFA's *Factbook* (under "Policy, trends, data, theory"), NCFA is embroiled in the adoption controversy on the side of privacy, having advocated very successfully in many states to prevent the opening of sealed records. Wherever you stand on that issue, NCFA's website is a window into the power politics of adoption regulation, and offers a wealth of information for both professionals and parents.

**North American Council on Adoptable Children.**  Online at www.nacac .org. On land at 970 Raymond Avenue, Suite 106, St. Paul, MN 55114. By phone at 651-644-3036.

Founded in 1974 by adoptive parents in Minnesota, the North American Council on Adoptable Children is committed to meeting the needs of waiting U.S. children and the families who adopt them. The NACAC website holds a wealth of valuable information for professionals and for people considering adoption. Their "How to Adopt" section and their "Table of Adoption Types" are fabulous— clear, concise, informative.

**Pact, An Adoption Alliance.**  Online at www.pactadopt.org. On land at 4179 Piedmont Avenue, Suite 330, Oakland, CA 94611. By phone at (510) 243-9460. Also offering the toll-free Birth Parent Line at (800) 750-7590, and the toll-free Adoptive Parent Peer Support Line at 888-448-8277.

I have the greatest respect for the founders of Pact—two adoptive mothers of children of color who, in 1991, recognized a need for information and support for adoptive families of color (same-race and transracial) and set out to fill the need. They have done an admirable job. Although Pact is located in Oakland, California (so you are unlikely to attend their seminars if you live on the East Coast), they have built an invaluable website, full of sensitive, thoughtful, pragmatic advice and questions for birth parents, adoptive parents, and adoptive children of color. They also have a bookstore and a newsletter. Hats off to the women who have done this wonderful work.

## International Adoptions

All of these organizations (except for the professional organization, the Joint Council on International Children's Services) are founded and run by adoptive parents. The websites all have that "home-grown" feel to them, and reveal quite a range of organizational capacities: some are highly responsive, some a little slower on the uptake. All offer important connections and information for people adopting internationally, and demonstrate terrific goodwill and commitment on the part of the parent volunteers who run them.

**Adopting from Korea** www.adoptkorea.com

**Adopt Vietnam** www.adoptvietnam.org

**Comeunity: Adoptive Parenting Support** www.comeunity.com

**Eastern European Adoption Coalition** www.eeadopt.net

**Families with Children from Vietnam** www.fcvn.org

**Families for Russian and Ukrainian Adoption** www.frua.org

**Friends of Korea** www.friendsofkorea.org

**Joint Council on International Children's Services.** Online at www.jcics.org. On land at 117 South Saint Asaph Street, Alexandria, VA 22314. By phone at 703-535-8045.

JCICS is one of the oldest and largest professional associations for licensed, nonprofit, international adoption agencies. As stated on its website, JCICS's mission is to advocate on behalf of children in need of permanent families and to promote ethical practices in intercountry adoption. Begun over twenty-five years ago as a grassroots affiliation among professionals, JCICS now represents over 200 organizations who work in fifty-one countries around the globe and support over 75 percent of all children adopted internationally by U.S. citizens. The greatest asset of the website for parents is the amazing information provided on adoption issues in fifty-eight sending countries. Click on the button for any country and get the latest information available.

**Parent Network for the Post-Institutionalized Child** www.pnpic.org

**Also see Pact, An Adoption Alliance,** which is specifically dedicated to families raising children of color through domestic or international adoptions. The full listing for **Pact** is in the previous section.